ESSENTIAL LATIN

To Morgan
Illegitium non carbicondum.
Mum & Dad

ESSENTIAL LATIN

The language and life of ancient Rome

G. D. A. Sharpley

London and New York

This edition first published 2000
by Routledge
11 New Fetter Lane, London EC4P 4EE

Simultaneously published in the USA and Canada
by Routledge
29 West 35th Street, New York, NY 10001

Reprinted 2000, 2002

Routledge is an imprint of the Taylor & Francis Group

© 2000 G. D. A. Sharpley
First published 1994 by Bristol Classical Press
under the title 'Latin Better Read Than Dead'

Typeset in Times by The Florence Group, Stoodleigh, Devon
Printed and bound in Great Britain by St Edmundsbury Press

British Library Cataloguing in Publication Data
A catalogue record for this book is available from the British Library

Library of Congress Cataloging in Publication Data
Sharpley, G. D. A.
Essential Latin : the language and life of ancient Rome /
G. D. A. Sharpley.
p. cm.
1. Latin language–Grammar. 2. Latin language–Grammar–Problems,
exercises, etc. 3. Rome–Civilization–Problems, exercises, etc.
I. Title.
PA2087.5.S53   1999
478.2'421–dc21   99–18324
CIP

ISBN 0–415–21319–3 (hbk)
ISBN 0–415–21320–7 (pbk)

CONTENTS

v

PREFACE

Essential Latin is an introduction to the language and civilisation of ancient Rome. It is intended both for individuals who wish to discover (or rediscover) Latin, and for colleges and universities in need of material for short courses of one year or less. A brief course like this inevitably has limitations, and is unlikely to satisfy all the needs of all students. My hope is that there is something, at least, for everyone.

The reading material is taken from the works of ancient authors, and selected to illustrate the history, politics and society of Rome. This has proved highly stimulating, but also challenging – beginners should not be too anxious if they are unable to analyse each excerpt down to the last letter: there are plenty of exercises for that. The lexical help and translations in the appendix will help beginners to negotiate a passage through these authentic texts; and later they can return to apply their improved knowledge to sentences that may have caused uncertainty. The grammar is introduced in stages, and reinforced with exercises that include cartoons to lighten the struggle; there are also studies of English words derived from Latin.

A course that combines a Latin primer with an introduction to ancient civilisation is perhaps unusual, though this concept has evolved over several years of teaching Latin to students who attended purely by choice. Teachers of modern languages have impressed upon me the need to bring the learning out of the classroom and place it in a practical context. Of course, Latin will no longer buy us our daily bread or help us to find the Colosseum; but there remains a practical reason for studying the language, and for studying the historical context that frames it.

People have different reasons for joining Latin courses – to understand historical documents, inscriptions, law, scientific jargon, the roots of English, what 'caldo' means on an Italian tap, or simply to satisfy a curiosity. The sheer variety of these aims, despite good intentions, undermines our efforts to make a cogent and irresistible case for Latin's return to the curriculum.

If there is one compelling reason, it has to be the literature. These ancient poems, histories, letters and speeches are now a part of our own tradition, a cultural heritage we share with much of the modern world. Far from being 'too narrow' or 'out of touch', they conceal a range of interests to invigorate any modern curriculum: architecture, art, drama, poetry, administration, engineering, law, politics, social organisation, argument, grammar, presentation skills, ethnic studies, history, linguistics, philosophy and religion can all be counted amongst them.

Teachers' note

Newcomers to Latin and its grammar should seek the guidance of a teacher. Teachers are advised to give plenty of help during the reading of the texts, so that enjoyment of the Latin is not impaired by slow progress. They are also asked to note that a few of the texts contain constructions and forms that are not explained in advance.

Traditional language courses tend to explain points of grammar and syntax before they appear in reading passages. The approach in this book resembles more modern methods, although the careful study of grammar and syntax remains as important here as anywhere else. It has simply not been feasible – whether or not desirable – to introduce students to all the linguistic forms and rules before they appear in the authentic passages. So when teachers meet ablative absolutes, jussive subjunctives or indirect statements, they should resist the temptation to explain these to beginners, or even to name them. True beginners will be frightened away by too much linguistic jargon, though they will settle for a simple translation; this will allow them to concentrate on those parts of the text containing linguistic points they have covered. As more advanced syntactical explanations are reached later in the book, previous chapters will furnish a ready supply of examples for discussion and comparison.

The above is meant as guidance rather than instruction, for course teachers are the best judges of what their students want. Much will depend on whether the book is for beginners, false beginners or those seeking practice and revision. Adult and postgraduate classes often mix true with false beginners (just to keep the numbers up), and when a student with rusty school Latin greets an *ut* clause like a long-lost friend, a newcomer can be expected to raise an eyebrow.

ACKNOWLEDGEMENTS

I am very grateful to Mark Espiner, Niall Rudd, P. O'R. Smiley and J. M. Will for their contributions to the first edition (*Latin – Better Read than Dead*); to David Miller for many practical suggestions and improvements to this edition; to my students for their helpful comments; to Andy Riley for his excellent cartoons; to friends and family for their enthusiasm and support; and most of all to Sarah Sharpley and our daughters, Rebecca, Meg and Flora.

INTRODUCTION

Latin and English

Latin and English belong to separate groups of the Indo–European family of languages. English is a Germanic language, beginning life relatively recently when the Anglo–Saxons left the continent of Europe to settle in Britain. Latin is an Italic language, and from Latin developed the Romance languages (French, Italian, Portuguese, Spanish and Romanian). There is another group in western Europe, the Celtic languages, which include Welsh, Cornish, Breton and Gaelic. The Italic, Germanic and Celtic groups have a certain amount in common, such as widely-used and recent additions like *computer* or *telephone*, and also words which have been part of man's basic vocabulary for thousands of years: the ancient pronunciation of **mater** and **pater** is much closer to English *mother* and *father* than 'mayter' and 'payter' of recent times might suggest; our word *wool* does not appear to be similar to Latin **lana**, but a connection is offered by Welsh *gwlan*. These are cognate words, related by virtue of a common Indo–European ancestor. Most similarities between English and Latin, however, have come about through derivation, directly from Latin or through French. For example, *two* and **duo** are cognates, *dual* and *duet* are derivatives. The derivation of Latin words has been happening since the Romans were first in occupation of northern Europe, as a result of conquest, trade, religious influence, science, learning and, most recently, technological innovation.

At the time of the Roman occupation of Britain, a few words passed from Latin into the British languages and were later taken up by the Anglo–Saxons. Other words were borrowed by Anglo–Saxons while they were still on the continent. The German tribes were not under direct Roman rule, but many came into contact with Rome either through trade or military service. Some of the words to pass into English during this period are: *street* (*straet*) **strata via**; *wine* (*win*) **vinum**; *port* **portus**. Welsh, being a British language, was more directly influenced by Roman occupation, and thus contains many Latin words (e.g. Welsh equivalents of the above examples: *ystrad*, *gwin* and *porth*). Welsh *ffenestr* (*window*) survives from **fenestra**, but *fenester*, which appeared in old English, is no longer with us.

Many of the Latin words which passed into English after the Romans left Britain had military or commercial meanings, and, after the arrival of Christianity, religious ones. Beside words of a purely religious character, the Church introduced words of a learned and scientific nature (during this period all learning, science and scholarship remained within churches and monasteries). Examples of Latin words taken into English from AD 450 until the Norman Conquest are: *monk* (*munuc*), **monachus**; *minster* (*mynster*), **monasterium** (*monastery* appears much later); *purse* (*purs*), **bursa**; *camel*, **camelus**; *heretic* (*eretic*), **haereticus**; *creed* (*creda*), **credo**; *pope* (*papa*), **papa**; *saint* (*sanct*), **sanctus**; *note* (*not*) **nota**; *paper*, **papyrus**; *school* (*scol*), **schola**; *-chester*, *-caster*, and *-cester*, **castra** (*a camp*); *cup* (*cupp*), **cuppa**.

Some of these words have not survived, or were replaced at a later date by others which were reborrowed from Latin, directly or through Old French. In the period after the Norman Conquest up until the Renaissance, many French words derived from Latin passed into English. There are also words derived directly from Latin: *admit, arbitrator, cause, client, collect, combine, complete, conclude, confide, conviction, diocese, discuss, eccentric, equal, equator, expedition, explicit, imaginary, immortal, import, legitimate, library, locust, memorandum, prima facie, psalm, requiem, simile, subpoena*, etc. With some words, it is difficult to know whether they came to English through French or directly from Latin (e.g. *distant, impression, execution*), although to some extent this must have varied according to the period and education of individual users. Several words taken from French were later refashioned on Latin models (e.g. suffixes *-tioun, -cioun* and *-sioun* became *-tion* and *-sion*), while others kept the French form, such as *custody* (*custodie*) from **custodia**, and *family* (*familie*) from **familia**.

During the sixteenth and seventeenth centuries, as a result of the Renaissance, scholars and writers coined a large number of new words modelled on Latin originals (not all of which survived), and imported several whole Latin words. Moreover, some existing English words which had been derived from Latin through Old French were at this time sidelined in favour of words more closely modelled on the Latin originals. As time passed, the new formations developed marginally different meanings from the old ones: *purvey* and *provide* (**provideo**), *strait* and *strict* (**strictus**), *count* and *compute* (**computo**), *sure* and *secure* (**securus**), *ray* and *radius* (**radius**), *poor* and *pauper* (**pauper**).

During the Renaissance, the meanings of certain words which had previously been derived from Latin were altered to bring them into line with the meanings of their classical models: in the fourteenth century, an *oration* was a petition, but was later used to mean a formal speech, similar to **oratio**; likewise *discipline* in the thirteenth century meant correction, but in the sixteenth century took on the original Latin sense of control over conduct (**disciplina**); *prefer* was used in the sixteenth century to mean put something forward, on the model of **praefero**, but the word had already appeared two centuries earlier to mean set before others, the usage which is more common today.

Not content with making new words and giving new meanings to ones already in use, scholars of the period also tampered with the spelling of words derived through French: *doute* became *doubt* (**dubium**), *dette* became *debt* (**debitum**), and *receit* became *receipt* (**receptum**). Some of these changes had already occurred in

France before the words entered English, for example *caitiff* became *captif (captive)* on the model of **captivus**.

In the sixteenth and seventeenth centuries, several Latin words passed into English in their classical form, and some arrived later. Here are a few examples:

16th century:	**aborigine, alias, area, circus, exit, genius, virus**
17th century:	**agenda, arena, premium, rabies, squalor, status**
18th century:	**alibi, bonus, deficit, extra, ultimatum**
19th century:	**consensus, ego, omnibus, referendum**
20th century:	**computer*, facsimile*, video**

       *These words had been used before the twentieth century, a *facsimile* being a likeness, and *computer* a person who counts.

Before the Renaissance, English absorbed Latin nouns and anglicised them. But words imported later came complete with their plural forms, with the result that we now have *curriculum* and *curricula*, *agendum* and *agenda*, and yet *circuses* not **circi**, *spectators* not **spectatores**, and *areas* not **areae**.

Some Latin imports remain in English as the same parts of speech they were in Latin (e.g. *creator* and *genius* are nouns, *stet* a verb). Others change their function (e.g. *alias*, *alibi* and *interim* were Latin adverbs and are now nouns). There are also Latin verbs which survive in English as nouns: *recipe, affidavit, deficit, exit, veto, caveat, ignoramus* and *video*. Latin gerundives (e.g. *memorandum, agenda, dividend, reverend*), almost always kept the orginal Latin sense of obligation (**agenda**: *things which must be done*).

Suffixes were formed from Latin models, such as *-ate*, which was an adjectival ending (e.g. *obstinate, desperate*), but now is more commonly used for verbs (e.g. *liberate, frustrate*). This ending comes from the past participle **liberatum, frustratum**. There are many other suffixes too, including the adjectival endings *-ible* and *-able* from **-ibilis** and **-abilis**, and some are added to non-Latin stems (e.g. *laughable, comfortable*). Prefixes figure in the importing of whole words, and are also added separately (e.g. *post-, trans-, inter-, contra-, sub-, pre-*). For a list of prepositions and prefixes, see page 141.

Today, Latin's influence is often seen in technical subjects, in jargon or pompous affectation. This might be expected of a language which has long been the vehicle for learning, science, law and officialdom. Yet Latin has also given us countless everyday words, and in the entire history of English, no other language has had, or continues to have, as much influence on our vocabulary.

A guide to pronunciation

The alphabet

The Latin alphabet is almost identical to ours: **i** and **v** served both as consonants (English 'j' and 'v'), and vowels ('i' and 'u'); there was no written 'w' in Latin – but its sound was made by the consonantal **v**.

   The practice until relatively recently was to write the consonantal **i** as a 'j', although the current convention is to write both the consonant and vowel as **i**. In some texts (including this one) you will find a 'v' for the consonantal **v** and a 'u' for the vowel (e.g. **vider<u>u</u>nt**); in others the letter 'u' is used for both (e.g. **<u>u</u>ider<u>u</u>nt**). Romans themselves wrote everything in upper case:

> **IVLIVS (Iulius,** or **Julius)**
> **VETVRIA (Veturia)**

The current convention is to use lower case (except for proper names), even to begin a sentence.

Letter sounds

a   (short) as in 'c<u>a</u>p'
ā   (long) as in 'f<u>a</u>ther'
ae as in 'f<u>i</u>ne'
au as in 'h<u>ou</u>se'
b   as in English (**bs** and **bt** are pronounced 'ps' and 'pt')
c   as in 'c<u>at</u>' (not '<u>ch</u>air' or '<u>c</u>eiling')
ch like English 'k', with a sharper expulsion of breath
d   as in English
e   (short) as in 'm<u>e</u>t'
ē   (long) as in 'm<u>a</u>te'
ei as in 's<u>ay</u>'
eu two sounds run together 'e–oo'
f   as in English
g   as in 'g<u>o</u>t' ('gn' at the beginning of a word is pronounced 'n', and in the middle of a word 'ngn')
h   as in English
i   (short) as in 'l<u>i</u>p'
ī   (long) as in 'k<u>ee</u>p'
i   (consonant: sometimes written as a 'j') like English 'y'
l   as in English

m as in English at the beginning or in the middle of words; a final 'm' should be pronounced with the lips open, as a nasalisation of the preceding vowel

n as in English

ng as in 'anger' (not 'hangar')

o (short) as in 'n<u>o</u>t'

ō (long) as in 'n<u>o</u>te' (as pronounced by Scots and Welsh)

oe as in '<u>oi</u>l'

p as in English

ph as in 'p', with a sharper expulsion of breath

qu as in '<u>qu</u>it'

r always trilled with the tip of the tongue

s as in 'ga<u>s</u>' (not 'ha<u>s</u>')

t as in English (and even closer to French 't')

th as in 't', with a sharper expulsion of breath

u (short) as in 'p<u>u</u>ll'

ū (long) as in 'p<u>oo</u>l'

v (sometimes written as a 'u') like English 'w'

x as in English

y (short) as in French 't<u>u</u>'

ȳ (long) as in French 's<u>ur</u>'

z as in English

Quantity and stress

A vowel marked 'long' with a macron (‾) does not mean that the syllable should necessarily be *stressed* (though it often is). Latin had a stress accent similar to our own: the penultimate syllable of a word is stressed if it is long, e.g. **ómnes, vivámus**; but if that syllable is short, then the previous (antepenultimate) one is stressed, e.g. **ómnibus, vívimus**. Words of two syllables carry the stress on the first syllable, whether it is long or short (**páter**), and monosyllabic words are also stressed, if only negligibly so in the case of some minor words (e.g. **ad, et**). The force of the stress will no doubt have varied according to how the word was being used, the speaker, region and period.

Latin poetry before and after the classical period was based on rhythms created by stressed syllables – similar to our own poetry. Classical Latin verse had rhythms borrowed and refined from Greek poetry, in which rhythm was measured by the quantities of syllables (long or short), not by the weight of stress. Virgil, Horace and other classical Latin poets were at the mature end of a process of harnessing these Greek quantities to the natural sounds of their own language.

Medieval Latin verse, of the spontaneous sort, reverted to rhythms of stress only. There were also metrical compositions, in most cases rather studied imitations, of which very few managed to recover the easy and natural interplay of quantity and stress that we can hear in the rhythms of their classical models.

Numbers

1	I	ūnus		11	XI	ūndecim
2	II	duo		12	XII	duodecim
3	III	trēs		13	XIII	tredecim
4	IV	quattuor		14	XIV	quattuordecim
5	V	quīnque		15	XV	quīndecim
6	VI	sex		16	XVI	sēdecim
7	VII	septem		17	XVII	septendecim
8	VIII	octō		18	XVIII	duodēvīgintī
9	IX	novem		19	XIX	ūndēvīgintī
10	X	decem		20	XX	vīgintī

21	XXI	ūnus et vīgintī		101	CI	centum et ūnus
22	XXII	duo et vīgintī		126	CXXVI	centum vīgintī sex
29	XXIX	ūndētrīgintā		200	CC	ducentī-ae-a
30	XXX	trīgintā		300	CCC	trecentī-ae-a
40	XL	quadrāgintā		400	CCCC	quadringentī-ae-a
50	L	quīnquāgintā		500	D	quīngentī-ae-a
60	LX	sexāgintā		600	DC	sescentī-ae-a
70	LXX	septuāgintā		700	DCC	septingentī-ae-a
80	LXXX	octōgintā		800	DCCC	octingentī-ae-a
90	XC	nōnāgintā		900	DCCCC	nōngentī-ae-a
98	IIC	octō et nōnāgintā		1000	M	mīlle, *indecl.*
99	XCIX	ūndēcentum				(*plural:* mīlia)
100	C	centum				

Names

Praenōmen	Nōmen	Cognōmen
individual name	***gēns**/clan*	***familia***
Mārcus	Tullius	Cicerō
Publius	Vergilius	Marō
Gāius	Iūlius	Caesar

In addition to these names a prominent Roman might assume another name (**agnōmen**), perhaps the name of the family that adopted him, or an honorary title:

'Coriolānus'	(Gnaeus Marcius)
'Africānus'	(Publius Cornēlius Scīpiō)
'Magnus'	(Gnaeus Pompēius)

Praenōmina are often abbreviated:

A.	Aulus	M.	Mārcus	Ser.	Servius
C.	Gāius	M'.	Mānius	Sp.	Spurius
Cn.	Gnaeus	P.	Publius	T.	Titus
D.	Decimus	Q.	Quīntus	Ti(b).	Tiberius
L.	Lūcius	S(ex).	Sextus		

Daughters had no peculiar **praenōmina**, but were called by the name of the **gēns** in which they were born. If there were two, they were distinguished as **māior** and **minor**; if more than two, by **tertia, quārta**, etc.

1 EARLY ROME

Nouns: subjects and objects

agricola taurum fugat
the farmer chases/is chasing the bull

The Latin word for *chases*, **fugat**, appears at the end of the sentence. *The farmer*, **agricola**, comes first, and *the bull*, **taurum**, is second.

The farmer is the active one, the person doing the chasing, and so is the subject. *The bull* is the object, because he is on the receiving end, i.e. he is being chased.

agricolam taurus fugat
the bull chases/is chasing the farmer

Now *the bull* is the subject, while *the farmer* has become the object. To make this clear, the English words have been moved. The Latin words, however, have not changed their position, but their endings.

The Latin for *farmer* as subject is	**agrico<u>la</u>**
and as object	**agricol<u>am</u>**
The Latin for *bull* as subject is	**taur<u>us</u>**
and as object	**taur<u>um</u>**

English also has a few words which change according to whether they are subject or object: *she/her, he/him, I/me, we/us, they/them, who/whom*. These words are all pronouns, words which are used in the place of nouns.

Vocabulary

Words like **agricola**:

nauta	*sailor*
puella	*girl*
dea	*goddess*
fēmina	*woman*
poēta	*poet*

Words like **taurus**:

servus	*slave*
dominus	*master*
deus	*god*
equus	*horse*

Practice A

With the help of the pictures, complete the words and translate:

1 **puell . . . . equ . . . . fugat.**   2 **serv . . . . domin . . . . fugat.**

3 **naut**. . . . . . . **femin**. . . . . . . **fugat**.   4 **de**. . . . . . . **poet**. . . . . . . **fugat**.

The cases

The technical name for these different endings of a noun is 'case'. Each case has a particular function: it may be to show that the noun is the subject or object. The subject ending is called the <u>nominative</u> case, and the object ending is called the <u>accusative</u> case. There are other cases too:

The genitive case

The English preposition *of* is used to translate the genitive case:

    e.g. **taurus agricol<u>ae</u>**   *the bull <u>of</u> the farmer*

We might leave out *of* and use an apostrophe instead: 'the farmer's bull'. Centuries ago, before the Norman Conquest, English had a genitive ending too. The 'e' of the genitive ending '-es' has since given way to the apostrophe.

    taurus agricol<u>ae</u>
    the bull <u>of</u> the farmer (the farmer's bull)

    oculus taur<u>i</u>
    the eye <u>of</u> the bull (the bull's eye)

    equus puell<u>ae</u>
    the horse <u>of</u> the girl (the girl's horse)

The dative case

The dative case is used for the indirect object. The English preposition *to* is commonly used (and sometimes *for*):

agricola tauro faenum dat
the farmer gives/is giving hay to the bull

femina equum puellae ostentat
the woman shows/is showing the horse to the girl

Note that in each of the above two examples there are two objects, one direct (accusative), the other indirect (dative).

The ablative case

The most common use of the ablative is instrumental (*by, with*) or with a preposition (e.g. **in**). English prepositions used to translate this case are: *by, with, from, in, on*.

agricola cum equo ambulat
the farmer walks/is walking with the horse

agricola a tauro videtur
the farmer is seen by the bull

agricola in equo est
the farmer is on the horse

femina equum faeno pascit
the woman feeds/is feeding the horse with hay

servus e villa ambulat
the slave walks/is walking from (out of) the villa

Practice B

With the help of the pictures, complete the words and translate:

1 **agricol. . . . . cum taur. . . . .
ambulat.**

2 **equus in vill. . . . . est.**

3 **puella tauri faenum equ. . . . .
dat.**

4 **poeta agricolae taur..... deo dat.**

Summary

Latin nouns change endings according to their function in the sentence. These endings are defined as cases:

Case	Function	**fēmina** *woman*	**servus** *slave*
Nominative	subject	**fēmina**	**servus**
Accusative	object	**fēminam**	**servum**
Genitive	*of*	**fēminae**	**servī**
Dative	*to, for*	**fēminae**	**servō**
Ablative	*in, on, with, from, by*	**fēminā**	**servō**

See p. 159 for examples of these and other uses of the cases.

Reading notes

Pronunciation

Latin **au** is similar to h*ou*se; the **v** is pronounced like our *w*; **i** (vowel) as in l*i*p (short) or l*ea*p (long); **i** (consonant, e.g. **Iulius**) as the English *y*; **ae** similar to the English *eye*; **c** and **g** are both hard, as in *c*ake, *g*ate, not in *g*ender or *ch*ali*c*e.

Macrons are used in the vocabularies and grammatical tables to mark long vowels. See p. xiii for more information. There is a cassette available from the publisher with readings of all the Latin passages.

Order of words

Writers put words in the order they want you to read them. A verb generally comes at the end of a sentence, and one traditional method is to scan ahead and identify this before turning to the other words. This procedure is obviously not a natural one, and should only be followed as a last resort. As far as possible, take the words in the order they were written, which will lead to a certain amount of juggling with possibilities – and some rather odd English! As the sense becomes clear you can rephrase your translation in more appropriate idiom:

e.g. **agricolam taurus fugat**

agricolam	*the farmer* (object)
taurus	*the bull* (does something to) *the farmer*
fugat	*The bull chases/is chasing the farmer.*

Articles and 'is'

There are no Latin words for 'the' or 'a': add them to your English translation as appropriate. Also, 'is' in Latin is **est**. But the Latin equivalent of 'is walking' is **ambulat** without **est**, for 'is walking' is the equivalent of 'walks'.

Missing subjects

If there is no subject noun, the subject (in English, a pronoun) is implied in the verb:

e.g. **taurum fugat**   *he/she chases/is chasing the bull*

Capital letters

This book adopts the convention of not using capital letters, except for proper names.

Identifying cases

In the first few chapters you will be given the case of a word, from which you can determine the word's function. The names of the cases will be abbreviated to nom., acc., gen., dat. and abl., and pl. indicates a plural ending.

Authentic texts

The Latin texts have been taken from ancient authors. Very little of the original Latin has been altered, although in a few selections some words have been omitted, altered, or added to complete the context.

Myth, legend and history

Origins are often defined for us by the limits of what we can see. Rome emerges from obscurity as a collection of villages which grow together and become a satellite of Etruria, a powerful culture to the north. 510 BC is the traditional date of the expulsion of the last king, Tarquin, and the beginning of the republic. The king was replaced by a pair of leaders (consuls), whose length of office was restricted to one year. Clearly there was a fear of power concentrated in a single authority for any length of time.

This moment in their history had great significance for later Romans, as it marked the end of Etruscan domination and the beginning of an independent republic. Free from patriotism or nostalgia, we might say that it was a political struggle of a kind that frequently recurs, followed by a compromise of power-sharing between the leading families. But this perspective was too prosaic for Roman historians, who worked within a different set of conventions to those of the twentieth century. Their readers had no novels, films, newspapers or television. They didn't want a set of scant statistics or incomplete details to herald the dawn of the Roman era. Today's historian might well wonder at the first two books of Livy's history of Rome, with all their biographical excitement and facts interwoven with myths and legends; but that was precisely what his readership expected of him.

A myth is by definition untrue, while a legend has factual origins which are distorted in the telling and retelling of the story. There is a clear difference in meaning, as a hapless newspaper editor once discovered when he published an obituary of a local dignitary and described the man's kindness as a 'myth'.

Myths, though untrue, are not always meant to mislead. They are valuable as symbols or moral paradigms, and are often an articulate if implausible way of perceiving the world. Greek historians had already borrowed the theatre's tendency to make a metaphor of life, not simply hold up a mirror. Much later Oscar Wilde was to say, with some mischief, 'the ancient historians gave us delightful fiction in the form of fact; the modern novelist presents us with dull facts under the guise of fiction' (*The Decay of Lying*).

Roman historians admired and imitated the standards of accuracy and impartiality set by the Greek historian Thucydides, who wrote an account of the war between Athens and Sparta in fifth-century Greece. Yet the more immediate legacy was that left by later Greek historians, who were as much interested in an episode's dramatic, literary and moralising potential as in its historical importance. The story of Brutus condemning his sons to death (No. 8) has both dramatic suspense and a moral message of exemplary parental behaviour.

Roman historians absorbed these Greek historiographical conventions, adding to them a taste for biography, with its natural inclination to extremes, and raised the moralising element to the grander level of national interest, public duty, and Rome.

1   The most famous of Rome's ancestors is the Trojan prince Aeneas. He escapes from Troy after the city has fallen to the Greeks, and after a perilous journey westwards he and his companions reach Italy.

urbem Romam condiderunt atque habuerunt initio Troiani.

Sallust, *Bellum Catilinae* 6, 1

atque *and*	**Rōmam** [acc.] *(of) Rome*
condidērunt *(they) founded*	**Trōiānī** [nom. pl.] *Trojans*
habuērunt *(they) had, held*	**urbem** [acc.] *city*
initiō [abl.] *beginning*	

2   Formal ties are made with the indigenous Italians.

Lavinia Latini filia Aeneae in matrimonium data est.

Livy, I, 1, ix

Aenēae [dat.] *Aeneas*	**Latīnī** [gen.] *Latinus*
data est *was given*	**Lāvīnia** [nom.] *Lavinia*
fīlia [nom.] *daughter*	

3   Romulus is equally well known to us as founder of Rome, and he is credited with being a descendant of Aeneas. It is Romulus who founds the city of Rome, after slaying his brother Remus. The name of Romulus is given to the new city.

urbs conditoris nomine appellata est.

Livy, I, 7, iii

appellāta est *was called*	**nōmine** [abl.] *name*
conditōris [gen.] *founder*	**urbs** [nom.] *city*

4   As leader of the new community, he appoints a group of advisers.

centum creat senatores. patres appellati sunt.

Livy, I, 8, vii

appellātī sunt *were called, given the title*	**creat** *he appoints*
centum *hundred*	**patrēs** *fathers* (complement: see p. 159)

9

5 History begins to emerge from the mists of myth and legend with the overthrow of the royal house of Tarquin in the sixth century.

urbem Romam a principio reges habuerunt.

Tacitus, *Annals* I, 1, i

ā prīncipiō [abl.]   *from the beginning*
habuērunt   *(they) had, held*
rēgēs [nom.]   *kings*

Rōmam [acc.]   *(of) Rome*
urbem [acc.]   *city*

6 Tarquinius Superbus was the last of the kings of Rome.

Tarquinius Superbus regnavit annos quinque et viginti.

Livy, I, 60, iii

annōs quīnque et vīgintī   *for five and twenty years*

rēgnāvit   *ruled*

7 In place of the king, two consuls were appointed.

duo consules inde creati sunt, Lucius Iunius Brutus et Lucius Tarquinius Collatinus.

Livy, I, 60, iv

creātī sunt   *were appointed*

inde   *then*

8 Brutus condemns his sons to public execution, after they and other aristocrats are discovered plotting to bring back Tarquin.

stabant deligati ad palum consulis liberi.

Livy, II, 5, vi

cōnsulis [gen.]   *the consul*
dēligātī ad pālum   *bound to a stake*

līberī [nom.]   *the children*
stābant   *stood*

9 The struggle with Etruria is remembered for the heroic deeds of individuals.

pons iter paene hostibus dedit, ni unus vir fuisset, Horatius Cocles.

Livy, II, 10, ii

dedit   *gave*
fuisset   *had been*
hostibus [dat.]   *enemy*
iter [acc.]   *route, passage*

nī   *if not*
paene   *almost*
pōns [nom.]   *bridge*
ūnus vir [nom.]   *one man*

10   Cloclia is one of several Roman girls taken hostage by the Etruscans. She helps her comrades to escape and leads them back to Rome.

Cloelia Tiberim tranavit sospitesque omnes ad propinquos restituit.

Livy, II, 13, vi

ad [+acc.]   *to*
omnēs [acc.]   *everyone*
propinquōs [acc.]   *relatives*
-que   *and* (to be understood before the word to which it is suffixed)

restituit   *restored*
sospitēs [acc.]   *safe*
Tiberim [acc.]   *River Tiber*
trānāvit   *swam across*

Vocabulary

TEXT

Rōma   *Rome*
fīlia   *daughter*
vir   *man, husband*
   (acc.: **virum**, like **servus**)
annus   *year*
ūnus   *one*
duo   *two*
quīnque   *five*
vīgintī   *twenty*
centum   *hundred*
omnēs   *all, everyone*

atque
et
ac } *and*
-que
est, sunt   *is, are*
   (with a participle:
   was, were, e.g. **est**
   factus: *was made*)
rēgēs   *kings*
urbs   *city* (acc.: **urbem**)

NOUNS

amīca   *friend* (female)
nauta   *sailor*
dea   *goddess*
agricola   *farmer*
puella   *girl*
vīlla   *villa, farm*
fēmina   *woman*
poēta   *poet*

amīcus   *friend* (male)
deus   *god*
dominus   *master*
equus   *horse*
servus   *slave*
taurus   *bull*
Augustus   *Augustus*
Brūtus   *Brutus*
Iūlius   *Julius*

VERBS

fugat *chases*	**dat** *gives*
ambulat *walks*	**habet** *has*
est *is*	**videt** *sees*

PREPOSITIONS

With the accusative

in   *into, on to*
ad   *to, towards*

With the ablative

in   *in, on*
cum   *with*
ā, ab   *from, by*
ē, ex   *out of, from*

The prepositions **in** and **ad** governing the accusative case imply some movement, whereas with the ablative they describe a location only.

e.g.   **in vīllam** [acc.]   *into the villa*
   in vīllā [abl.]*   *in the villa*

The prepositions **ā** and **ē** are never used before a vowel (where **ab** and **ex** are used).

* Long vowels are marked by macrons only in vocabulary lists and grammatical tables. For reference see pp. 146–158 (endings) and pp. 201–214 (vocabulary).

Exercises

1   Identify the case of each underlined word and translate:

(a)   **agricola servum fugat.**
(b)   **Augustus taurum habet.**
(c)   **Tiberius feminam videt.**
(d)   **Iulius in Britannia est.**
(e)   **poeta cum nauta ambulat.**
(f)   **villa Tiberii est in Italia.**
(g)   **Tiberium in Britanniam Iulius fugat.**
(h)   **nauta deo taurum dat.**

2   Choose the correct alternative in each sentence and translate:

(a)   **filia ad** [agricolam/agricola] **ambulat.**
(b)   **dominus servo** [equum/equo] **dat.**
(c)   **nauta Augustum in** [Britanniam/Britannia] **videt.**
(d)   **Iulius cum** [amico/amici] **ambulat.**
(e)   **filia** [Augustum/Augusti] **equum in Italia habet.**

3   What do the expressions **in memoriam** and **ad infinitum** mean?

4   The Latin word **duo** is similar to its English counterpart *two*: both words are derived from a common ancestor. What English words are derived from **duo**?

5   What English words are derived, or part-derived, from **annos, urbem, omnes, initio, unus** and **deligati**?

2 CARTHAGE

Singular and plural

Latin nouns have different endings to indicate the plural (as do English nouns, e.g. *farmers, women*). Once again, these endings vary according to the function of the word in the sentence:

tauri agricolas vident	*the bulls see the farmers*
tauros agricolae vident	*the farmers see the bulls*
tauros agricola videt	*the farmer sees the bulls*

The verb **vident** loses the **n** in the third example, because there is a <u>singular</u> subject:

> A verb ending **... -nt** has a plural subject.
> A verb ending **... -t** has a singular subject.

Practice

With the help of the pictures, complete the words and translate:

1 **agricol. . . . . taur. . . . .
vide. . . . .**

2 **agricol. . . . . taur. . . . .
vide. . . . .**

3 **amici poetae taur. . . . . non
vide. . . . .**

4 **naut. . . . . de. . . . . vide. . . . .**

Neuter nouns

femina is a feminine noun, while **servus** is masculine. Most nouns which end **-a**, like **femina**, are feminine (**agricola, nauta** and **poeta** are exceptions). Nouns which end **-us**, like **servus**, are usually masculine.

A third category is the neuter noun, of which an example, **vinum** (*wine*), is added to the table below. Most of the endings of **vinum** are the same as those of **servus**.

15

Neuter nouns have the same endings in the nominative and accusative cases, and so you will not know from a neuter ending whether it is subject or object: the context will help you resolve any difficulty. All neuter plurals end in **-a** in the nominative and accusative.

Summary of nouns

Case	Function		Singular	
Nominative	subject	**servus**	**fēmina**	**vīnum**
Accusative	object	**servum**	**fēminam**	**vīnum**
Genitive	*of*	**servī**	**fēminae**	**vīnī**
Dative	*to, for*	**servō**	**fēminae**	**vīnō**
Ablative	*in, on, with, from, by*	**servō**	**fēminā**	**vīnō**

Case	Function		Plural	
Nominative	subject	**servī**	**fēminae**	**vīna**
Accusative	object	**servōs**	**fēminās**	**vīna**
Genitive	*of*	**servōrum**	**fēminārum**	**vīnōrum**
Dative	*to, for*	**servīs**	**fēminīs**	**vīnīs**
Ablative	*in, on, with, from, by*	**servīs**	**fēminīs**	**vīnīs**

Reading notes

Some of the endings could imply a number of different possible cases:

> e.g.　**servo**: dat. or abl. singular.
> **feminae**: gen. or dat. singular, or nom. plural.

Use the context to identify the right ending:

> e.g.　**servus vinum feminae dat.**

> *The slave*　(subject: **servus** can only be nominative.)
> *wine*　(subject or object: we already have a subject, so probably object.)
> *of/to the woman*　(genitive or dative; **feminae** could also be nominative plural, i.e. subject, but we already have **servus** as subject.)

gives   (**dat** confirms the subject is singular.)

'*The slave gives wine to* (possibly *of*) *the woman.*'

Carthage in history and myth

History relates how Hannibal travelled over the Alps with his elephants and arrived in Italy causing surprise and panic in Rome; similar, say, to the shock the English might have felt had the Spanish Armada beached in Scotland and walked unnoticed into York.

This was not the first conflict into which Rome had been drawn; but none of the previous ones had been on this scale. Rome's development from small city-state to a centre of some importance in the Italian peninsula was the result of military successes, and also of less aggressive diplomatic alliances, and protective ventures. But not everyone wanted friendship with Rome. The growth of her influence soon brought her into contact with north Africa, where Carthage, the established power in the region, already had strong trading links and a powerful navy to guard them.

So long as Roman advances were confined to the Italian peninsula, Carthage could ignore them. But in the early part of the third century BC, Rome's sphere of influence reached the southern parts of Italy and from there to Sicily, and conflict became inevitable. The ensuing Punic wars lasted about a hundred years, and Rome's final victory could not have been easy to foresee. First she had to overcome her inexperience in naval warfare, and later the morale-sapping defeats inflicted by Hannibal, who, if his peers in Carthage had given him their full support, would probably have completed what he set out to do.

His eventual defeat signalled the end for Carthage, and greatly empowered Rome. Now her acquisitive instincts were turned eastwards across the Adriatic to Greece, where cultural and diplomatic ties had already been made. The Greek cities had once been independent states, but during the fourth century had fallen under the rule of Macedonia. At the end of the third century, the Greeks asked Rome to help them win back their independence, a request she readily responded to. And so the empire continued to grow.

Virgil's story of Dido and Aeneas in the *Aeneid* symbolises the conflict with Carthage and Rome's ultimate victory. Jupiter's desire for Aeneas to leave Carthage gives the seal of divine approval to Rome's destiny. It also lends a sharp edge to the story. Aeneas has to sail away because the gods wish him to; we recognise this but cannot entirely condone it. Dido certainly does not. We can excuse him on the grounds of divine manipulation, but Aeneas is no puppet, for the gods interfere more to jog his memory than dictate his behaviour. On another level the gods' behaviour serves as a metaphor, to enhance – not replace – human feelings and responses. Necessity (from the plot of the story) may be presented as a divine plan, but such is Virgil's art that the human characters always act in the belief that they are free agents taking their own decisions, often after great moral struggle.

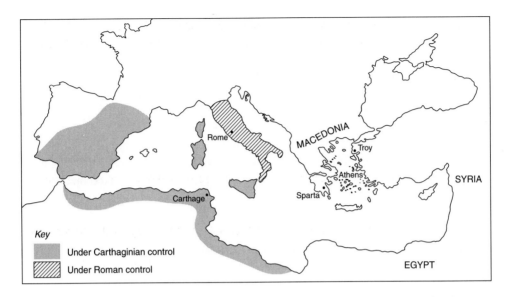

Map of the Mediterranean, c.270 BC

There is nothing supernatural or odd about Aeneas' behaviour. The encounter in Carthage is a welcome relief after the perils of his journey, and he lets himself fall into a dreamy romance. In all too human a manner, he forgets himself and then does much damage in his waking.

Aeneas calls to mind the behaviour of other mythical heroes, such as Theseus' desertion of Ariadne, and Jason's treatment of Medea. These were characters whom Virgil had known from Greek literature, and the poet would have encouraged readers to make such associations. Greece gave Roman writers a cultural heritage, which they openly acknowledged by deliberately reworking Greek ideas.

1 Livy reflects upon the significance of the war against Hannibal's Carthaginians.

> **bellum maxime omnium memorabile erat.**
>
> Livy, XXI, 1, i

bellum [nom.] *war*   **maximē** *most*
erat *was*   **omnium** [gen.] *of all*

2 Hannibal reaches the summit of the Alps.

> **nono die in iugum Alpium perventum est.**
>
> Livy, XXI, 35, iv

Alpium [gen.] *Alps*   **nōnō** [abl.] *ninth*
diē [abl.] *day*   **perventum est** *they reached*
iugum [acc.] *summit, ridge*

18

3 With hostile tribesmen and the extreme conditions causing acute difficulties, Hannibal tries to lift Carthaginian morale by pointing out the land ahead of them.

Hannibal militibus Italiam ostentat.

Livy, XXI, 35, viii–ix

mīlitibus [dat.] *soldiers*

ostentat *shows*

4 The Romans were not expecting war in Italy. Several defeats cause confusion and panic in the city.

Romae cum ingenti terrore ac tumultu concursus populi in forum est factus.

Livy, XXII, 7, vi

concursus [nom.] *rush*
cum [+abl.] *with*
est factus *was made*
ingentī [abl.] *huge, great*

populī [gen.] *people*
Rōmae *in Rome*
terrōre [abl.] *terror, fear*
tumultū [abl.] *noise*

5 After an overwhelming Carthaginian victory at Lake Trasimene, Hannibal avoids a quick assault on Rome.

hac pugna pugnata, Romam profectus est, nullo resistente; in propinquis urbis montibus moratus est.

C. Nepos, *Hannibal 5*

hāc pugnā pugnātā *after fighting this battle*
montibus [abl.] *mountains*
morātus est *(he) delayed*
nūllō resistente *with no one resisting*

profectus est *he set out*
propinquīs [abl.] *neighbouring*
Rōmam [acc.] *(to) Rome*
urbis [gen.] *city*

6 Maharbal, a Carthaginian officer, urges his general to be bolder.

vincere scis, Hannibal, victoria uti nescis.

Livy, XXII, 51, iv

nescīs *you do not know (how to)*
scīs *you know (how to)*
ūtī [with its object in the abl.] *to make use of*

victōriā [abl.] *victory*
vincere *to conquer*

7 Virgil's story of Dido and Aeneas symbolises the destinies of the two cities. For a while the gods are unable to agree whether Aeneas should stay with Dido in Carthage or move on and found Rome. They contrive a thunderstorm, which scatters a hunting party of Carthaginians and Trojans, and brings Dido and Aeneas together in a cave, alone.

speluncam Dido dux et Troianus eandem deveniunt.

Virgil, *Aeneid* IV, 165–6

dēveniunt *come*	**eandem** [acc.] *the same*
dux et Trōiānus [nom.] *and the Trojan leader*	**spēluncam** [acc.] *cave*

8 Jupiter does not wish the new city to end up on the wrong side of the Mediterranean, and sends Mercury to persuade Aeneas to leave Carthage and set out for Rome.

Ascanio-ne pater Romanas invidet arces?

Virgil, *Aeneid* IV, 234

arcēs [acc. pl.] *citadels*	**-ne** introduces a question
Ascaniō [dat.] *Ascanius* (Aeneas' son)	**pater** [nom.] *father*
invidet *begrudges*	**Rōmānās** [acc. pl.] *Roman*

9 Aeneas prepares to sail. Dido is enraged by his casual behaviour, and he tries to appease her.

Italiam non sponte sequor.

Virgil, *Aeneid* IV, 361

sequor *I follow, make for*	**sponte** *by choice*

10 He fails, and Dido sends him on his way.

i, sequere Italiam ventis, pete regna per undas.

Virgil, *Aeneid* IV, 381

ī *go!*	**sequere** *follow! chase!*
per [+acc.] *across*	**undās** [acc. pl.] *waves*
pete *seek!*	**ventīs** [abl. pl.] *winds*
rēgna [acc. pl.] *realms, land*	

11 Dido takes her own life – to the Romans, a proper and dignified end. Later in the poem Aeneas meets her spirit when he visits the underworld.

... Phoenissa recens a vulnere Dido
errabat silva in magna.

Virgil, Aeneid VI, 450–1

errābat *was wandering*	**recēns** [nom.] *fresh*
magnā [abl.] *great, large*	**silvā** [abl.] *wood*
Phoenissa ... Dīdō [nom.] *Phoenician Dido*	**vulnere** [abl.] *wound*

12 Aeneas addresses her, but she does not answer.

tandem corripuit sese atque inimica refugit.

Virgil, Aeneid VI, 472

corripuit sēsē *(she) hurried away*	**refūgit** *fled back*
inimīca [nom.] *hostile, in an unfriendly manner*	**tandem** *at last*

Vocabulary

TEXT

nōn *not*	**urbis** [gen.] *city*
quod *because*	**per** [+acc.] *through, across,*
Ītalia *Italy*	*by means of*
pater *father*	**-ne** *introduces a question*
diēs *day(s)*	

NOUNS

fīlius *son*	**Graecia** *Greece*
populus *people*	**bellum** *war*
annus *year*	**forum** *forum*
Tiberius *Tiberius*	**imperium** *power*
aqua *water*	**rēgnum** *kingdom*
fīlia *daughter*	**faenum** *hay*

VERBS

With a singular subject	With a plural subject
amat *loves, likes*	amant *love, like*
ambulat *walks*	ambulant *walk*
audit *hears*	audiunt *hear*
bibit *drinks*	bibunt *drink*
capit *takes, captures*	capiunt *take, capture*
dat *gives*	dant *give*
dīcit *says, tells*	dīcunt *say, tell*
dūcit *leads, brings*	dūcunt *lead, bring*
est *is*	sunt *are*
facit *makes, does*	faciunt *make, do*
fugat *chases*	fugant *chase*
habet *has*	habent *have*
laudat *praises*	laudant *praise*
mittit *sends*	mittunt *send*
ōrat *begs*	ōrant *beg*
venit *comes*	veniunt *come*
videt *sees*	vident *see*

Exercises

1 Identify the case of each underlined word and translate:

   (a) Iulius in <u>forum</u> venit.
   (b) filius in <u>villa</u> est.
   (c) femina cum <u>puellis</u> est.
   (d) Tiberius e <u>villa</u> ambulat.
   (e) filius <u>Augusti</u> in Italia est.
   (f) <u>vinum</u> servus bibit!

2 Identify the correct form of each verb and translate:

   (a) puella aquam equo [dat/dant].
   (b) dea poetam [audit/audiunt].
   (c) servi non vinum [bibit/bibunt].
   (d) dominus filiam [laudat/laudant].
   (e) servus taurum ad aquam [ducit/ducunt].
   (f) nautae poetam in foro [videt/vident].

3 Translate into Latin:

   e.g.   *The master leads the slaves.*
   Answer: **dominus servos ducit.**

(a) The slave sees a woman.
(b) The farmer praises his sons.
(c) The daughter hears Julius.
(d) Hannibal captures Italy.
(e) The slave begs the master.
(f) The girls love the poet.
(g) Augustus has power.

4 **Exit** and **exeunt** are used to describe action on a stage. What is the difference between the two?

5 The following words and expressions are all used today. Can you identify the cases of the underlined words?

in <u>loco</u> parentis, anno <u>domini</u>, in <u>toto</u>, <u>via</u>, ad <u>infinitum</u>, per <u>annum</u>

6 Identify Latin words in this chapter which are ancestors of:

video, suburb, transmit, rebellion, factory, bib

3 GREECE

Adjectives

Look again at the endings of **femina, servus** and **vinum** in the previous chapter, and compare the endings of the three nouns with the adjective **bonus** (*good*):

Case	Singular			Plural		
	masculine	*feminine*	*neuter*	*masculine*	*feminine*	*neuter*
nom.	**bonus**	**bona**	**bonum**	**bonī**	**bonae**	**bona**
acc.	**bonum**	**bonam**	**bonum**	**bonōs**	**bonās**	**bona**
gen.	**bonī**	**bonae**	**bonī**	**bonōrum**	**bonārum**	**bonōrum**
dat.	**bonō**	**bonae**	**bonō**	**bonīs**	**bonīs**	**bonīs**
abl.	**bonō**	**bonā**	**bonō**	**bonīs**	**bonīs**	**bonīs**

The feminine endings of **bonus** are identical to those of **femina**, the masculine to **servus**, and the neuter to **vinum**.

Adjectives have equivalent case-endings to the nouns they qualify:

e.g.   **femina <u>bona</u> servo vinum dat**
the <u>good</u> woman gives the wine to the slave

femina <u>bono</u> servo vinum dat
the woman gives the wine to the <u>good</u> slave

femina servo <u>bonum</u> vinum dat
the woman gives the <u>good</u> wine to the slave

An adjective is said to 'agree with' its noun. The adjective's ending must conform in three ways:

1   Case (nom., acc., etc.)

2 Number (singular or plural)
3 Gender (masculine, feminine or neuter)

est and sunt

1 The verb *to be* is followed by the nominative case, not the accusative:

e.g. **Iulius amicus est**   *Julius is a friend*
ignavus est Tiberius   *Tiberius is cowardly*
in foro sunt duo servi   *there are two slaves in the forum*

2 **est** and **sunt** are sometimes used with a dative to show possession:

e.g. **est Iulio taurus**   *Julius has a bull (lit. 'a bull is to Julius')*

Practice

Fill each gap with the correct form of **bonus–a–um**, and translate:

1 **vir . . . . . vinum non bibit.**

2 **puella faenum equis . . . . . dat.**

3 **servus . . . . . vinum videt.**

4 **Augustus feminas . . . . . laudat.**

Reading notes

The vocative case

There is an additional case, the 'vocative', which shows that someone is being addressed:

> **vincere scis, <u>Hannibal</u>**
> *you know how to conquer, <u>Hannibal</u>*

> **<u>o miseri</u>, quae tanta insania, <u>cives</u>?**
> *<u>O wretched citizens</u>, why such madness?*

The form is the same as the nominative, singular and plural, except for nouns like **taurus** which end **-e** in the vocative singular (or, in a few instances, **-i**):

> **tu regere imperio populos, <u>Romane</u>, memento**
> *you, <u>Roman</u>, remember to rule the nations with your power*

The vocative is by nature conspicuous, and often preceded by **o** or **meus–a–um** (*my*):

> **o mi Attice . . .**
> *O my Atticus . . .*

26

vivamus, mea Lesbia ...
let us live, my Lesbia ...

Identifying the case

For the next few chapters, the nouns and adjectives listed in the vocabularies will give all the possible cases an ending could imply, and the final choice is yours:

e.g. 'nom./acc.' means the word could be nominative or accusative.

The gender of a noun (m., f. or n.) may be added to help you identify an adjective in agreement.

The legacy of Greece

The present day owes a debt to ancient Greece, and in particular to fifth-century Athens, which was governed by the world's first democracy (**demos**: *people*, **kratos**: *power*). To Athenians, democracy meant more than turning out once in a while to vote; it meant active participation in public life and debate (our word *idiot* is derived from **idiotes**, someone who keeps to himself).

The Greeks loved a good argument. We can see this in their literature, from the dawn of their civilisation, the poems of Homer, throughout their classical period, the histories, plays, and the dialogues of Plato. This was an extraordinarily creative period, not only for literature but also for architecture and other arts. In Athens the whole community enjoyed this creativity; the whole community breathed life into it. There was nothing elitist or self-consciously alternative in their enthusiasms, no distinction between highbrow and tabloid interests. The cultural achievements of Athens in the late fifth and early fourth centuries remain unique.

At her most powerful, Athens controlled many of the smaller states in and around the Aegean Sea. Greece wasn't a single unified country, but a collection of separate city-states, of which the strongest were Athens and Sparta. These two fought a long-drawn-out war in the last few decades of the fifth century, and weakened each other enough for Philip of Macedon to subdue all the Greek cities during the following century.

The distant conquests of his son, Alexander the Great, created a new Greek-inspired culture throughout the Near East, in Egypt, and all around the eastern Mediterranean. This is known as the 'Hellenistic' culture. Works of art and literature were deliberately imitative of the classical period, and it was this Hellenistic culture that the Romans inherited. Visitors to Greece liked what they saw and read, and with no similar culture at home in Italy, eagerly made Hellenistic criteria of good taste their own.

Thus Virgil's story of Aeneas quite deliberately invited association with the *Odyssey* and the *Iliad*, the epic poems of Homer. Virgil's contemporary, the poet

Horace, could think of no better achievement than his adapting of Greek verse-forms to the requirements of Latin lyric. The modern concept of originality would have been meaningless to these Latin writers. They had a strong sense of form and a liking for Greek models, and the success of their work depended upon the use they made of what they annexed. The *Aeneid* has echoes of Greece on every page, yet remains a triumph of Italian creativity and the Latin language.

1 After the defeat of Carthage, Rome's empire-builders were tempted eastwards to Greece, which at this time was under the control of the kingdom of Macedonia.

pacem Punicam bellum Macedonicum excepit.

Livy, XXXI, 1, vi

bellum [nom./acc.] *war*
excēpit *took the place of*
Macedonicus–a–um *Macedonian*

pācem [acc.] *peace*
Pūnicus–a–um *Carthaginian*

2 After the defeat of the Macedonians, Rome was hailed as a liberator. A Roman victory over the Macedonians was reported to the Greeks at the Isthmian Games in 196 BC.

audita voce praeconis gaudium fuit.

Livy, XXXIII, 32, vi

audītā vōce *the voice having been heard*
fuit *there was*

gaudium [nom./acc.] *joy*
praecōnis [gen.] *herald*

3 Many Romans were genuinely attracted to Greek culture and lifestyle, though for some people this interest was just another exercise in public relations. Rome had to control Greece if she was to counter the eastern threat from Syria – where Hannibal had taken refuge.

Hannibal patria profugus pervenerat ad Antiochum.

Livy, XXXIV, 60, ii

Antiochum [acc.] *Antiochus* (king of Syria)
patria/patriā [nom./abl.] *country*

pervēnerat *had come*
profugus [nom.] *fugitive*

4 When the Romans first encountered Greek culture, they cast themselves as poor country cousins.

**Graecia capta ferum victorem cepit et artis
  intulit agresti Latio.**

Horace, *Epistles* II, 1, 156–7

agrestī [dat./abl.] *rustic*
artīs [acc. pl.] *arts*
cēpit *captivated*
ferus-a-um *wild*

Graecia capta [nom.] *Greece, when captured*
intulit *brought*
Latiō [dat./abl.] *Latium*
victōrem [acc.] *conqueror*

5 Some people, according to Pliny, believed that civilisation, literature, and even the cultivation of crops originated in Greece.

**in Graecia primum humanitas, litterae, etiam fruges inventae esse
creduntur.**

Pliny, *Letters* VIII, 24, 2

crēduntur *are believed*
etiam *even*
frūgēs [nom. pl./acc. pl.] *crops*
hūmānitās [nom.] *civilisation*

inventae esse *to have been discovered*
litterae [nom. pl.] *literature*
prīmum *first of all*

6 There were Romans who felt that such refinements as Greece had to offer were out of keeping with their own traditional values. These people wanted to retain a simple and uncomplicated lifestyle, and, like Cato below, complained about those who grew too fond of Greece.

**iam nimis multos audio Corinthi et Athenarum ornamenta laudantes
mirantesque.**

Livy, XXXIV, 4, iv

Athēnārum [gen.] *Athens*
audiō *I* (Cato) *hear*
Corinthī [gen.] *Corinth*
iam *now*
laudantēs [nom. pl./acc. pl.] *praising*

mīrantēs [nom. pl./acc. pl.] *admiring*
multōs (**multus–a–um**) *many (people)*
nimis *excessively*
ōrnāmenta [nom. pl./acc. pl.] *ornaments*

7 This resistance was not successful, but a hundred years later we find Cato's attitude echoed by the historian Sallust.

**at populo Romano numquam scriptorum copia fuit, quia optimus
quisque facere quam dicere malebat.**

Sallust, *Bellum Catilinae* 8, 5

at *but*

cōpia/cōpiā [nom./abl.] *abundance*

29

dīcere *to talk*
facere *to do*
fuit [+dat. to show possession] *there was*
mālēbat *preferred*
numquam *never*
optimus quisque [nom.] *all the best people*

populō [dat./abl.] *people*
quam *than*
quia *because*
Rōmānō [dat./abl.] *Roman*
scrīptōrum [gen. pl.] *writers*

---

8 Virgil recognised Greek mastery of the arts.

**excudent alii spirantia mollius aera
(credo equidem), vivos ducent de marmore vultus.**

Virgil, *Aeneid* VI, 847–8

aera [nom. pl./acc. pl.] *bronze statues*
alīī [nom. pl.] *others*
crēdō equidem *indeed I believe it*
dē [+abl.] *from*
dūcent *they will bring*

excūdent *shall hammer out*
marmore [abl.] *marble*
mollius *more delicately*
spīrantia [nom. pl./acc. pl.] *breathing*
vīvōs vultūs [acc. pl.] *living faces*

---

9 Yet Romans had qualities of their own.

**tu regere imperio populos, Romane, memento
(hae tibi erunt artes), pacique imponere morem,
parcere subiectis et debellare superbos.**

Virgil, *Aeneid* VI, 851–3

dēbellāre *to subdue*
erunt *will be*
hae artēs [nom.] *these skills, qualities*
imperiō [dat./abl.] *power, empire*
impōnere *to impose*
mementō *remember!*
mōrem [acc.] *way of life*
pācī [dat.] *peace*

parcere [+dat.] *to spare*
populōs [acc. pl.] *peoples*
regere *to rule, guide*
Rōmāne i.e. vocative singular
subiectīs [dat. pl./abl. pl.] *the conquered*
superbōs [acc. pl.] *the proud*
tibi [dat.] *to you, your*
tū [nom.] *you* (sing.)

---

10 Cicero had only praise for the culture of Greece. But he was less sure about the Greeks themselves. He once claimed that evidence given in court by Greek witnesses could not be relied upon.

**sed sunt in illo numero multi boni, docti, pudentes et etiam
impudentes, illiterati, leves. verum tamen hoc dico de toto genere
Graecorum: tribuo illis litteras, do multarum artium disciplinam.
testimoniorum religionem et fidem numquam ista natio coluit.**

Cicero, *Pro Flacco* IV, 9

artium [gen. pl.]   *arts*
coluit   *has cultivated*
dē [+abl.]   *concerning*
disciplīnam [acc.]   *knowledge*
dō   *I give, grant*
doctī (**doctus–a–um**)   *learned*
etiam   *also*
fidem [acc.]   *reliability*
Graecōrum [gen. pl.]   *Greeks*
hoc dīcō   *I make this point*
illīs [dat. pl./abl. pl.]   *them*
illō [abl.]   *that*
ista nātiō [nom.]   *that nation*
levēs [nom. pl./acc. pl.]   *frivolous*

litterās [acc. pl.]   *literature*
multārum [gen. pl.]   *much, many*
multī (**multus–a–um**)   *many (people)*
numerō [dat./abl.]   *number*
numquam   *never*
pudentēs [nom. pl./acc. pl.]   *scrupulous*
religiōnem [acc.]   *awe, sacredness*
sed   *but*
tamen   *however*
testimōniōrum [gen. pl.]   *evidence, testimony*
tōtō genere [abl.]   *whole race*
tribuō   *I concede*
vērum   *but*

11   Before Aeneas escaped from Troy, a few Greeks had entered the city concealed in the famous Wooden Horse. They opened the gates to the invading army, which then sacked the city. Virgil's story of Laocoon urging the Trojans not to trust the Greeks must have struck a contemporary note.

> **Laocoon ardens summa decurrit ab arce,**
> **et procul 'o miseri, quae tanta insania, cives?**
> **quidquid id est, timeo Danaos et dona ferentis.'**

Virgil, *Aeneid* II, 41–2; 49

ardēns [nom.]   *raging, burning*
Danaōs [acc. pl.]   *Greeks*
dēcurrit   *runs down*
dōna [nom. pl./acc. pl.]   *gifts*
et   *even*
ferentīs [acc. pl.]   *bearing*
id [nom./acc.]   *that* (i.e. the wooden horse)

īnsānia [nom.]   *madness*
ō miserī cīvēs   *o wretched citizens*
procul   *from afar*
quae tanta   *why such*
quidquid [nom./acc.]   *whatever*
summā arce [abl.]   *from the topmost citadel*
timeō   *I fear*

12   The art and literature of the Greeks were not the only examples of their creativity to influence Roman society. Professional skills outside soldiery and law were not very highly thought of, and Roman aristocrats tended to employ Greeks as their doctors, accountants, architects, artists and teachers. Actors were often Greek, and so too were singers, athletes and performers of various kinds. There was a mixture of snobbery and resentment towards Greeks, because the Romans' military and administrative power was combined with a sense of cultural inferiority; and because Greeks were displacing less gifted Italians in profitable occupations. The complaining persona adopted by the poet Juvenal, who was writing around AD 120, has something in common with an Alf Garnett or Basil Fawlty.

grammaticus, rhetor, geometres, pictor, aliptes,
augur, schoenobates, medicus, magus – omnia novit
Graeculus esuriens.

Juvenal, Satire III, 76–78

alīptēs [nom.] *masseur*
augur [nom.] *soothsayer*
ēsuriēns [nom.] *hungry*
geometrēs [nom.] *surveyor*
Graeculus *little Greek*
grammaticus [nom.] *teacher*

magus [nom.] *sorcerer*
medicus [nom.] *doctor*
omnia nōvit *is a proper know-all*
pictor [nom.] *painter*
rhētor [nom.] *professor*
schoenobatēs [nom.] *tightrope artist*

13 Juvenal is not impressed by Greek acting skills.

natio comoeda est. rides, maiore cachinno
concutitur; flet, si lacrimas conspexit amici,
nec dolet . . ./. . . si dixeris 'aestuo', sudat.

Juvenal, Satire III, 100–102; 103

aestuō *I am hot*
amīcī [gen./nom. pl.] *friends*
cōmoedus–a–um *given to acting*
concutitur *he is shaken*
cōnspexit *he has seen*
dīxeris *you say*
dolet *he grieves*
flet *he weeps*

lacrimās [acc. pl.] *tears*
māiōre cachinnō [abl.] *louder laughter*
nātiō [nom.] *country* (i.e. Greece)
nec *and . . . not*
rīdēs *you smile*
sī *if*
sūdat *he sweats*

Vocabulary

TEXT

pācem [nom.: **pāx**] *peace*
patria *country*
dōnum *gift*
cīvēs *citizens*
amīcī *friends*
fuit *was*
erunt *will be*
timeō *I fear*
cēpit *captured, took*
dē [+abl.] *from, about*

tū *you* (singular)
tibi *to you* (singular)
id *that*
alīī *some, others*
sed *but*
etiam *also, even*
numquam *never*
nec *and not*
quam *than*
sī *if*

ADJECTIVES

bonus–a–um   *good*

malus–a–um   *bad*

magnus–a–um   *great, large*

parvus–a–um   *small*

multus–a–um   *much, many*

avārus–a–um   *greedy*

fōrmōsus–a–um   *beautiful*

ignāvus–a–um   *cowardly*

laetus–a–um   *happy*

grātus–a–um   *pleasing*

pius–a–um   *dutiful*

īrātus–a–um   *angry*

Exercises

1   Identify the case, gender and number of each underlined word and translate:

(a)   **vinum gratum est.**

(b)   **poeta feminam formosam videt.**

(c)   **servus filium ignavum domini non amat.**

(d)   **agricola cum servis ambulat.**

(e)   **multi viri in villa sunt.**

2   Change the underlined words into the plural (you may need to alter other words too). Translate the new version into English:

(a)   **femina donum filio dat.**

(b)   **nauta laetus amicum videt.**

(c)   **puella equum habet.**

(d)   **vir aquam cum servo bibit.**

(e)   **taurus in villam agricolam fugat.**

(f)   **Augustus filium pium audit.**

3   Translate into Latin:

(a)   Marcus is a dutiful son.

(b)   Julia hears the pleasing poet.

(c)   Many slaves are walking in the forum.

(d)   Augustus has many gifts (say: many gifts are to Augustus).

(e)   Masters do not praise cowardly slaves.

(f)   The farmer does not chase an angry bull.

4   **Optimum** and **maximum** were once Latin adjectives in the neuter singular. How would you account for the endings of **errata**, **media** and **et cetera**?

5   From which famous conqueror of the east is the name *Sikhander* derived?

6   Identify derivatives of **magnus, multus** and **avarus**.

33

4 CICERO

Verbs: subjects and pronouns

The commonest verb-endings are **-t** (singular subject) and **-nt** (plural subject). The subject may be a noun, or the subject may be implied in the verb, which we would translate with a pronoun:

e.g. **Marcus taurum videt**   *Marcus sees the bull*
     taurum videt   *he sees the bull*

Verbs also have endings for the subject pronouns *I, you* and *we*:

	1st person	*I*	–o, –m, –i
Singular	2nd person	*you* (singular)	–s, –isti
	3rd person	*he, she, it*	–t
	1st person	*we*	–mus
Plural	2nd person	*you* (plural)	–tis
	3rd person	*they*	–nt

A verb's ending helps you identify the subject. It may also indicate the verb's tense:

The tenses

Present	*I see, I am seeing*
Future	*I shall see, I am going to see*
Imperfect	*I saw (frequently/continuously), I was seeing*
Perfect	*I saw (momentarily/briefly), I have seen*
Future Perfect	*I shall have seen*
Pluperfect	*I had seen*

The verb-ending also indicates the kind of action being described:

e.g.   *I see you*   (ordinary action)
        I may see you   (potential action)

and whether the verb is active or passive:

e.g.   *I see you*   (active)
        I am seen by you   (passive)

Personal pronouns and adjectives

Pronouns are used in place of nouns (the Latin word **pro** means *in place of*). A personal pronoun is sometimes included as a subject, even though it may already be implied in the verb's ending. This use of a pronoun is for greater emphasis:

e.g.   **Ciceronem vidisti**   *You have seen Cicero*
        tu Ciceronem vidisti   <u>*You*</u> *have seen Cicero*

Case	I/me	you (s.)	we/us	you (pl.)
nom.	**ego**	**tū**	**nōs**	**vōs**
acc.	**mē**	**tē**	**nōs**	**vōs**
gen.	**meī**	**tuī**	**nostrum**	**vestrum**
dat.	**mihi**	**tibi**	**nōbīs**	**vōbīs**
abl.	**mē**	**tē**	**nōbīs**	**vōbīs**

The Latin words for *he, she, they, him, her,* and *them* will be seen later.

The possessive adjectives (*my, your,* etc.) have the same endings as **bonus–a–um** (see p. 149):

meus, mea, meum	*my*
tuus, tua, tuum	*your* (one person)
noster*, nostra, nostrum	*our*
vester*, vestra, vestrum	*your* (more than one)

*The nominative masculine singular ends **-er**, otherwise the endings are the same as **meus** and **tuus**.

esse *to be*

esse *to be*	present	future	imperfect	perfect
I	sum	erō	eram	fuī
you (s.)	es	eris	erās	fuistī
he, she, it	est	erit	erat	fuit
we	sumus	erimus	erāmus	fuimus
you (pl.)	estis	eritis	erātis	fuistis
they	sunt	erunt	erant	fuērunt

See p. 25 for notes on uses of **esse**.

Practice

Add one of the following to each speech-bubble: **meum, te, vos, nostrum**

36

Reading notes

Sometimes the English prepositions we normally associate with Latin cases are not idiomatic in a translation:

e.g. **pecuniae cupido**
pecuniae [genitive: '*of money*'] **cupido** [nominative: '*desire*'] becomes 'a desire _for_ money' – though we might say 'a love _of_ money'.

novarum rerum studium
novarum rerum is genitive, though we would say 'an eagerness _for_ political innovations'.

The fall of the republic

In the second and first centuries BC, Rome added Sicily, Spain, North Africa, Greece, Asia Minor, Gaul and Egypt to her empire. Former consuls were appointed provincial governors, and the character of Rome changed from dominant city-state to the capital of the known world.

This growth of power played a part in the downfall of the republic. Political leadership by a pair of consuls whose term of office lasted only a year – and much of that spent in competition with each other for military distinction – was a system better suited to conquering new territories than looking after existing ones. Success in battle brought more prestige than prudent administration, the results of which might not be enjoyed until a consul was long out of office. So the provinces began to suffer from inconsistent and short-lived directives from Rome.

Another problem was the increase in wealth. The copious flow of goods and luxuries imported from the new territories distracted Roman noblemen from their cherished virtues of austerity and simplicity, and the era that later generations considered one of the greatest in history, the classical period, filled some writers of the time with distaste. They wrote longingly of the old days of manly virtues and self-sufficiency, and despised the decadent consumerism of their day.

This nostalgic longing for a golden past became something of a literary convention, and it is no doubt naïve to suppose that previous generations of Romans had been incorruptible. We know much less about the earlier period. But in the first century BC the evidence certainly points to widespread corruption. Bribery was not only rife, it was acceptable; political intrigue and double-dealing were a matter of course. Such were the stakes in the political struggles of the world's fastest-growing power. And much of its new wealth was in the hands of traders, to whom the conservative senate was slow to concede power. This created a political tension that was not going to disappear by being ignored.

The senate soon lost control over its armies, which were posted on the fringes of the empire at great distances from the capital and were led by powerful and ambitious generals. Throughout the first century BC, there were a number of civil wars: Sulla against Marius, Pompey against Caesar, and Antony against Octavian. From the last conflict, Octavian (later 'Augustus') emerged as the **princeps** of the Roman empire, and the transfer of authority from the senate to one man marked the beginning of imperial rule.

1 Pessimism and nostalgia were widespread during the first century BC.

primo magis ambitio quam avaritia animos hominum exercebat.

Sallust, *Bellum Catilinae* 11, 1

primo pecuniae, deinde imperii, cupido crevit. avaritia fidem, probitatem, ceterasque artes bonas subvortit.

Sallust, *Bellum Catilinae* 10, 3–4

nec vitia nostra nec remedia pati possumus.

Livy, *Praefatio*, ix

ambitiō [nom.] *ambition*
animōs [acc. pl.] *minds*
artēs [nom. pl./acc. pl.] *arts, qualities*
avāritia/avāritiā [nom./abl.] *greed*
bonās (bonus-a-um) *good*
cēterās (cēterus-a-um) *other*
crēvit *grew*
cupīdō [nom.] *desire*
deinde *then, next*
exercēbat *exercised*
fidem [acc.] *trust*
hominum [gen. pl.] *men*

imperiī [gen.] *power*
magis *rather*
nec ... nec *neither ... nor*
patī *to suffer*
pecūniae [gen./dat.] *money*
possumus *we are able*
prīmō *at first*
probitātem [acc.] *honesty*
quam *than*
remedia [nom. pl./acc. pl.] *cures*
subvortit *ruined*
vitia [nom. pl./acc. pl.] *vices, defects*

2 For the poet Catullus, there was no time like the present.

vivamus, mea Lesbia, atque amemus,
rumoresque senum severiorum
omnes unius aestimemus assis!

Catullus, 5, 1–3

aestimēmus *let us value*
amēmus *let us love*
atque *and*
Lesbia *i.e. his girlfriend*
omnēs [nom. pl./acc.pl.] *all*

rūmōrēs [nom. pl./acc. pl.] *gossip*
senum [gen. pl.] *old men*
sevēriōrum [gen. pl.] *austere, strict*
ūnius ... assis *at one penny*
vīvāmus *let us live*

3 In 65 BC, Cicero stood for the consulship. Not an aristocrat, his claims rested on his reputation as an outstanding orator. When Catiline, the candidate for the other consulship, faced charges of misgovernment, Cicero thought he should help him.

> **hoc tempore Catilinam, competitorem nostrum, defendere cogitamus. iudices habemus quos voluimus, summa accusatoris voluntate.**

> Cicero, *Ad Atticum* I, 2

accūsātōris [gen.] *prosecutor*
Catilīnam [acc.] *Catiline*
cōgitāmus *we are contemplating*
competītōrem [acc.] *fellow candidate*
dēfendere *to defend*
habēmus *we have*

hōc tempore [abl.] *this time*
iūdicēs [nom. pl./acc. pl.] *judges*
quōs [acc.] *whom*
summā voluntāte [abl.] *the utmost good will*
voluimus *we wanted*

4 In fact Cicero did not take the brief. Catiline failed in his attempt to become consul, and so attempted to take power by less legitimate means. He exploited the political tension arising from the sudden growth of a wealthy middle class and the impoverishment of certain aristocrats. He offered to cancel all debts, which won him support from those in difficulties.

> **cuncta plebes, novarum rerum studio, Catilinae incepta probabat.**

> Sallust, *Bellum Catilinae* 37, 1

cūncta (cūnctus-a-um) *all, whole*
incepta [nom. pl./acc. pl.] *initiative*
novārum rērum [gen.] *political innovations*

plēbēs [nom.] *ordinary people*
probābat *approved of*
studiō [dat./abl.] *eagerness*

5 Catiline's initiatives gained some momentum. Cicero, who had been elected consul, stood in his way.

> **neque interea quietus erat, sed omnibus modis insidias parabat Ciceroni.**

> Sallust, *Bellum Catilinae* 26, 1

Cicerōnī [dat.] *Cicero*
erat *he was*
īnsidiās [acc.] *ambush*
intereā *meanwhile*

modīs [dat. pl./abl. pl.] *ways, methods*
neque *and not*
omnibus [dat. pl./abl. pl.] *all, every*
parābat *he prepared*

6 Cicero believed in the republic's system of government by the senate; but not all the senators themselves were well disposed towards him. He was a **novus homo**

(a 'new man' was the first member of his family to hold the consulship), while Catiline, an aristocrat, enjoyed good relations with a number of leading men. Catiline and his supporters were confident enough to attend meetings of the senate, but soon found Cicero's eloquence a powerful enemy.

> **o tempora, o mores! senatus haec intellegit, consul videt: hic tamen vivit. vivit? immo vero etiam in senatum venit.**

Cicero, *In Catilinam* I, 1

etiam *even*	**ō tempora** *what times!*
haec [nom./acc.] *these things*	**senātus/senātūs** [nom./gen.] *senate*
hic *this man*	**tamen** *still*
immō vērō *why*	**venit** *he comes*
intellegit *understands*	**videt** *sees*
ō mōrēs *what moral standards!*	**vīvit** *lives*

7 He identifies Catiline's cronies.

> **hic, hic sunt in nostro numero, patres conscripti.**

Cicero, *In Catilinam* I, 4

hīc *here*	**patrēs cōnscrīptī** [voc.] *senators*
numerō [dat./abl.] *number, midst*	

8 Cicero rounded on Catiline.

> **quotiens me consulem interficere conatus es!**

Cicero, *In Catilinam* I, 6

cōnātus es *you have tried*	**interficere** *to kill*
cōnsulem [acc.] *consul*	**quotiēns** *how many times*

9 Catiline withdrew from Rome to gather provincial support. Cicero imprisoned and executed five of his agents left in Rome. Catiline's rebellion was crushed in Italy. Cicero then sought to justify his peremptory treatment of the five conspirators.

> **ego vitam omnium civium, quinque hominum amentium ac perditorum poena, redemi.**

Cicero, *Pro Sulla* XI, 33

āmentium [gen. pl.] *crazed*	**omnium cīvium** [gen. pl.] *all the citizens*
hominum [gen. pl.] *men*	**perditōrum** [gen. pl.] *desperate*

poena/poenā [nom./abl.] *punishment*
quīnque *five*

redēmī *I have saved*
vītam [acc.] *life*

10 Cicero sensed that the survival of the republic would need the support of the influential Pompey, a respected general. Although Pompey appreciated his interest, and recognised the usefulness of his eloquence, the general had ties and obligations to other individuals, like Julius Caesar. He remained lukewarm about Cicero's success against Catiline, and Cicero did not hide his resentment of this.

aliquam in tuis litteris gratulationem exspectavi.

Cicero, *Ad Familiares* V, 7, 3

aliquam [acc.] *some*
exspectāvī *I expected*

grātulātiōnem [acc.] *thanks*
litterīs [dat./abl.] *letter*

11 Pompey may have wished he himself had been asked to resolve the Catilinarian crisis, although more to the point is the offence he might have caused elsewhere by publicly praising Cicero's success. At any event Cicero soon made an enemy of another aristocrat, Publius Clodius, a friend and protégé of Julius Caesar. Clodius had caused a scandal by disguising himself as a woman and participating in the women's festival of Bona Dea, held at his patron's house. In the subsequent court case, Clodius was acquitted after bribing the jurors, but not before Cicero destroyed his alibi. Resentment ran deep, and though Pompey tried to reassure Cicero that Clodius would not seek revenge, Cicero remained doubtful.

Clodius inimicus nobis. Pompeius confirmat eum nihil esse facturum contra me. mihi periculosum est credere, ad resistendum me paro.

Cicero, *Ad Atticum* II, 21, 6

ad resistendum *for resistance*
cōnfirmat *assures*
contrā [+acc.] *against*
crēdere [+dat.] *to believe*
eum ... esse factūrum *that he will do*

inimīcus–a–um *hostile*
mē parō *I am preparing myself*
nihil *nothing*
perīculōsus–a–um *dangerous*

12 Pompey misled Cicero.

Pompeius de Clodio iubet nos esse sine cura.

Cicero, *Ad Atticum* II, 24, 5 [Oct. 59 BC]

cūra/cūrā [nom./abl.] *care, anxiety*
dē [+abl.] *concerning*
esse *to be*

iubet *orders*
sine [+abl.] *without*

13   Clodius was elected tribune, and in 58 BC took his revenge. With Cicero's executions of the Catilinarians in mind, he introduced a law banishing those who put citizens to death without a trial. Cicero sought help from Pompey and other friends and colleagues, but none was forthcoming. Under considerable threats and duress from Clodius, he left Rome, and in exile revealed his despair to his friend, Atticus.

> **utinam illum diem videam, cum tibi agam gratias quod me vivere coegisti!**
>
> Cicero, *Ad Atticum* III, 3 [April 58 BC]

agam grātiās [+dat.] *I might give thanks*	**quod** *because*
coegistī *you compelled*	**utinam** *if only*
cum *when*	**videam** *I might see*
illum diem [acc.] *that day*	**vīvere** *to live*

14   On his return, Cicero renewed his enmity towards the Clodii. In court he diverted the attention of judges from a client's crime to the involvement of the infamous Clodia (sister of Clodius and probably 'Lesbia' in Catullus' poems).

> **res est omnis in hac causa nobis, iudices, cum Clodia, muliere non solum nobili verum etiam nota.**
>
> Cicero, *Pro Caelio* 13

est . . . cum [+abl.] *rests with, depends on*	**nōn sōlum . . . vērum etiam** *not only . . .*
hāc causā [abl.] *this case*	*but also*
iūdicēs *gentlemen of the jury*	**nōtus-a-um** *well–known, notorious*
muliere [abl.] *woman*	**omnis** [nom./gen.] *whole*
nōbilī [dat./abl.] *noble, well-born*	**rēs** [nom.] *matter*

15   Caesar tried to elicit Cicero's support. He was a shrewd political tactician as well as a good general, and he recognised the value of Cicero's talent and contacts. He also appeared to have some genuine affection for Cicero (and had become a friend of Cicero's brother). Here Caesar writes to Cicero.

> **in primis a te peto ut te videam.**
>
> Cicero, *Ad Atticum* IX, 6A

in prīmīs *first of all*	**ut** *that, so that*
petō *I seek*	**videam** *I may see*

16   During Caesar's dictatorship, Cicero withdrew from public life and concentrated on his studies and writing. Hundreds of his letters have survived, some with public consumption in mind, others more intimate. He confided in Atticus his joy at the murder of Caesar, but confesses it was short-lived when Antony emerged from the dictator's shadow.

> **o mi Attice, vereor ne nobis Idus Martiae nihil dederint praeter laetitiam.**

Cicero, *Ad Atticum* XIV, 12

dederint *have given*	**nihil** *nothing*
Īdūs Mārtiae [nom.] *Ides of March*	**ō mī Attice** *my dear Atticus*
laetitiam [acc.] *joy*	**praeter** [+acc.] *except*
nē *that*	**vereor** *I fear*

17 Cicero tried to keep on good terms with Antony, as he made clear to his personal secretary, Tiro, in 44 BC.

> **ego tamen Antoni amicitiam retinere sane volo, scribamque ad eum, sed non antequam te videro.**

Cicero, *Ad Familiares* XVI, 23, 2

amīcitiam [acc.] *friendship*	**sānē** *certainly*
antequam *before*	**scrībam** *I shall write*
Antōnī [gen.] *Antony*	**tamen** *however*
eum *him*	**vīderō** *I see*
retinēre *to keep*	**volō** *I want*

18 There were some obstacles to cooperation with Antony. In the first place Antony had been adopted by one of the conspirators Cicero had executed some twenty years before. More significant for Cicero was Antony's marriage to Fulvia, formerly the wife of Clodius. In August 44 BC, Cicero delivered the first of his speeches against Antony (*The Philippics*). To begin with, his tone was critical but conciliatory, and ever hopeful of a return to the republic. When Antony showed his contempt, Cicero produced another speech, with all the vigour of old.

> **defendi rem publicam adulescens, non deseram senex; contempsi Catilinae gladios, non pertimescam tuos.**

Cicero, *Phil.* II, 46

adulēscēns [nom.] *a young man*	**gladiōs** [acc. pl.] *swords*
contempsī *I scorned*	**pertimēscam** *I shall fear*
dēfendī *I defended*	**rem pūblicam** [acc.] *republic*
dēseram *I shall abandon*	**senex** [nom.] *old man*

19 Caesar's heir (by adoption), Octavian, though still in his teens, became the focus of Cicero's efforts to restore the constitution. The following words are taken from Cicero's letter to Trebonius, who was killed by Antony's men before he had a chance to read it (43 BC).

> **puer egregius est Caesar.**
>
> Cicero, *Ad Familiares* X, 28, 3

ēgregius–a–um *outstanding*   **puer** [nom.] *boy*

20 Brutus, one of Caesar's assassins, did not share Cicero's enthusiam for Octavian, and he made his reservations clear to Cicero's friend, Atticus, in 43 BC.

> **licet ergo patrem appellet Octavius Ciceronem, referat omnia, laudet, gratias agat, tamen illud apparebit, verba rebus esse contraria.**
>
> Cicero, *Ad Brutum* I, 17, 5

apparēbit *will be apparent*   **licet** *although*
appellet *may call*   **patrem** [acc.] *father*
ergō *so, therefore*   **rēbus** [dat. pl./abl. pl.] *actions*
grātiās agat *may give thanks*   **referat** *may refer*
illud *that*   **tamen** *however*
laudet *may praise*   **verba ... esse** *that his words are*

21 Brutus was right. Octavian agreed terms with Antony and divided the world between them. Antony went east to Egypt while Octavian remained in Rome. To gain this strategic advantage, Octavian was forced to make concessions, one of which was Cicero. He died at the hands of Roman troops while half-heartedly attempting flight to Greece. His head and hands (which had written *The Philippics*) are said to have been nailed up in the forum, and Fulvia to have stuck a hairpin through his tongue. The following was written some sixty years later.

> **omnis posteritas Ciceronis in te** (i.e. Antony) **scripta mirabitur, tuum in eum factum exsecrabitur; citiusque e mundo genus hominum quam Cicero cedet.**
>
> Velleius Paterculus II, 66

cēdet *will fade away*   **in** *into, against*
Cicerōnis [gen.] *Cicero*   **mīrābitur** *will admire*
citius *more quickly*   **mundō** [dat./abl.] *world*
eum [acc.] *him*   **omnis** [nom.] *all*
exsecrābitur *will curse*   **posteritās** [nom.] *posterity*
factum [nom./acc.] *deed*   **quam** *than*
genus [nom./acc.] *race*   **scrīpta** [nom. pl./acc. pl.] *writings*

Vocabulary

TEXT

prīmō *at first*

hic *this (man)*

hīc *here*

tamen *however*

ergō *so, therefore*

puer *boy*

vīta *life*

sine [+abl.] *without*

intereā *meanwhile*

NOUNS AND ADJECTIVES

cēna *dinner*

fortūna *fortune*

culīna *kitchen*

magister *master, teacher*

saevus–a–um *cruel*

acerbus–a–um *bitter*

ager *field*

vir *man, husband*

hortus *garden*

fātum *fate*

prīmus–a–um *first*

superbus–a–um *proud*

NUMBERS 1–10

ūnus *one*

duo *two*

trēs *three*

quattuor *four*

quīnque *five*

sex *six*

septem *seven*

octō *eight*

novem *nine*

decem *ten*

PREPOSITIONS

inter [+acc.] *among*

post [+acc.] *after*

contrā [+acc.] *against*

ante [+acc.] *before*

Exercises

1   If the underlined words were translated into Latin, what would be
their tense?

*Every morning during his tutorial the emperor would lie on the couch
and <u>throw</u> fruit at the philosopher. The philosopher <u>stood</u> still and was
not troubled by the emperor's poor aim.*

*One day the door suddenly <u>opened</u> and the emperor's mother swept
into the room, only to intercept a rather soft peach. With remarkable
dignity the matron of Rome wiped the battered fruit from her neck,
removed her cloak and gave it to a slave.*

'I was trying to put it in the bucket,' stammered the young autocrat.
'Are you going to give me your attention for a moment?' said his
mother, ignoring his apologies.

2   Identify the case of each underlined word and translate:

(a)   **princeps primus erat Augustus.**
(b)   **pater mihi erat Iulius.**
(c)   **nos servi Augusto grati sumus.**
(d)   **poeta non me sed feminam formosam amat.**
(e)   **amicus patriae est Augustus.**
(f)   **Cleopatra tuum vinum bibit.**

3   Translate into Latin:

(a)   Our teacher does not see you (*singular*).
(b)   Friends (**o** *with the vocative – see p. 26*), the woman is not
      drinking our water, but your wine.
(c)   You (*pl.*) are greedy, and we are angry.
(d)   Julia, your son is chasing us.
(e)   I will not have proud slaves (*use* **erunt** *with the dative*).

4   Cicero spent much of his leisure reading Greek literature and philos-
    ophy. His own philosophical writings did not contribute many new
    ideas but were more a synthesis of Greek ones, adapted to a Roman
    outlook on life. By his reworking of Greek ideas, Cicero made Latin a
    vehicle for philosophical discussion, and many of the abstract words
    he used have since passed into English with slight changes of form
    and meaning:

    e.g. **libertas, humanitas, constantia, moderatio**

    Find similar Latin words in this chapter from which you can identify
    English descendants.

5   What do **ante meridiem, post meridiem, inter alia** and **curriculum
    vitae** mean?

6   *September* is now the ninth month of the year. What were *September,
    October, November* and *December* when they were first introduced?

5 AUGUSTUS

Verbs

There are four main types (for all the endings see pp. 150–158):

1   Verbs like **paro, parare** (e.g. **am<u>a</u>t, ambul<u>a</u>nt, par<u>a</u>mus**).
2   Verbs like **moneo, monere** (e.g. **hab<u>e</u>mus, vid<u>e</u>nt, mon<u>e</u>t**).
3   Verbs like **mitto, mittere** (e.g. **bib<u>i</u>t, mitt<u>u</u>nt**).
4   Verbs like **audio, audire** (e.g. **aud<u>i</u>t, ven<u>iu</u>nt**).

Principal parts

A dictionary shows four key parts of a verb, which are called principal parts. These are formed from the first person of the present tense (**paro**, I prepare), the infinitive (**parare**, to prepare), the first person of the perfect tense (**paravi**, I prepared), and the supine, or the neuter form of the past participle (**paratum**, having been prepared):

Present	**parō**	**moneō**	**mittō**	**audiō**
Infinitive	**parāre**	**monēre**	**mittere**	**audīre**
Perfect	**parāvī**	**monuī**	**mīsī**	**audīvī**
Supine	**parātum**	**monitum**	**missum**	**audītum**

If a verb has principal parts like **paro–are**, then it belongs to the first group (or conjugation), if like **moneo–ere** to the second, if like **mitto–ere** to the third, and if like **audio–ire** to the fourth.

Practice A

With the help of the table on p. 150, translate:

(a) **paramus**   (e) **audivit**
(b) **mittemus**   (f) **monuisti**
(c) **monetis**   (g) **parabatis**
(d) **mittit**   (h) **audietis**

Nouns

The following nouns belong to the same group as **servus**, with the same endings outside the nominative case:

Case	Singular		
	boy	*man, husband*	*master, teacher*
nom.	puer	vir	magister
acc.	puerum	virum	magistrum
gen.	puerī	virī	magistrī
dat.	puerō	virō	magistrō
abl.	puerō	virō	magistrō

Case	Plural		
	boy	*man, husband*	*master, teacher*
nom.	puerī	virī	magistrī
acc.	puerōs	virōs	magistrōs
gen.	puerōrum	virōrum	magistrōrum
dat.	puerīs	virīs	magistrīs
abl.	puerīs	virīs	magistrīs

Practice B

Identify the correct form of each verb and translate:

1   **pueri magistrum non**
    . . . .
    [audio–ire: imperfect**].**

2 **vir servum in amphitheatrum**
    . . . . [mitto–ere:
    perfect**].**

3   **domina irata dominum**
    . . . . [mitto–ere:
    future**].**

4 servus Neronem

. . . .

[moneo–ere: future**].**

Reading notes

To translate a Latin adjective (or participle – see p. 103) you may need more than the equivalent English adjective:

> **cuncta discordiis civilibus fessa**
> *all things exhausted by civil strife* (i.e. *all things that were exhausted . . .*)

> **dictaturam mihi delatam**
> *the dictatorship offered to me* (i.e. *the dictatorship that had been . . .*)

> **cohortes decimatas pavit**
> *he fed the decimated cohorts* (i.e. *he decimated the cohorts and fed them . . .*)

Augustus

Antony and Octavian were joined by Lepidus in a triangle of power, a triumvirate. As happened to the earlier triumvirate of Pompey, Caesar and Crassus, this became increasingly less secure, until 31 BC when the issue was resolved in Octavian's favour at the sea battle of Actium off southern Greece. A few years later, Octavian took the title 'Augustus'.

Augustus turned out to be a shrewd politician and an imaginative administrator. At the moment of Antony's defeat, and after decades of internal conflict, few would have anticipated the forty-four years of his political supremacy. He had the gift of political timing, and made the most of his luck. As the Romans might have put it, he was favoured by the goddess Fortuna. According to Suetonius (whose tempting stories leave a little to be substantiated), Augustus was able to predict the outcome of a naval engagement from the behaviour of a small fish. Implausible as it may seem, such sign-reading was an integral part of religious belief.

His successes no doubt had more to do with strategy than with the spasms of a fish, but this was too prosaic an explanation for historians like Suetonius, whose myths, at least, we can tell at a glance. Decades of civil war, often brutal, had brought the people of Italy to such a state of fear and insecurity that anyone with the authority to bring peace and law would be welcomed, regardless of the consequences to the constitution of the republic.

But Augustus was careful to maintain the constitution, in appearance at least. If the senate lost authority to the **princeps**, it still retained the functions, privileges and facade of government. He avoided the image of king or dictator, preferring to be seen as the first citizen, **primus inter pares**. The senators may have resented the new role of the **princeps**, but others welcomed it. Augustus developed a much-needed administrative system for the empire, and employed people from different backgrounds to manage it. Moreover, he made Italians feel part of Rome and didn't neglect the interests of the distant provinces.

A statesman as well as a politician, Augustus sensed that his own political fate was wrapped up in the destiny of Rome: he secured his position by being seen as the bringer of peace, security and optimism. He realised that a new age needed to draw upon the strengths of the past. Traditional practices that had become almost obsolete were reintroduced: stricter discipline was restored to the army; forgotten rituals were observed, temples were repaired and new ones built. The morality of family life was revitalised: there were incentives for having children, and penalties for divorce; adoption was discouraged; children could not be abandoned (at least not before they were three years old). The once-fashionable depraved excesses of the aristocracy were severely censured – a message that apparently failed to reach his own daughter, Julia.

He offered support to writers and poets, especially if they had something to say about his revival of Rome. He wasn't so unsubtle as to insist on obsequiousness, but expected them to share his vision and enthusiasm. Virgil, Horace and Livy were among those who thrived under his patronage.

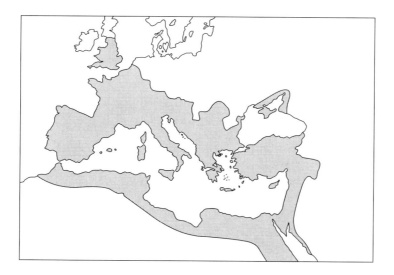

The Roman Empire at its greatest extent (second century AD)

51

1 Augustus emerged as **princeps** after the failure of the triumvirate.

> **Lepidi atque Antonii arma in Augustum cesserunt, qui cuncta discordiis civilibus fessa nomine principis sub imperium accepit.**
>
> Tacitus, *Annals* I, 1

accēpit (accipiō–ere) *he received*
Antōnīī [gen.] *Antony*
arma [nom. pl./acc. pl.] *weapons (armed forces)*
cessērunt in ... (cēdō–ere) *passed into the hands of ...*
cūncta ... fessa [nom./acc.] *everything exhausted*

discordīīs cīvīlibus [dat.pl./abl.pl.] *civil strife*
Lepidī [gen.] *Lepidus*
nōmine [abl.] *name*
prīncipis [gen.] *'princeps'*
quī [nom.] *who*
sub imperium *into his control*

2 He avoided obvious symbols of power.

> **dictaturam mihi delatam et a populo et a senatu non recepi.**
>
> Augustus, *Res Gestae* 5

dēlātus–a–um *offered*
dictātūram [acc.] *dictatorship*

et ... et *both ... and*
recēpī (recipiō–ere) *I accepted*

3 He punished his opponents.

> **qui parentem meum trucidaverunt, eos in exilium expuli.**
>
> Augustus, *Res Gestae* 2

eōs [acc.] *them, those men*
expulī (expellō–ere) *I banished*

quī [nom.] *who*
trucīdāvērunt (trucīdō–āre) *murdered*

4 According to Suetonius, Augustus was savagely vindictive.

> **scribunt quidam trecentos ad aram Divo Iulio extructam Idibus Martiis hostiarum more mactatos.**
>
> Suetonius, *Augustus* 15

āram [acc.] *altar*
dīvō (dīvus–a–um) *divine*
extructus–a–um *constructed*
hostiārum [gen. pl.] *sacrificial victims*
Iūliō [dat./abl.] *(in honour of) Julius*

mactātōs *were slaughtered*
mōre [abl.] *manner, custom*
quīdam [nom.] *some (people)*
scrībunt (scrībō–ere) *they write*
trecentōs [acc.] *three hundred men*

5   He renewed former traditions, religious, social and moral.

> **multa exempla maiorum reduxi.**
>
> Augustus, Res Gestae 8

māiōrum [gen. pl.]   *ancestors*   **redūxī (redūcō–ere)**   *I brought back*

6   Temples were rebuilt.

> **aedes sacras vetustate conlapsas aut incendio absumptas refecit,**
> **easque et ceteras opulentissimis donis adornavit.**
>
> Suetonius, Augustus 30

absūmptus–a–um   *consumed*   **eās et cēterās** [acc.]   *these and the rest*
adōrnāvit (adōrnō–āre)   *decorated*   **incendiō** [dat./abl.]   *fire*
aedēs [nom. pl./acc. pl.]   *shrines*   **opulentissimus–a–um**   *most lavish*
aut   *or*   **refēcit**   *he restored*
dōnīs [dat. pl./abl. pl.]   *gifts*   **vetustāte** [abl.]   *age*

7   The new era is to be celebrated.

> **nunc est bibendum, nunc pede libero**
> **pulsanda tellus.**
>
> Horace, Odes I, XXXVII, 1–2

līber–a–um   *free, unfettered*   **pede** [abl.]   *foot*
nunc est bibendum   *now there is to be*   **tellūs pulsanda**   *the earth is to be beaten*
  drinking   *(danced upon)*

8   Augustus was anxious to restore the numbers, self-respect and morality of his own social class. Suetonius suggests he was not the perfect model ...

> **adulteria quidem exercuisse ne amici quidem negant.**
>
> Suetonius, Augustus 69

adulteria [nom. pl./acc. pl.]   *acts of adultery*   **nē ... quidem**   *not even*
amīcī [gen./nom. pl.]   *friends*   **negant (negō–āre)**   *deny*
exercuisse   *that he practised*   **quidem**   emphasises the preceding word

9   ... but leaders allegedly need some licence.

> **consilia adversariorum per cuiusque mulieres exquirebat.**
>
> Suetonius, Augustus 69

ESSENTIAL LATIN

adversāriōrum [gen. pl.] *opponents*
cōnsilia [nom. pl./acc. pl.] *plans*
cūiusque [gen.] *each person*

exquīrēbat (exquīrō–ere) *he discovered*
mulierēs [nom. pl./acc. pl.] *women, wives*

10 Augustus worked hard himself . . .

ipse ius dixit assidue et in noctem nonnumquam.

Suetonius, *Augustus* 33

assiduē *assiduously*
dīxit *he administered*
ipse *he himself*

iūs [nom./acc.] *justice*
noctem [acc.] *night*
nōnnumquam *sometimes*

11 . . . and expected similar standards from others.

cohortes, si quae loco cessissent, decimatas hordeo pavit.

Suetonius, *Augustus* 24

cessissent (cēdō–ere) *had withdrawn*
 (in battle)
cohortēs [nom. pl./acc. pl., f.] *troops*
decimātus–a–um [agrees with **cohortēs**]
 decimated

hordeō [dat./abl.] *barley*
locō [dat./abl.] *place, position*
pāvit (pāscō–ere) *he fed*
quae *any*
sī *if*

12 He reorganised the administration of the empire.

exiit edictum a Caesare Augusto, ut describeretur universus orbis.

St Luke, *New Testament* 2, 1 (Trans. Jerome)

dēscrīberētur *should be registered*
ēdictum [nom./acc.] *decree*
exiit (exeō–īre) *went out*

ūniversus orbis *the whole world*
ut *that*

13 People outside the senatorial body, and even former slaves, were given opportunities within the new administration. But corruption and abuse of power by new 'civil servants' was discouraged:

Augustus, quod Thallus pro epistula prodita denarios quingentos accepisset, crura ei fregit.

Suetonius, *Augustus* 67

accēpisset (accipiō–ere) *he had received*
crūra [nom. pl./acc. pl.] *legs*
dēnāriōs [acc.] *denarii*

eī [dat.] *him* (dative of possession)
epistula/epistulā [nom./abl.] *letter*
frēgit *(he) broke*

54

prō [+abl.] *in return for*
prōditus–a–um *disclosed, 'leaked'*

quīngentōs [acc.] *five hundred*
quod *because*

---

14 Augustus was not fond of comedians.

Hylan pantomimum in atrio domus suae flagellis verberavit.

Suetonius, *Augustus* 45

ātriō [dat./abl.] *hall*
domus/domūs [nom./gen.] *house, home*
flagellīs [dat. pl./abl. pl.] *whips*
Hylan [acc.] *Hylas*

pantomīmum [acc.] *pantomime artist*
suae [gen./dat.] *his own*
verberāvit (verberō–āre) *he beat*

---

15 But he was kinder to poets. They in turn were grateful for his support, and welcomed the widespread relief after decades of civil war. Anchises prophesies the rule of Augustus to his son Aeneas.

hic vir, hic est, tibi quem promitti saepius audis,
Augustus Caesar, divi genus, aurea condet
saecula.

Virgil, *Aeneid* VI, 791–3

audīs (audiō–īre) *you hear*
Augustus Caesar [nom.] *Augustus Caesar*
aurea saecula [nom./acc.] *golden age*
condet (condō–ere) *(who) will found*

dīvī genus *offspring of a god*
prōmittī *being promised*
quem [acc.] *whom*
saepius *quite often*

---

16 Augustus may have wanted to be identified, in part at least, with Virgil's Aeneas; but other characters are also suggested by the poem's hero. Mark Antony's bid for sole power came from the east – where Aeneas' wanderings had started – and it was Antony who fell for that other African queen, whose famously manipulative and seductive charms the mythical Dido must have echoed, Cleopatra.

arma virumque cano, Troiae qui primus ab oris
Italiam fato profugus Lavinaque venit
litora.

Virgil, *Aeneid* I, 1–3

arma [nom. pl./acc.pl.] *weapons*
canō (canō–ere) *I sing of*
fātō [dat./abl.] *fate*
Lāvīnus–a–um *Latin*

lītora [nom. pl./acc. pl.] *shore*
ōrīs [dat. pl./abl. pl.] *lands, shore*
virum [acc.] *man*

17 In AD 8, the poet Ovid was banished by Augustus for participating (it seems) in some kind of conspiracy. But the publication of the *Ars Amatoria* some years earlier was also held against him. The princeps was in no mood to tolerate witty erotic poetry only a few months after his own daughter, Julia, had been banished for licentious behaviour. Now in exile, Ovid wistfully recalls the final moments before his exile.

> **iam prope lux aderat, qua me discedere Caesar**
> **finibus extremae iusserat Ausoniae.**

Ovid, Tristia I, 3, 5–6

aderat (adsum–esse) *was present*
Ausoniae [gen./dat.] *Ausonia* (i.e. Italy)
discēdere (discēdō–ere) *to depart*
fīnibus [dat. pl./abl. pl.] *limit, boundary*
iam *now, already*

iusserat (iubeō–ēre) *had ordered*
lūx [nom.] *day*
prope *almost*
quā [abl.] *which*

18 Cicero is said to have had a dream in which the young Octavian appeared as the future ruler of Rome.

> **M. Cicero somnium pristinae noctis familiaribus forte narrabat: puer**
> **facie liberali demissus e caelo catena aurea ad fores Capitoli**
> **constitit eique Iuppiter flagellum tradidit; deinde repente Augusto**
> **viso, affirmavit ipsum esse.**

Suetonius, Augustus 94

affirmāvit (affirmō–āre) *he declared*
Augustō vīsō *on seeing Augustus*
aureus–a–um *golden*
Capitōlī [gen.] *the Capitol* (temple)
catēna/catēnā [nom./abl.] *chain*
cōnstitit (cōnsistō–ere) *he stood*
deinde *then*
dēmissus (est) *was sent down*
eī [dat.] *him*
faciē [abl.] *face*

familiāribus [dat. pl./abl. pl.] *friends*
forēs [nom. pl./acc. pl.] *door*
forte *by chance*
ipsum esse *him to be the one*
līberālī [dat./abl.] *noble*
narrābat (narrō–āre) *was recounting*
prīstinus–a–um *previous*
repente *suddenly*
somnium–ī *dream*
trādidit (trādō–ere) *he handed over*

Vocabulary

TEXT

quidem *indeed*
iam *now, already*
nunc *now*
vel *or*
aut *or*
eōs *them*
quī *who*

cōnsilium *plan, advice*
epistula *letter*
gladius *sword*
lūdus *game*
nē *so that not, lest*
senātus *senate*
ut *so that, as*

VERBS

	Present	Infinitive	Perfect	Supine
prepare	parō	parāre	parāvī	parātum
chase	fugō	fugāre	fugāvī	fugātum
love	amō	amāre	amāvī	amātum
beg	ōrō	ōrāre	ōrāvī	ōrātum
watch	spectō	spectāre	spectāvī	spectātum
give	dō	dare	dedī	datum
sail	nāvigō	nāvigāre	nāvigāvī	nāvigātum
blame	culpō	culpāre	culpāvī	culpātum
praise	laudō	laudāre	laudāvī	laudātum
warn	moneō	monēre	monuī	monitum
see	videō	vidēre	vīdī	vīsum
fear	timeō	timēre	timuī	–
have	habeō	habēre	habuī	habitum
teach	doceō	docēre	docuī	doctum
hold	teneō	tenēre	tenuī	tentum
sit	sedeō	sedēre	sēdī	sessum
send	mittō	mittere	mīsī	missum
seek	petō	petere	petīvī	petītum
lead	dūcō	dūcere	dūxī	ductum
say	dīcō	dīcere	dīxī	dictum
rule	regō	regere	rēxī	rēctum
write	scrībō	scrībere	scrīpsī	scrīptum
drink	bibō	bibere	bibī	–
hear	audiō	audīre	audīvī	audītum
come	veniō	venīre	vēnī	ventum

Exercises

1   Change the underlined words into the plural (you may need to alter other words too), and translate your answer:

   (a)   <u>agricola</u> taurum vidit.
   (b)   <u>donum</u> est puellae.
   (c)   saeva <u>mihi</u> est fortuna.
   (d)   Augustum–ne <u>tu</u> audivisti?
   (e)   <u>filiam</u> Augusti laudabam.
   (f)   <u>magister</u> in forum pueros ducet.

2   Change the tense of each verb as directed, and translate your answer:

   (a)   servus in culina <u>sedet</u> (FUTURE).
   (b)   pueri in amphitheatro ludos <u>spectant</u> (IMPERFECT).
   (c)   Augustus nobis in foro <u>dicit</u> (FUTURE).
   (d)   femina puellas in horto <u>videt</u> (PERFECT).
   (e)   agricolae consilium Augusti <u>audiunt</u> (PERFECT).
   (f)   non Iuliae gratus <u>est</u> poeta (IMPERFECT).

3   Translate the underlined words into Latin:

   (a)   The Romans often <u>watched</u> the games in the amphitheatre.
   (b)   Antony <u>will lead</u> his forces against Rome.
   (c)   Iulius <u>has written</u> a letter.
   (d)   Aristotle <u>used to teach</u> Alexander the Great.
   (e)   The emperor <u>will warn</u> us all.
   (f)   The farmer <u>would come</u> to see us every day.

4   Translate into Latin:

   (a)   We heard the woman's advice.
   (b)   Augustus came to the amphitheatre.
   (c)   The master is greedy, the slaves are lazy.
   (d)   The gods will not drink bitter wine.
   (e)   The farmer works in the field, the woman works in the garden, but the slave drinks wine in the kitchen.

5   What is a *perambulator* usually called?

6   What does *culture* mean when it forms part of *agriculture* and *horticulture*?

7   What do *culinary* and *puerile* mean?

8   Identify English derivatives from the <u>supine</u> forms of some of the verbs listed in the vocabulary section of this chapter (e.g. 'oration' – **oratum**, 'spectator' – **spectatum**).

9   What is the original meaning of *decimated*, and how is it used today?

6 THE FAMILY

Nouns

Look back at the passages and their vocabulary lists, and identify the following:

1 Nouns like **femina** in the accusative singular, in the genitive or dative singular, in the ablative singular, in the nominative plural, and in the accusative plural.

2 Nouns like **servus** or **vinum** in the accusative singular, the genitive singular, and the dative or ablative singular.

3 Nouns like **servus** in the nominative plural, and in the accusative plural.

4 Any five nouns in the genitive plural.

5 Any five nouns in the dative or ablative plural.

6 Neuter nouns like **vinum** in the nominative or accusative plural.

Nouns like **femina** belong to the first group (or *declension*), **servus** and **vinum** belong to the second declension. There are five declensions in all. You have already met many nouns from the third and fourth declensions, and a few from the fifth:

Singular	*3rd declension*	*4th declension*	*5th declension*
nom.	various	**-us** (n. **-ū**)	**-ēs**
acc.	**-em** (n. **-us**)	**-um** (n. **-ū**)	**-em**
gen.	**-is**	**-ūs**	**-eī/-ēī**
dat.	**-ī**	**-uī (-ū)**	**-eī/-ēī**
abl.	**-e (-ī)**	**-ū**	**-ē**

Plural			
nom.	-ēs (n. -a)	-ūs (n. -ua)	-ēs
acc.	-ēs/-īs (n. -a)	-ūs (n. -ua)	-ēs
gen.	-um	-uum	-ērum
dat.	-ibus	-ibus	-ēbus
abl.	-ibus	-ibus	-ēbus

For the all the declensions, see pp. 146–147. On pp. 159–163 there is a summary of the different uses of the cases, followed on p. 164 with an index of endings: this index gives all possible functions an ending can imply.

Note that nouns are identified by two of their cases: the nominative and genitive.

e.g. **servus–i, femina–ae, vinum–i,**
pater–tris, civis–is, dux–cis, tempus–oris,
gradus–us, manus-us, res, rei.

The nominative and genitive together tell you which declension a noun belongs to. From that information you can identify other endings.

Practice A

To which declensions do these nouns belong?

(a) **opus–eris** (*work*)　　　　(c) **mater–tris** (*mother*)
(b) **exercitus–us** (*army*)　　　(d) **dies, diei** (*day*)

Practice B

Give the genitive singular form of each underlined word:

(a) **in loco parentis**　　　　(c) **ante meridiem**
(b) **o tempora, o mores!**　　(d) **per annum**

Practice C

With help from the nominative and genitive forms shown in brackets, identify the correct endings:

1 **equus est in villa . . . . .** [pater, patris]**.**

2 **dux . . . . .** [civis, civis] **ad agros mittit.**

3 **puella donum in . . . . .** [manus, manus] **pueri vidit.**

4 **cives . . . . .** [dux, ducis] **non timent**

Family ties

The grim practice of abandoning unwanted children happened frequently enough for rulers to legislate against it. In some cases the parents were just too poor to afford the cost of bringing up a child. For others, the socialites and the ambitious, children were an extra burden they could do without. If the rudimentary methods of contraception (always female) failed to work, the next step was to induce a miscarriage, sometimes with serious consequences. When that failed, the final rejection by parents of their children was to abandon them. Girls suffered more frequently than boys, who could later earn an income and wouldn't cost parents a dowry. It is no wonder that so many ancient plays used the plot of the abandoned child who is rescued and brought up by others, then sold or otherwise separated from his adoptive parents, and eventually recognised as being free-born. For the ancient audience there was nothing remote or quaint about this kind of comedy of errors.

If the pleasures of family life were lost on some Romans, the instinct for wanting an heir remained. Adoption was the convenient alternative, and was frequently practised. Augustus himself was adopted by his great-uncle, Julius Caesar, and he later adopted Tiberius to secure the succession. This meant that some degree of choice was exercised in the preferment of imperial power, although such decisions were not always taken with the interests of the state primarily in mind.

Like adoption, divorce and remarriage were commonplace. Children would remain with their father, and in some cases never saw their mother again. By the time Cicero's daughter Tullia was in her early thirties, she was separated from her third husband. This was an unfortunate but not unusual marital statistic from the latter half of the first century BC. When Augustus came to power, he identified the reinforcement of the family unit as a remedy for society's ills. Abandonment of children, divorce and adoption were all discouraged, particularly among the senatorial class, whose numbers had dwindled in the civil wars.

The **paterfamilias** (father of the family) was the formal head of the household, while the **matrona** would supervise day-to-day activities and often the education of the children. A father even had the right to execute his offspring, though this was seldom exercised. He was also entitled to sell them into slavery, which in extreme cases he might do to avoid his (and their) starvation. A mother had less legal authority over her young, and a widow had to depend on her children for support.

Family in the sense of all the relatives, like a Scottish *clan*, was **gens**. The **familia** included not only the immediate family but the entire household, including the slaves. From early republican days, Roman society encouraged social patronage: a man would have a patron, **patronus**, for whom he would vote, run errands, and perform all kinds of services, depending on the patron's social position. In return a dependant, **cliens**, could expect legal and financial support and various other favours. In the period of the empire, many clients were former slaves.

Romans much admired the quality of **pietas**, which was the sense of duty to family, country and gods. **Pietas** included good will and support between patron and client. Today's mafia hoodlum may not have *piety* in the Christian sense, but he does have **pietas**. The word **patronus** has much in common with *patron*, and perhaps even more with the Italian *padrone* (*godfather*). The idea of *family* in Sicily and New York has its roots in the **familia** of ancient Rome.

1   In Terence's play *The Lady from Andros*, a man finds his long-lost daughter.

> **propero ad filiam. illam me credo haud nosse.**
>
> Terence, *The Lady from Andros* 951–2

crēdō–ere *believe*	**illam . . . nōsse** *that she knows*
haud *not*	**properō–āre** *hurry*

2   Nero was adopted by his stepfather, the emperor Claudius.

> **Nero undecimo aetatis anno a Claudio adoptatus est.**
>
> Suetonius, *Nero* 7, 1

aetās, aetātis *age, life*	**ūndecimus–a–um** *eleventh*

3   Agricola's mother discouraged her son from reading too much philosophy.

> **Agricola prima in iuventa studium philosophiae acrius, ultra quam concessum Romano ac senatori, hausisset, ni prudentia matris incensum ac flagrantem animum coercuisset.**
>
> Tacitus, *Agricola* 4

ācrius *too/more keenly*	**iuventa–ae** [f.] *youth*
animus–ī [m.] *spirit, temperament*	**nī** *if not*
coercuisset *had restrained*	**philosophia–ae** *philosophy*
concessum *(was) conceded*	**prūdentia–ae** *good sense*
flagrantem [acc.] *burning*	**senātor–ōris** *senator*
hausisset *he would have plunged into*	**studium–ī** *pursuit, study*
incēnsus–a–um *inflamed*	**ultrā quam** *more than*

4   The theme of family versus state was popular with historians, for they could point to moral paradigms and focus upon personal suffering: Brutus, the legendary creator of the republic, executed his sons for plotting to bring back the king (see Chapter 1, no. 8). The conflict of loyalty in the case of Coriolanus was also between family and state, but here the state was not Rome. Coriolanus had sided with the enemy, and members of his own family were Rome's final defence:

> **Veturia, mater Coriolani, et Volumnia, duos parvos ferens filios, in castra hostium ibant. ubi ad castra ventum est, nuntiatumque Coriolano est adesse ingens mulierum agmen, primum multo obstinatior adversus lacrimas muliebres erat. dein familiarium quidam inter ceteras cognoverat Veturiam: 'nisi me frustrantur,' inquit, 'oculi, mater tibi coniunxque et liberi adsunt.'**

Livy II, 40

adesse (adsum–esse) *that … was present*	**inquit** *he said*
adversus [+acc.] *against*	**inter** [+acc.] *among*
agmen–inis *crowd*	**lacrima–ae** *tear*
castra–orum *camp*	**līberī–ōrum** *children*
cēterus–a–um *other*	**muliebrēs** [acc. pl., f.] *female*
cognōverat *had recognised*	**mulier–is** *woman*
coniūnx–gis *spouse*	**multō obstinātior** *much more stubborn*
dein *then*	**nisi** *unless*
duōs [acc.] *two*	**nūntiātum est** *it was announced*
familiāris–is *attendant*	**oculus–ī** *eye*
ferēns *carrying*	**parvus–a–um** *small*
frūstrantur *deceive*	**prīmum** *at first*
hostēs–ium *enemy*	**quīdam** [nom.] *one*
ībant (eō, īre) *they were going*	**ubī** *when*
ingēns *huge*	**ventum est** *they came* (lit.: *it was come*)

5 Horace reminds his contemporaries of the bravery of Regulus, who was captured by the Carthaginians during the Punic wars and sent home to negotiate a ransom for his fellow-prisoners. In spite of pleas from his family and friends, he urged the senate to reject all terms, and returned to his captors:

> **atqui sciebat quae sibi barbarus**
> **tortor pararet. non aliter tamen**
>   **dimovit obstantes propinquos**
>   **et populum reditus morantem,**
>
> **quam si clientum longa negotia**
> **diiudicata lite relinqueret,**
>   **tendens Venafranos in agros**
>   **aut Lacedaemonium Tarentum.**

Horace, Odes III, 5, 49–56

atquī *and yet*
cliēns–tis *client*
dīiūdicātā līte *a case having been decided*
dīmōvit (dīmoveō–ēre) *he removed*
Lacedaemonius–a–um *Lacedaemonian*
  (Spartan)
morantem [acc.] *delaying*
negōtium–ī *affair, business*
non aliter . . . quam *in just the same way . . . as*
obstantēs *blocking his path*
parāret (parō–āre) *was preparing*

propinquus–ī *relative*
reditūs [acc. pl.] **(reditus-ūs)** *return*
relinqueret *he were leaving*
sciēbat (sciō–īre) *he (Regulus) knew*
sī *if*
sibi *for him*
Tarentum–ī *Tarentum* (in southern Italy)
tendēns *hastening*
tortor–ōris *torturer*
Venāfrānus–a–um *Venafran* (suburb of
  Rome)

6 After the death of Cicero's daughter (45 BC), Servius Sulpicius wrote to him and criticised his personal grief at a time of political oppression (Caesar's dictatorship).

> **quid te commovet tuus dolor intestinus? ea nobis erepta sunt, quae hominibus non minus quam liberi cara esse debent, patria, honestas, dignitas, honores omnes. at vero malum est liberos amittere. malum; nisi peius est, haec sufferre et perpeti.**

> Cicero, *Ad Familiares* IV, 5, ii, iii

āmittō–ere *lose*
at vērō *but indeed*
cārus–a–um *dear*
commovet (commoveō–ēre) *disturbs*
dēbent (dēbeō–ēre) *ought*
dignitās–tātis *prestige*
dolor–ōris *grief*
ea *those things*
ērepta sunt *have been snatched*
haec *these things*
homō–inis *man*
honestās–tātis *reputation*
honor–ōris *public honour*

intestīnus–a–um *private*
līberī–ōrum *children*
malus–a–um *bad*
minus *less*
nisi *except*
nōbīs *from us*
patria–ae *country*
pēius *worse*
perpetī *to endure*
quae [nom. pl.] *which*
quid *why*
sufferre *to suffer*

7 In imperial times it was not the theme of family and state, but the struggles within the same (imperial) family which interested the historians. Tacitus recounted Nero's poisoning of Britannicus (AD 55), Claudius' natural son:

> **ita venenum cunctos eius artus pervasit, ut vox pariter et spiritus raperentur. facinori plerique hominum ignoscebant, antiquas fratrum discordias et insociabile regnum aestimantes.**

> Tacitus, *Annals* XIII, 16, 17

aestimantēs *putting it down to*
artus–ūs [m.] *limb*
cūnctus–a–um *all*
ēius *his*

facinus–oris *crime*
frāter–tris *brother*
ignōscēbant [+dat.]
(īgnōscō–ere) *they forgave*

65

īnsociābile *impossible to be shared*
ita ... ut *in such a way ... that*
pariter *at the same time*
pervāsit (pervādō–ere) *pervaded*
plērīque hominum *most people*

raperentur (rapiō–ere) *were taken*
rēgnum–ī *kingdom*
spīritus–ūs *breath*
venēnum–ī *poison*
vōx–cis *voice*

8 Virgil idealises the role of the mother.

> (mater) cinerem et sopitos suscitat ignis
> noctem addens operi, famulasque ad lumina longo
> exercet penso, castum ut servare cubile
> coniugis et possit parvos educere natos.

> Virgil, *Aeneid* VIII, 410–13

addēns *adding*
castus–a–um *chaste*
cinis–eris *ash*
coniūnx–gis *husband*
cubīle–is [n.] *couch, bed*
ēdūcō–ere *bring up*
exerceō–ēre *put to work*
famula–ae *maidservant*
ignīs [acc. pl.] *flames*
longus–a–um *long*

lūmen-inis *light*
nātus–ī *son*
nox–ctis *night*
opus–eris *work, working hours*
parvus–a–um *small*
pēnsum–ī *weight (of wool)*
servō–āre *keep*
sōpītus–a–um *sleeping*
suscitō–āre *revive*
ut ... possit *so that she can*

9 Pliny advises a father not to be too strict with his son.

> castigabat quidam filium suum, quod paulo sumptuosius equos et
> canes emeret. huic ego, iuvene digresso, 'heus tu, numquamne
> fecisti quod a patre corripi posset? "fecisti", dico? non interdum
> facis, quod filius tuus, si repente pater ille, tu filius, pari gravitate
> reprehendat?'

> Pliny, *Letters* IX, 12

castigō–āre *punish*
corripī posset *could be blamed*
dīcō–ere *say*
emeret *he was buying*
facis (faciō–ere) *you do*
fēcistī (faciō–ere) *you have done*
gravitās–tātis *sternness*
heus *hey!*
huic *to this man*
ille *he*
interdum *sometimes*

iuvene dīgressō *after the boy departed*
numquam *never* (**-ne** introduces a question)
parī [abl.] *equal*
paulō *a little*
quīdam [nom.] *some fellow*
quod *because/(that) which*
repente *suddenly*
reprehendat *he would scold*
sūmptuōsius *too extravagantly*
suum *his*
tuus–a–um *your*

10   The poet Martial complains that his casual manner in the presence of his patron, Caecilianus, has cost him a few coins.

> **mane salutavi vero te nomine casu**
> **nec dixi dominum, Caeciliane, meum.**
> **quanti libertas constet mihi tanta, requiris?**
> **centum quadrantes abstulit illa mihi.**

Martial, Epigrams VI, 88

abstulit (auferō–erre) *has taken away*
cāsū *by chance*
centum *hundred*
dīxī (dīcō–ere) *I said*
dominus–ī *master, boss, sir*
illa [nom.] *that*
lībertās–tātis *licence*
māne *this morning*

mihi [dat.] *me* (see p. 161)
nōmen–inis *name*
quadrantēs *coins*
quantī . . . cōnstet *how much . . . costs*
requīris (requīrō–ere) *you want to know*
salūtāvī (salūtō–āre) *I greeted*
tantus–a–um *such, so great*
vērus–a–um *real*

11   Clients could be fickle.

> **nemo te ipsum sequitur, sed aliquid ex te. amicitia olim petebatur,**
> **nunc praeda; mutabunt testamenta destituti senes, migrabit ad aliud**
> **limen salutator.**

Seneca, Epistulae Morales 19, 4

aliquid *some advantage*
aliud [nom./acc., n.] *other*
dēstitūtus–a–um *lonely*
līmen–inis [n.] *door, threshold*
migrō–āre *move*
mūtō–āre–āvī–ātum *to change*
nēmō *no one*
nunc *now*

ōlim *once, previously*
petēbātur (petō–ere) *was sought*
praeda–ae *loot, plunder*
salūtātor–ōris *visitor*
senex–is *old man*
sequitur *follows*
tē ipsum *you yourself*
testāmentum–ī *will*

Vocabulary

TEXT

postquam *after*
ēius *his, her*
quia *because*
ubī *where, when*
nisi, nī *unless, if not, except*
vērō *but, indeed*

vērum *but, however*
vērus–a–um *real, true*
nōnne *surely*
quod *because, which*
quīdam *a certain (person)*
igitur *therefore*
inter [+acc.] *among*

NOUNS

anima–ae *soul, breath*
animus–ī *spirit, courage*
oculus–ī *eye*
castra–ōrum *camp*
nōmen–inis *name*
homō–inis *man*
canis–is *dog*
māter–tris *mother*
soror–ōris *sister*
frāter–tris *brother*
senātor–ōris *senator*
gladiātor–ōris *gladiator*

mīles–itis *soldier*
hostēs–ium *enemy*
dux–cis *leader*
facinus–oris *crime*
corpus–oris *body*
mūnus–eris *gift*
exercitus–ūs *army*
gemitus–ūs *groan*
senātus–ūs *senate*
rēs, reī *thing*
diēs, diēī *day*
rēs pūblica* *republic*

*Note that **pūblica** is an adjective agreeing with **rēs**.

Exercises

1   Choose the correct word for each gap, identify its case, and translate:

canes, matrem, ducem, hostium, gemitu

(a) **servi . . . . . fugant.**
(b) **cives . . . . . laudabant.**
(c) **pater . . . . . culpat.**
(d) **gladiator ducem . . . . . audiebat.**
(e) **dux . . . . . ad Africam navigabat.**

2   Identify the case of each underlined word and translate:

(a) **<u>milites</u> ex castris pueros fugabant.**
(b) **magna erant servi <u>facinora</u>.**
(c) **servus <u>munus</u> Ciceronis vidit.**
(d) **Marcus <u>gemitus</u> hostium audiebat.**

(e) **sorores** Iulii in Gallia habitant.

3 Translate into Latin:

(a) The boys walk with the father.
(b) We saw the bodies of the gladiators.
(c) The dogs were watching Marcus' dinner.
(d) The brothers will send a letter to the senate.
(e) Great are the gifts of the gods.
(f) You senators used to love the republic!

4 What is the connection between:

pendulum, pending, pensive and *pension*?

7 SOCIETY

Verbs: active and passive

Most of the verbs you have seen so far have been active:

e.g. **agricola taurum fugat**   *the farmer chases the bull*

When the verb is passive, the object of the active verb becomes the subject:

e.g. **taurus ab agricola fugatur**   *the bull is chased by the farmer*

There is no significant change in meaning, but just in emphasis.

	Active	Passive
3rd person singular (*he, she, it*)	**-t**	**-tur**
3rd person plural (*they*)	**-nt**	**-ntur**

Note how the subject of the active verb (above: **agricola**) has changed in the passive expression to the ablative: **ab agricola** *by the farmer*.

Practice A

Make each verb passive, and change any other words to keep the sense; then translate:

e.g. **agricola taurum in horto videt**
taurus ab agricola in horto videtur
the bull is seen in the garden by the farmer

1   **mater pueros monet.**

2 **Augustus canem in villam fugat.**
3 **femina gladiatores laudat.**
4 **cives senatorem audiunt.**

Perfect passive

This is formed from the past participle with **est** (plural: **sunt**):

e.g. **agricola a tauro <u>fugatus est</u>**
the farmer <u>was chased</u> by the bull

The past participle is formed from the supine, with endings identical to **bonus–a–um**. It agrees with its subject noun:

e.g. (above) **agricol<u>a</u> ... fugat<u>us</u>**   (masculine, singular)

Practice B

Add the correct form of the past participle to complete each sentence, and translate:

e.g. **cena a puellis ..... est.**   [paro–are, paravi, paratum]
      cena a puellis <u>parata</u> est.
      The dinner was prepared by the girls.

1 **hostes a Caesare ..... sunt.**   [vinco–ere, vici, victum]
2 **puer a Seneca ..... est.**   [doceo–ere, docui, doctum]
3 **epistula a matre ..... est.**   [mitto–ere, misi, missum]
4 **vinum Britannico a servo ..... est.** [do–are, dedi, datum]

Past participles

Past participles without **est** or **sunt** agree with their nouns as adjectives do, and are <u>passive</u>:

e.g. **serv<u>us</u> a femina vis<u>us</u> e villa venit**
the slave, having been seen by the woman, came out of the villa

senator muner<u>a</u> fratri dat<u>a</u> vidit
the senator saw the gifts which had been given to his brother

Practice C

Complete the endings of the participles and translate:

e.g. **captivi in amphitheatrum . . . . . a gladiatoribus caesi sunt.
[duco–ere, duxi, ductum]
captivi in amphitheatrum <u>ducti</u> a gladiatoribus caesi sunt**
*The prisoners were brought into the amphitheatre and were killed by
the gladiators.*

1 **puellae in agros . . . . . matrem non viderunt.
[mitto–ere, misi, missum]**

2 **taurus militem in agro . . . . . fugavit.
[video–ere, vidi, visum]**

3 **magister puero . . . . . munus dedit.
[laudo–are, laudavi, laudatum]**

Occupations and status

The very poor at least had the freedom to sell themselves into slavery to reduce
their debt. Not all those who remained free had voting rights, but only those who
were citizens, a status not granted to all provincials until the later years of the
empire. This was a cause of discontent, since provincials fought in campaigns, risking
their lives and the loss of property in their absence.

There were three classes of citizens: plebeians, equestrians (knights) and
senators. The vast majority of people were plebeians. Equestrians had to have
400,000 sesterces to qualify, a sum which excluded all but the richest of citizens (an
equestrian was originally defined as one who could afford his own horse while
serving in an army). Senatorial families were limited to aristocratic **gentes** (clans)
like the Claudii or Iulii. During the early republican period almost all political
power lay in the hands of the senators. They performed duties as magistrates, judges,
diplomats, military officers and priests. Senators weren't paid for their services, nor
did they need to be. Although they held the notion of commerce somewhat in
contempt, most of them had business agents who managed their investments in
construction, farming and other profitable enterprises.

The equestrians (knights) grew in power along with the growth of trading opportunities around the expanding empire. They made up the 'middle class', but were
few in number and vastly richer than the average plebeian. In the early republic,
plebeians had struggled with patricians (senators) for political rights, and had gained
some concessions, including their own council and officers.

These social divisions were formal, and defined by privileges such as preferential
seats at a theatre. There was some mobility from one grade to another, although
few plebeian businessmen would have amassed the wealth required to join the

equestrians. Some talented equestrians broke through into public and senatorial life: Cicero's equestrian family had been involved in local politics in his home town of Arpinum.

Slavery was the usual destination for prisoners of war, criminals, debtors, and the offspring of slaves. If you were fortunate, you belonged to someone who wanted to protect his investment and enjoy your loyalty or even affection. If you weren't so lucky you might end up working on a large estate or in a mine where life-expectancy was cheerlessly short.

Another class of person emerged from the process of enslavement: **libertini** (freedmen). From slavery to liberty was the greatest social leap of all, and the talent and ingenuity of freedmen would often earn them the envy and contempt of other citizens. Some achieved positions of considerable importance: Nero's freedmen, Pallas and Narcissus, were highly influential, and they benefited from the distrust between emperor and senate.

1   In the early days of the republic, leading men owned and farmed their own land.

> **in agris erant tum senatores.**
>
> Cicero, *De Senectute* XVI, 56

2   Cato (second century BC) was asked what he believed to be the best occupation.

> **'bene pascere'; quid secundum: 'satis bene pascere'; quid tertium: 'male pascere'; quid quartum: 'arare'; et cum ille, qui quaesierat, dixisset: 'quid faenerari?', tum Cato: 'quid hominem,' inquit, 'occidere?'**
>
> Cicero, *De Officiis* II, 25, 89

arō–āre *plough*	**quaesierat (quaerō–ere)** *had asked*
bene *well*	**quārtus–a–um** *fourth*
cum … tum *when … then*	**quid faenerārī** *what of moneylending*
dīxisset (dīcō–ere) *had said*	**quid occīdere** *what about murdering*
homō–inis *person*	**satis** *enough*
male *badly*	**tertius–a–um** *third*
pāscō–ere *raise livestock*	

3   Roman poets inherited the pastoral tradition from the Greeks, and so farming was perceived to be not only respectable but also a pleasure.

> **beatus ille qui procul negotiis,**
> **ut prisca gens mortalium,**
> **paterna rura bobus exercet suis**
> **solutus omni faenore;**

libet iacere modo sub antiqua ilice,
modo in tenaci gramine.

Horace, *Epodes* II, 1–4, 23–24

beātus–a–um *happy*
bōbus [abl. pl. of bōs, bovis] *ox*
faenus–oris *interest payment*
gēns–tis [f.] *race*
grāmen–inis *grass*
iaceō–ēre *lie*
īlex–icis *oak-tree*
libet *it is pleasing*
modo *now*
mortālis–is *mortal*

negōtium–ī *business*
omnī [dat./abl.] *all*
paternus–a–um *ancestral*
prīscus–a–um *ancient*
procul [+abl.] *far from*
rūra exerceō–ēre *work the land*
solūtus–a–um *released*
tenācī [dat./abl.] *clinging*
ut *as*

4 This fantasy of rural life appealed most to city-dwellers, who had little experi-
ence of farming's hardships. Varro had practical advice for serious farmers.

neque enim senes neque pueri callium difficultatem ac montium
arduitatem atque asperitatem facile ferunt.

Varro, *Rerum Rusticarum* II, 10, 3

arduitās–tātis *steepness*
asperitās–tātis *unevenness*
callis–is *footpath*
difficultās–tātis *difficulty*
enim *for*

facile *easily*
ferunt *bear, endure*
mōns–tis *mountain*
neque ... neque *neither ... nor*
senex–is *old man*

5 Making money from commerce was despised by the aristocracy – unless you
did so on a large scale.

mercatura autem, si tenuis est, sordida putanda est; sin magna et
copiosa, non est vituperanda. omnium autem rerum ex quibus
aliquid acquiritur, nihil est agri cultura melius, nihil uberius, nihil
dulcius, nihil homine libero dignius.

Cicero, *De Officiis* I, 42, 151

acquīritur *is acquired*
ager, agrī *field*
aliquid *something*
cōpiōsus–a–um *abundant*
cultūra–ae *tilling*
dignius* [+abl.] *more worthy*
dulcius* *sweeter*
ex quibus *from which*
melius *better*

mercātūra–ae *business, profit*
omnium [gen. pl.] *all*
putandus–a–um *to be reckoned*
rēs, reī *thing*
sīn *but if*
tenuis [nom.] *insignificant*
ūberius* *more fruitful*
vituperandus–a–um *to be disparaged*

(*) Look for an ablative for the point of the comparison (**agrī cultūrā**: *than agriculture*).

6 There were many slaves in ancient Rome. Some belonged to the state, but the majority were owned by private citizens. The infrequency of rebellion suggests that the kind of treatment described below did not happen very often.

> **hic frangit ferulas, rubet ille flagello,**
> **hic scutica.**
>
> > Juvenal, *Satire* VI, 479–480

ferula–ae *cane*	**hic ... ille** [nom.] *this (slave) ... that (slave)*
flagellum–ī *whip*	**rubeō–ēre** *be red*
frangō–ere *cause to break*	**scutica–ae** *strap*

7 Vedius Pollio, a friend of Augustus, was especially cruel.

> **invenit in hoc animali documenta saevitiae Vedius Pollio eques**
> **Romanus vivariis earum immergens damnata mancipia.**
>
> > Pliny the Elder, *Natural History* IX, 39

in hōc animālī *in this animal* (lamprey)	**immergēns** [nom.] *plunging*
damnātus–a–um *condemned*	**inveniō–īre–vēnī–ventum** *find*
documentum–ī *example, demonstration*	**mancipium–ī** *slave*
eārum [gen.] *them* (the lampreys)	**saevitia–ae** *cruelty*
eques–itis *knight*	**vīvārium–ī** *pond, aquarium*

8 Some domestic slaves were given their freedom. A **libertus**, however, would often stay with the **familia**. If he were talented, loyal, and important to the household, such a 'release' might amount to no more than acknowledgement of his role or a sign of affection. Cicero was fond of his secretary, Tiro, and Pliny showed his concern for the health of his **libertus**, Zosimus.

> **nihil aeque amorem incitat et accendit quam carendi metus.**
>
> > Pliny, *Letters* V, 19

accendō–ere *stimulate*	**incitō–āre** *arouse*
aeque *as much, equally*	**metus–ūs** *fear*
amor–ōris *love, affection*	**nihil** *nothing*
carendī *of losing*	**quam** *than, as*

9 Farm slaves had a meaner existence than domestic ones, but they could expect some care and protection, for they were after all an investment.

> **gravia loca utilius est mercenariis colere quam servis.**

Varro, Rerum Rusticarum I, 17, 3

colō–ere *cultivate*	**mercēnārius–ī** *mercenary, hired hand*
gravia [neut. pl.] *difficult*	**quam** *than*
locus–ī [pl. **loca**, n.] *place*	**ūtilius** [neut.] *more profitable*

10 Some of the poorer citizens were not much better off than slaves, but their slender hold on liberty made them appreciate it all the more keenly. In this street-level account of life in the first century AD, a hired man complains about the weight of the luggage he is carrying.

> **'quid vos,' inquit, 'iumentum me putatis esse aut lapidariam navem? hominis operas locavi, non caballi. nec minus liber sum quam vos, etiam si pauperem pater me reliquit.' nec contentus maledictis tollebat subinde altius pedem et strepitu obsceno simul atque odore viam implebat.**

Petronius, Satyricon 117

altius *higher*	**pauper–is** *poor man*
caballus–ī *horse*	**pēs, pedis** *foot*
impleō–ēre *fill*	**putō–āre** *think*
iūmentum–ī *pack-animal*	**relīquit (relinquō–ere)** *left*
lapidārius–a–um *stone-carrying*	**simul** *simultaneously*
locāvī (locō–āre) *I contracted, took on*	**strepitus–ūs** *noise*
maledictum–ī *abuse*	**subinde** *then*
nāvis–is *ship*	**tollō–ere** *raise*
opera–ae *task*	

11 At the other end of the social scale were the senators. Below them were ranked the equestrians, who achieved this status by virtue of their wealth. 400,000 sesterces was the requisite sum – part of which Pliny was prepared to lend a fellow-townsman to help him qualify:

> **est autem tibi centum milium census. offero tibi ad implendas equestres facultates trecenta milia nummum.**

Pliny, Letters I, 19

ad implendās *to be made up*	**equestrēs facultātēs** *property qualification for the knights*
cēnsus–ūs *assets*	**offerō–erre** *offer*
centum mīlium *of 100,000 sesterces*	**trecenta mīlia nummum** *300,000 sesterces*

12 Pliny dined with a man who gave guests food and wine according to their social status. Another guest asked him if he approved.

> **animadvertit, qui mihi proximus recumbebat, et, an probarem,**
> **interrogavit. negavi. 'tu ergo,' inquit, 'quam consuetudinem**
> **sequeris?' 'eadem omnibus pono; ad cenam enim, non ad notam**
> **invito cunctisque rebus exaequo, quos mensa et toro aequavi.'**
> **'etiamne libertos?' 'etiam; convictores enim tunc, non libertos puto.'**
> **et ille: 'magno tibi constat.' 'minime.' 'qui fieri potest?' 'quia scilicet**
> **liberti mei non idem quod ego bibunt, sed idem ego quod liberti.'**

Pliny, *Letters* II, 6

aequāvī (aequō–āre) *I have made equal*
an *whether*
animadvertō–ere *notice*
bibō–ere *drink*
cēna–ae *dinner*
cōnsuetūdō–inis *custom, habit*
convīctor–ōris *table-companion*
cūnctus–a–um *all*
eadem [nom./acc.] *the same things*
ergō *therefore*
etiam *even*
exaequō–āre *regard as equal*
fierī *to be (done)*
idem [nom./acc.] *the same*
invītō–āre *invite*
lībertus–ī *freedman*
magnō cōnstat *it costs much*

mēnsa–ae *table*
minimē *not at all*
negāvī (negō–āre) *I said no*
nota–ae *social grading*
pōnō–ere *put*
probārem (probō–āre) *I approved*
proximus–a–um *nearest*
quī *how*
quia *because*
quod *which*
recumbō–ere *recline*
rēs, reī *thing*
scīlicet *of course*
sequeris *you follow*
torus–ī *couch*
tunc *then*

Vocabulary

TEXT

bene *well*
quid *what*
tunc *then*
tum *then*
nihil *nothing*
procul *far from/off*
autem *however*
saepe *often*

satis *enough*
silva–ae *wood*
mōns–tis *mountain*
senex–is *old man*
putō–āre, putāvī, putātum *think*
iaceō–ēre, iacuī, iacitum *lie down*
colō–ere, coluī, cultum *till*
relinquō–ere, relīquī, relictum *leave*

Past participles

āctus–a–um	*done*	(agō–ere)
audītus–a–um	*heard*	(audiō–īre)
amātus–a–um	*loved*	(amō–āre)
captus–a–um	*taken, captured*	(capiō–ere)
dictus–a–um	*said*	(dīcō–ere)
ductus–a–um	*led*	(dūcō–ere)
factus–a–um	*made, done*	(faciō–ere)
lātus–a–um	*brought*	(ferō, ferre)
laudātus–a–um	*praised*	(laudō–āre)
missus–a–um	*sent*	(mittō–ere)
monitus–a–um	*warned, advised*	(moneō–ēre)
parātus–a–um	*prepared*	(parō–āre)
scrīptus–a–um	*written*	(scrībō–ere)
victus–a–um	*conquered*	(vincō–ere)
vīsus–a–um	*seen*	(videō–ēre)

Exercises

1　Change each word in brackets into the past participle with the correct ending, and translate:

(a) **pueri a magistro** [laudo–are] **sunt**.
(b) **puella a poeta** [amo–are] **est**.
(c) **carmina ab imperatore** [audio–ire] **sunt**.
(d) **gladiatores in amphitheatrum** [duco–ere] **sunt**.
(e) **Caesar a femina** [moneo–ere] **est**.
(f) **vinum a servo** [video–ere] **est**.

2　Change each verb into the passive form, adapt other words as necessary, and translate your answer:

(a) **servus cenam parat**.
(b) **miles in amphitheatrum gladiatores ducit**.
(c) **senator epistulam scribit**.
(d) **femina canes culpat**.
(e) **pueri gladiatorem spectant**.
(f) **munera matri Iulius dat**.

3　Translate into Latin:

(a) The dinner was prepared in the kitchen.
(b) Rome has never been captured.

(c)   The enemy were conquered by Caesar.
(d)   The girls were praised by the mother.
(e)   A letter was written by the senator.
(f)   A bull was seen in the garden.

4   The past participles listed in the vocabulary above are simple forms, which can be compounded with certain prefixes:

e.g.   **captus – acceptus, receptus, susceptus, deceptus,** etc.
ductus – adductus, inductus, productus, conductus, etc.

What English words are related etymologically to compounds of these words:

dictus   factus   latus   missus
(e.g. **captus**: *accept, reception, deception*, etc.)

5   Identify English words derived from **relinquo–ere–liqui–lictum** and **puto–are–avi–atum**.

8 WOMEN

Pronouns

ille, illa, illud	*he, she, it* or *that* (demonstrative)
hic, haec, hoc	*he, she, it, this* (demonstrative)
is, ea, id	*he, she, it, that* (demonstrative)
qui, quae, quod	*who, which* (relative)
quis? quid?	*who? what?* (interrogative)

The above are the nominative forms of the pronouns. For all the endings, see pp. 147–8. **ille** and **hic** are demonstrative pronouns, emphasising *that* one there or *this* one here; **qui** can be either a relative pronoun which defines or describes, as in *the man who knew Caesar*, or an interrogative adjective, which asks a question, e.g. *what man has not heard of Caesar?*; the interrogative pronoun is **quis?** or **quid?** e.g. *who knows Caesar?*

hic, **ille** and **is** can serve as adjectives as well as pronouns, e.g. **hic equus**, *this* horse.

Subjunctive

The <u>indicative</u> mood of a verb is the one we have seen so far. This describes something which has happened, is happening or will happen:

e.g. **agricola ad villam venit**   *the farmer comes to the villa*

The <u>subjunctive</u> describes potential action:

Expressing a wish:

o agricola ad villam <u>veniat</u>!   *if only the farmer would come to the villa!*

Expressing a command:

agricola ad villam <u>veniat</u>!   *the farmer should come to the villa*

Expressing a condition that is unlikely to be fulfilled:

si agricola ad villam <u>veniat,</u> eum <u>videam</u>	*if the farmer were to come to the villa, I would see him*

Expressing purpose:

agricola ad villam venit ut nos <u>videat</u>	*the farmer comes to the villa that he may see us*

Expressing a reported command:

agricola nobis imperat ne ad villam <u>veniamus</u>	*the farmer orders us not to come to the villa*

(**impero–are** is followed by the dative, not the accusative)

Expressing a reported question:

agricola nos interrogat cur ad villam <u>veniamus</u>	*the farmer asks us why we are coming to the villa*

Expressing a fear:

timemus ne agricola in villam <u>veniat</u>	*we fear that the farmer may come into the villa*

Expressing prevention:

miles poetam impedit quominus <u>canat</u>	*the soldier prevents the poet from singing*

The subjunctive usually expresses potential action. There are exceptions, however, such as the use of the subjunctive with **cum** (*since, when, although*) to express something that happens, and also with **ut** to express a consequence or result:

cum agricola ad villam <u>veniat,</u> ipse te rogabit	*since the farmer is coming to the villa, he will ask you himself*
agricola ad villam tam celeriter venit ut nos <u>videat</u>	*the farmer comes to the villa so quickly with the result that he sees us*

Practice

Match each sentence with its illustration and translate:

(a) **si equus essem, faenum devorarem.**   Illustration no. . . . . .

(b) **cives ad amphitheatrum veniunt ut ludos spectent.**

                                                        Illustration no. . . . . .

(c) **magister rogat ubi Marcus sit.**   Illustration no. . . . . .

(d) **servi in agros veniant statim.**   Illustration no. . . . . .

1

2

3

4

possum, volo

The irregular verbs **posse** (*to be able*) and **velle** (*to wish*) are often used with the infinitive of another verb (for the endings of these two verbs, see pp. 153–4):

e.g. **femina poetam <u>audire</u> <u>potest</u>**   *the woman can hear the poet*

     quis poetam <u>audire</u> <u>vult</u>?   *who wants to hear the poet?*

Reading notes

The present subjunctive looks like the indicative, but with an **a** in the ending. The exception is the first conjugation (e.g. **parare**) which already has an **a** in the indicative, and so has an **e** instead. The imperfect subjunctive has the present infinitive as the stem: e.g. **venire–t** (*he/she might come*). For all the tenses of the subjunctive, see pp. 152–3. Note also the irregular present subjunctive of **sum**: **sim, sis, sit,** etc.

Women

Classical writers were fond of presenting what they imagined to be the typical woman of the early republican period as a model for contemporaries to emulate: she was hard-working, both in the fields and at home; she attended to the upbringing of her children, and she managed domestic affairs while her husband would be fighting in the army or participating in politics. This image, more often than not, was offered by way of a contrast to the behaviour of contemporary women who were preoccupied with self-amusement and idle recreation. Since, however, we only have records written by men, this evidence probably tells us as much about the men as it does about the women.

Girls were abandoned at birth more often than boys, for they were thought to be less valuable to the state and their parents. Those who escaped this fate grew up under the control of parents who might seek a quick opportunity to marry them off. Once married (some as young as thirteen), they virtually became the property of their husbands, who even had the right to inflict capital punishment – though not without permission of the in-laws. Such customs and attitudes survived through the classical period, and the glimpses we have of more liberated women, including sports-loving grandmothers and single hostesses, are recorded for their rarity as much as anything else. There was nothing approaching equality of status, in practice or even in theory.

Girls from poor families worked as laundresses, bakers, shopkeepers, nurses, mid-wives and in various other unenviable occupations. Those from wealthier families didn't follow careers in business or politics, as the men would, but managed the **familia**, which included slaves and other dependants as well as the immediate family. Education for a girl rarely meant anything beyond primary school, and a career in politics or business was unthinkable.

Some **matronae** grew to be very influential, according to the status of their **familia** or the rank of their husband. Livia, the wife of Augustus, managed many of his responsibilities in his later years; and Agrippina, the mother of Nero, had similar powers when he became emperor. Both women are portrayed by the historian Tacitus in a somewhat sinister light as power-brokers consumed by self-interest to the detriment of the state.

1 During the war with Carthage, women were forbidden to wear gold, multi-coloured clothing, or to ride in carriages except during festivals. When peace and prosperity returned, women asked for the law to be relaxed. The austere Cato warned his fellow-men against concessions (unsuccessfully).

> **volo tamen audire propter quod matronae consternatae procucur-rerint in publicum ac vix foro se et contione abstineant. extemplo, simul pares esse coeperint, superiores erunt.**

> Livy, XXXIV, 3, vi; iii

coeperint *they have begun*
cōnsternātus–a–um *agitated*
contiō–nis *assembly*
extemplō *immediately*
mātrōna–ae [f.] *lady, matron*
parēs *equal*

prōcucurrerint *have rushed forth*
propter quod *for what reason*
sē abstineant *they restrain themselves*
simul *as soon as*
vix *scarcely*
volō (velle) *I want*

2 Equality for women was, Cato argued, desirable – but parity with each other, not with men.

> **vultis hoc certamen uxoribus vestris inicere, Quirites, ut divites id habere velint quod nulla alia possit; pauperes, ne ob hoc ipsum contemnantur, supra vires se extendant?**

> Livy, XXXIV, 4, xv

certāmen–inis [n.] *competition*
contemnantur *they may be despised*
dīvitēs [adj.] *rich*
extendant *they may overreach*
id . . . quod *that . . . which*
īniciō–ere *impose*
nē *lest, in case*
nūlla alia *no other (woman)*

ob hoc ipsum *because of this very thing*
Quirītēs *fellow Romans*
sē *themselves*
suprā [+acc.] *beyond*
uxor–ōris *wife*
velint (volō, velle) *(they) may want*
vīrēs–ium *resources*
vultis (volō, velle) *you want*

3 Lucius Valerius did not agree.

> **matrem familiae tuam purpureum amiculum habere non sines, et equus tuus speciosius instratus erit quam uxor vestita.**

> Livy, XXXIV, 7, iii

amiculum–ī *cloak*
familia–ae *household*
īnstrātus–a–um *covered*

sinō–ere *allow*
speciōsius *more lavishly*
vestītus–a–um *clothed*

4 Women were perceived to be all but the property of fathers or husbands, particularly during the early years of the republic. The scene below is taken from a comedy (second century BC) and shows a wife appealing to her father for help in a marital quarrel. His unlikely response must have amused at least the men in the audience.

MATRONA:	ludibrio, pater, habeor.
SENEX:	unde?
MATRONA:	ab illo quoi me mandavisti, meo viro.
SENEX:	ecce autem litigium! quotiens tandem edixi tibi ut caveres neuter ad me iretis cum querimonia?
MATRONA:	qui ego istuc, mi pater, cavere possum?
SENEX:	men interrogas?
MATRONA:	nisi non vis.
SENEX:	quotiens monstravi tibi viro ut morem geras, quid ille faciat ne id observes, quo eat, quid rerum gerat.
MATRONA:	at enim ille hinc amat meretricem ex proxumo.
SENEX:	sane sapit atque ob istanc industriam etiam faxo amabit amplius.
MATRONA:	atque ibi potat.
SENEX:	tua quidem ille causa potabit minus? quando te auratam et vestitam bene habet, ancillas, penum recte praehibet, melius sanam est, mulier, mentem sumere.

Plautus, *Menaechmi* 771–80, 789–90

amplius *more so*
ancilla–ae *servant*
aurātus–a–um *in gold, jewellery*
autem *however*
cavērēs (caveō–ēre) *you should take care*
eat (eō, īre) *he goes*
ecce *oh! look!*
ēdīxī (ēdīcō–ere) *I have made clear*
ex proxumō *from next door*
faciat (faciō–ere) *he does*
faxō *I'll warrant*
hinc *from this house, here*
ibī *there*
id *that*
īrētis (eō, īre) *you should come*
istuc *to that end*
lītigium–ī *dispute*
lūdibriō habeor *I am an object of scorn*
mandāvistī (mandō–āre) *you entrusted*
melius *better*
mēn i.e. mē–ne . . . ?
mēns–tis *mind, outlook*
meretrīx–cis *prostitute*
minus *less*
mōnstrō–āre–āvī *show*

mōrem gerās [+dat.] *you should humour*
neuter *neither of you*
nisi nōn vīs *if you don't mind*
ob istanc *because of that*
observēs (observō–āre) *you should observe*
penus–ī *provisions*
possum, posse *be able*
pōtō–āre *to drink*
praehibeō–ēre *supply*
quandō *since*
querimōnia–ae *complaint*
quī *how*
quid rērum gerat *what he gets up to*
quidem *indeed* (stresses the word before)
quō *where*
quoi [cui] *to whom*
quotiēns *how many times*
rēctē *properly*
sānē sapit *he has good taste*
sānus–a–um *healthy, balanced*
sūmō–ere *take*
tandem *pray, I ask you*
tuā causā *on your account*
unde *who from?*
ut *that*

5 Friends and relatives would be expected to suggest suitable candidates for arranged marriages.

petis, ut fratris tui filiae prospiciam maritum.

Pliny, Letters I, 14

marītus–ī *husband*
petis (petō–ere) *you seek, ask*

prōspiciam (prōspiciō–ere) *I watch out for*

6 Women from poorer backgrounds would seldom have had a moment to themselves. By contrast, upper-class women were barred from professions and careers. Even literary criticism was frowned upon – if Juvenal is to be taken seriously.

illa tamen gravior, quae cum discumbere coepit,
laudat Vergilium.
cedunt grammatici, vincuntur rhetores, omnis
turba tacet.

Juvenal, Satire VI, 434–5, 438–9

cēdunt (cēdō–ere) *they give way*
coepit *begins*
cum *when*
discumbō–ere *recline at table*
grammaticus *teacher*
gravior *more troublesome*

illa [nom.] *she*
quae [f.] *who*
rhētor–oris *professor*
taceō–ēre *be silent*
turba–ae *crowd*
vincō–ere *vanquish*

7 Pliny, however, praises his wife's good taste in books (his own!).

meos libellos habet, lectitat, ediscit etiam.

Pliny, Letters IV, 19

ēdiscō–ere *learn by heart*
etiam *even*

lēctitō–āre *read repeatedly*
libellus–ī *book*

8 Many young mothers died in childbirth.

tristem et acerbum casum Helvidiarum sororum! utraque a partu,
utraque filiam enixa decessit. adficior dolore nec tamen supra
modum doleo; ita mihi luctuosum videtur, quod puellas honestis-
simas in flore primo fecunditas abstulit.

Pliny, Letters IV, 21

abstulit (auferō, auferre)   *has taken away*
acerbus–a–um   *bitter*
adficior   *I am afflicted*
cāsus–ūs   *misfortune*
dēcēdō–ere–cessī   *withdraw, die*
doleō–ēre   *grieve*
dolor–ōris   *grief*
ēnīxus–a–um   *having given birth to*
fēcunditās–tātis   *fruitfulness*
flōs–ris [m.]   *flower*

Helvidiārum sorōrum   *Helvidia sisters*
honestissimus–a–um   *most honourable*
ita ... quod   *in that*
lūctuōsus–a–um   *sorrowful*
partus–ūs   *birth*
suprā modum   *beyond measure*
trīstem [acc.]   *sad* (see p. 159: exclamation)
utraque   *each*
vidētur   *seems*

9   Romans were surprised by the British custom of greater equality between the sexes. Boudicca's speech before leading the British into battle was recorded (and rewritten) by the enemy's historian.

Boudicca, curru filias prae se vehens, solitum quidem Britannis feminarum ductu bellare testabatur; vincendum illa acie vel cadendum esse; id mulieri destinatum: viverent viri et servirent.

Tacitus, *Annals* XIV, 35, i, ii

aciēs–ēī   *battle*
bellō–āre   *go to war*
cadendum esse   *they must fall*
currus–ūs   *chariot*
dēstinātus–a–um   *fixed objective*
ductū (ductus–ūs)   *under the leadership*
mulier–is   *woman*
prae sē   *before her*

servīrent (serviō–īre)   *let (them) be slaves*
solitum [+dat.]   *(it was) customary for*
testābātur   *declared*
vehēns   *carrying*
vel   *or*
vincendum (esse)   *they must win*
vir–ī   *man*
vīverent (vīvō–ere)   *let (them) live*

10   The poet Ovid on the subject of make-up:

discite, quae faciem commendet cura, puellae:
et quo sit vobis forma tuenda modo.
nec tamen indignum: sit vobis cura placendi,
cum comptos habeant saecula nostra viros.

Ovid, *Medic. Faciei* 1–2, 23–4

commendō–āre   *enhance*
cōmptus–a–um   *well-groomed*
cum   *since*
cūra–ae   *care, attention*
discite (discō–ere)   *learn*
faciēs-ēī   *face*
fōrma–ae   *beauty*

indignus–a–um   *unworthy*
placendī   *of pleasing*
quō ... modō   *in what way, how*
saeculum–ī   *age, era*
sit   *may (it) be*
tuendus–a–um   *to be preserved*

Vocabulary

TEXT

inde, deinde	*then, next*
tandem	*at last, at length*
simul	*at the same time*
ibī	*there*
quandō	*when, at any time, since, seeing that*
minus	*less*
melius	*better*
ob [+acc.]	*because of*
propter [+acc.]	*because of*
sē	*himself, herself, themselves*
cūra–ae	*care, attention*
fōrma–ae	*shape, appearance, beauty*
uxor–ōris	*wife*
marītus–ī	*husband*
currus–ūs	*chariot*
nisi	*if not, except, unless*

CUM

+ noun in the abl.	*with*
+ subjunctive verb	*when*
	since
	although (occasional)
+ indicative verb	*when*
cum ... tum	*both . . . and, when . . . then*

UT

+ indicative verb	*as*
	when
	how (occasional)
	although (occasional)
+ subjunctive verb	*so that* (expressing purpose)
	(with the result) that
	to (he commanded him to . . .)
	if only (expressing a desire)
	how (occasional)

Please note:
1 **ut** and **cum** are more often used with the subjunctive than the indicative.
2 **nē** is normally used in place of **ut ... nōn**.

Exercises

1 Change the underlined noun to the correct form of **hic** and translate:

(a) **Fulvia est uxor <u>Antonii</u>.**
(b) **Caesar cum <u>Bruto</u> ambulat.**
(c) **<u>Clodia</u> est soror Clodii.**
(d) **<u>captivi</u> in amphitheatrum ducti sunt.**
(e) **poeta <u>munera</u> feminae dedit.**

2 Change the underlined noun to the correct form of **ille** and translate:

(a) **<u>Caesar</u> in Italiam cum exercitu veniet.**
(b) **Cicero <u>Fulviam</u> non amabat.**
(c) **<u>gladiatores</u> in amphitheatro vidimus.**
(d) **gemitus <u>captivorum</u> audire possumus.**
(e) **vis-ne videre <u>dominum</u>?**

3 Change the underlined noun to the correct form of **is** and translate:

(a) **taurus <u>agricolas</u> fugavit.**
(b) **Plinius libellos <u>feminae</u> dabat.**
(c) **Hannibal a <u>civibus</u> visus est.**
(d) **<u>bellum</u> est saevum.**
(e) **fratrem-ne <u>Ciceronis</u> audivistis?**

4 Complete each sentence with the correct form of **qui** (or **quis**) and translate:

(a) **..... epistulam misit?**
(b) **..... canis est in amphitheatro?**
(c) **a ..... Romani capti sunt?**
(d) **puer ..... amabas nunc adest.**
(e) **domina ..... poeta munera dedit in horto sedebat.**

5 Translate into English:

(a) **feminae, ut viros viderunt, ridebant.**
(b) **Graeci, ut dicunt, impudentes sunt.**
(c) **non sum tam ignavus ut illud faciam (<u>tam</u>: *so*).**
(d) **imperator nobis imperat ut ludos spectemus.**
(e) **venio ut te videam.**
(f) **Caesar cum Romam pervenisset Ciceronis epistulam legit.**
(g) **cum videbis, tum scies.**
(h) **hi, cum servi sint, Romae tamen amici.**

6 Identify Latin words (in this chapter) which are ancestors of *vehicle*, *voluntary* and *simultaneous*.

7   **ille** and **illa** came to mean *the* in medieval Latin. How have these words survived in other European languages?

8   What are the meanings of **id est** and **ad hoc**?

9 EDUCATION

More adjectives

As well as adjectives like **bonus–a–um**, there are adjectives like **omnis** (*all*, *every*), and **ingens** (*huge*). The endings of these adjectives are listed on p. 149.

Some adjectives have the same endings as **omnis**, except in the nominative: **acer** (*keen*), **celer** (*swift*), **felix** (*fortunate*), etc.

There are also adjectives like **bonus**, which have the nominative ending **-er**: **pulcher–chra–chrum** (*beautiful*) and **miser–era–erum** (*wretched*).

The comparative

maior (see p. 149) is the comparative form of **magnus** (i.e. *great__r__*) and other comparative forms have similar endings: **gratus** (*pleasing*), **gratior** (*more pleasing*); **tristis** (*sad*), **tristior** (*sadder*); **celer** (*quick*), **celerior** (*quicker*), etc.

The superlative

An adjective ending **-issimus**, **-errimus** or **-illimus** is the superlative form: **gratissimus** (*very/most pleasing*); **tristissimus** (*saddest*); **celerrimus** (*quickest*), etc. All superlatives decline like **bonus**.

Quam

This word can mean a number of different things: it can mean *how*, *whom* (acc. fem. of **qui**), *as* or *than*. With the comparative form of an adjective or adverb, **quam** means *than*:

> e.g. **Caesar est <u>maior quam</u> Pompeius**
> *Caesar is <u>greater than</u> Pompey*

91

Pompeius is the same case (here, nom.) as the person or object being compared (here, **Caesar**). You will also find a comparison made without **quam**, where the <u>ablative</u> is used to convey the meaning of *than*:

> e.g. **Caesar est <u>maior</u> <u>Pompeio</u>**
> *Caesar is <u>greater</u> <u>than</u> <u>Pompey</u>*

Practice A

Identify the comparative form of each adjective:

1 **puella est . . . . .**
 quam puer. [laetus–a–um]

2 **poeta est . . . . .**
 quam miles. [gratus–a–um]

3 **servus est . . . . .**
  senatore. [ignavus–a–um]

Imperatives

In the last chapter you met the subjunctive form, which can express a wish or an instruction:

> e.g. **nunc veniat**   *may he come now/he should come now*

The imperative form is more direct and less polite (see p. 156 for the endings):

> e.g. **nunc veni!**   *come now!*

Practice B

Add the missing imperative to each sentence and translate:

1 **[bibo, bibere]**

2 [do, dare]

Schools

During the early republic the objectives of an education were kept simple: children would learn literacy and arithmetic, and to speak aloud. Without today's technology, this last subject, oratory, was as indispensable to a greengrocer selling vegetables as to a lawyer pleading a case. Children would also learn how to fight and to farm, to sew and to cook – strictly according to gender.

Schools as centres of education didn't appear until the third century BC. Previously, children of wealthy citizens had been taught by tutors, who were usually slaves or freedmen. To set up a school, a freedman would approach several families to send their children to him, and then rent some space in the forum. There wasn't the concept of institution as there is with schools today, for you studied with a particular teacher, not at a particular school. Most schools amounted to little more than one class.

In the second century BC, once Rome had discovered Greek culture, the reading of Greek literature became common in schools. The study of rhetoric absorbed the practice of oratory, and young Romans were introduced to Greek thought, debate and scientific analysis. They read Greek plays and poetry, with attention to their didactic and exemplary content.

This development wasn't solely the result of discovering Greek literature; it also reflected the changing needs of the people. They were no longer citizen–farmers belonging to a small state, but rulers of a growing empire with a developing machinery of government, which required a skilled and literate civil service.

There was a certain amount of opposition to these Greek trends. We read of Cato who preferred to educate his son himself rather than entrust the duty to a slave. The subjects he taught were the old-fashioned ones of oratory, horse-riding, swimming and throwing a javelin.

Though Greek trends prevailed, by no means every child received an education, and the majority had little more than a basic grounding in numeracy and literacy. Some girls went to primary school (7–12 years) with the **litterator**, but only a few remained with the boys for the next stage with the **grammaticus** (12–16 years). A limited number of teenagers would go on to study with a **rhetor**. Athens was popular with the rhetors, so students like Cicero's son stayed in Athens to attend a particular rhetor's course. Athens has subsequently been recognised as the university town of the ancient world. In truth, it resembled more closely the early medieval universities in Europe where a professor, and not the place itself, attracted a following.

The Roman era is celebrated for feats of construction and engineering, though the aristocrats (those who set the curriculum) were not especially interested in these practical sciences. They preferred on the whole to occupy themselves with more abstract or literary studies. If there hadn't been a plentiful supply of cheap manpower, perhaps they would have been more curious about applied sciences, and might have developed more advanced forms of mechanisation.

The arts were not highly regarded either. Romans admired the finished works, but thought little of the artists themselves – perhaps an aspect of their sense of inferiority regarding Greece. Philosophy would be studied with the rhetor, and not before. We have already seen in the case of Agricola's mother the reluctance of patricians to discuss theories of power and their right to wield it.

1 Tacitus criticises the use of nurses and slaves to look after a baby.

> **at nunc natus infans delegatur Graeculae alicui ancillae, cui adiungitur unus aut alter ex omnibus servis, plerumque vilissimus nec cuiquam serio ministerio adcommodatus. horum fabulis et erroribus teneri statim et rudes animi imbuuntur; nec quisquam in tota domo pensi habet quid coram infante domino aut dicat aut faciat.**

Tacitus, *Dialogus De Oratoribus* 29

adcommodātus–a–um *suited*
adiungitur (adiungō–ere) *is attached*
alicui [dat.] *some*
alter *other*
ancilla–ae *maid*
animus–ī *mind*
cōram [+abl.] *in the presence of*
cui *to whom*
cuiquam [dat.] *any*
dēlēgātur (dēlēgō–āre) *is entrusted*
fābula–ae *myth*
Graeculus–a–um *little Greek*
hōrum [gen.] *these (people)*

imbuuntur (imbuō–ere) *are filled*
in tōtā domō *in the entire household*
īnfāns dominus *little master*
ministerium–ī *service*
nātus–a–um *born*
pēnsī habet *care a jot*
plērumque *very often*
quisquam [nom.] *anyone*
rudis–e *impressionable*
sērius–a–um *serious*
statim *immediately*
tener–a–um *tender*
vīlis–e *worthless*

2 Quintilian advises competition and encouragement for the young learner.

doceatur alius, cui invideat; contendat interim et saepius vincere se putet: praemiis etiam, quae capit illa aetas, evocetur.

Quintilian, *Elements of Oratory* I, 1, 20

aetās–tātis [f.] *age, age-group*
alius–a–ud *other*
capit (capiō–ere) *welcomes*
contendat (contendō–ere) *let him compete*
doceātur (doceō–ēre) *let . . . be taught*
ēvocētur (ēvocō–āre) *let him be encouraged*

interim *sometimes*
invideat [+dat.] **(invideō–ēre)** *he may envy*
praemium–ī *reward*
putet (putō–āre) *let him think*
saepius *more often than not*
vincere sē *that he wins*

3 A school would be small and privately owned, situated in the forum or busy street. The school day started early to take advantage of the peace and quiet – to Martial's dismay:

**quid tibi nobiscum est, ludi scelerate magister,
    invisum pueris virginibusque caput?
nondum cristati rupere silentia galli:
    murmure iam saevo verberibusque tonas.
vicini somnum non tota nocte rogamus:
    nam vigilare leve est, pervigilare grave est.
discipulos dimitte tuos. vis, garrule, quantum
    accipis ut clames, accipere ut taceas?**

Martial, *Epigrams* IX, 68, 1–4, 9–12

(per)vigilō–āre *be awake (all night)*
accipis (accipiō–ere) *you receive*
caput, capitis [n.] *creature*
clāmēs (clāmō–āre) *you shout*
cristātus–a–um *crested*
dīmitte (dīmittō–ere) *dismiss!*
discipulus–ī *student*
gallus–ī *cock*
garrule *you chatterbox*
gravis–e *serious*
invīsus–a–um *hated*
levis–e *not serious*
lūdus–ī *school*
murmur–is *growling*

nam *for*
nōndum *not yet*
quantus–a–um *as much as*
quid . . . est *why do you have it in for us?*
   (lit. what is it to you with us?)
rūpēre (rumpō–ere) *(they) have broken*
scelerāte magister *wretched teacher*
silentium–ī *silence*
somnum–ī *sleep*
taceās (taceō–ēre) *you are silent*
tonō–āre *thunder*
verber–is [n.] *whip*
vīcīnus–a–um *neighbour*
vīs *do you want (. . .?)*

4 A character from Petronius' *Satyricon* does not approve of the intellectual nature (Greek-inspired) of schooling.

iste, qui te haec docet, est mufrius, non magister. dicebat enim
magister, 'sunt vestra salva? recta domum; cave, circumspicias;
cave, maiorem maledicas.'

Petronius, Satyricon 58

cavē (caveō–ēre) *take care not to*
cavē maledīcās *don't be cheeky to*
circumspiciās (circumspiciō–ere) *look behind you*
docet (doceō–ēre) *teaches*
enim *for, you see*
iste *he*

magister–trī *teacher*
māior–ōris *senior*
mufrius–ī *mutton-head*
rēctā domum *go straight home*
salvus–a–um *safe*
vester–tra–trum *your*

5 Juvenal says that a teacher's life is not a happy one. After he has paid his
suppliers, landlord and cashier, there are the parents ...

rara tamen merces quae cognitione tribuni
non egeat. sed vos saevas imponite leges,
ut praeceptori verborum regula constet,
ut legat historias, auctores noverit omnes
tamquam ungues digitosque suos.

Juvenal, Satire VII, 228–232

cognitiō–nis *court order*
cōnstet [+dat.] **(cōnstō–āre)** *should be correct*
digitus–ī *finger*
egeat [+abl.] **(egeō–ēre)** *needs*
impōnite (impōnō–ere) *impose!*
legat (legō–ere) *he read*
lēx, lēgis *law*
mercēs–ēdis [f.] *pay*
nōverit (nōscō–ere) *be acquainted with*

praeceptor–ōris *teacher*
rārus–a–um *rare, unusual*
rēgula–ae *rule, standard*
tamquam *as though they were*
tribūnus–ī *tribune*
unguis–is *nail*
verbum–ī *word, speech*
vōs *i.e. the parents*

6 And what does the teacher get in return? No more than a sportsman gets in
a day.

'haec,' inquit, 'cures, et cum se verterit annus,
accipe, victori populus quod postulat, aurum.'

Juvenal, Satire VII, 242–243

accipe (accipiō–ere) *take!*
aurum–ī *gold*
cūrēs (cūrō–āre) *you should attend to*
haec *these matters*

inquit *he/she says*
postulō–āre *demand*
verterit (vertō–ere) *has turned*
victor–ōris *winning gladiator/charioteer*

7   Whatever little amount teachers were paid, a schooling was only for the children of the rich or of those prepared to make a sacrifice. Horace's father, a **libertinus** (freed slave), refused to send his son to the local school, where he might be teased by the children of local grandees. Instead, Horace went to school in Rome.

> **noluit in Flavi ludum me mittere, magni**
> **quo pueri magnis e centurionibus orti,**
> **sed puerum est ausus Romam portare.**

Horace, *Satire* I, 6, 72–73, 76

est ausus *he dared*
Flāvius the local schoolmaster
lūdus–ī *school*
nōluit (nōlō, nōlle) *he did not want*

ortus–a–um *born, descended*
portō–āre *take*
quō *(to) where (went)*
Rōmam *to Rome*

8   Cicero's son completed his education in Athens, from where he writes to his father's personal secretary, Tiro.

> **praeterea declamitare Graece apud Cassium institui; Latine autem**
> **apud Bruttium exerceri volo.**

Cicero, *Ad Familiares* XVI, 21, 5

apud [+acc.] *with*
dēclāmitō–āre *declaim*
exercērī (exerceō–ēre) *to be trained*

īnstituī (īnstituō–ere) *I have begun*
praetereā *moreover*

9   The young man was anxious to show his father how seriously he was taking his studies; so seriously that he needed help with some of the duties involved.

> **sed peto a te, ut quam celerrime mihi librarius mittatur, maxime**
> **quidem Graecus; multum mihi enim eripietur operae in exscribendis**
> **hypomnematis.**

Cicero, *Ad Familiares* XVI, 21, 8

enim *you see*
ēripiētur (ēripiō–ere) *will be taken*
in exscrībendīs hypomnēmatīs *in writing*
   out notes
librārius–ī *clerk, secretary*

maximē *especially*
mittātur (mittō–ere) *may be sent*
opera–ae *work*
quam celerrimē *as quickly as possible*
quidem *indeed*

Vocabulary

dum	*while, until*
forte	*by chance*
statim	*immediately*
nam	*for*
iste–a–ud	*that* (like **ille**)
quantus–a–um	*how much, how great* (pl.: *how many*)
fābula–ae	*story*
lūdus–ī	*school*
praemium–ī	*reward*
aurum–ī	*gold*
lēx, lēgis	*law*
legō–ere, lēgī, lēctum	*read*
discō–ere, didicī	*learn*
vincō–ere, vīcī, victum	*conquer, win*

ADJECTIVES LIKE OMNIS–E

omnis	*every, all*	trīstis	*sad*
mollis	*soft*	fidēlis	*faithful*
gravis	*serious, heavy*	levis	*light*
dulcis	*sweet*	humilis	*meek*
difficilis	*difficult*	facilis	*easy*
ūtilis	*useful*	turpis	*disgraceful*
brevis	*short*	illūstris	*famous*

ADJECTIVES LIKE INGĒNS

sapiēns	*wise*	praesēns	*present*

(and all present participles)

Comparative forms of adjectives

cruel	saevus	saevior	saevissimus
sad	trīstis	trīstior	trīstissimus
easy	facilis	facilior	facillimus

good	bonus	melior	optimus
bad	malus	pēior	pessimus
much, many	multus	plūs*	plūrimus

*plūs in the singular is used as a neuter noun.

99

ESSENTIAL LATIN

Exercises

1   Identify all possible cases of each of the following (and indicate the gender[s] and whether singular or plural):

(a) **tristi**   (e) **facilium**
(b) **magni**   (f) **mollis**
(c) **multa**   (g) **saevis**
(d) **breve**   (h) **avidum**

2   Find the correct endings of the words in brackets:

(a) [vinum–i] [acerbus–a–um] **erat**
the wine was bitter
(b) [gravis–e] [res–ei] **est fortuna**
fortune is a serious matter
(c) **femina** [dignus–a–um] **meliore viro erat**
the woman was worthy of a better husband
(d) [opus–eris] [difficilis–e] **perfecit**
he finished the difficult task
(e) [praemium–i] [humilis–e], **non** [superbus–a–um], **dentur**
rewards should be given to the meek, not to the proud.
(f) [imperator–oris] **sunt numquam** [laetus–a–um]
emperors are never cheerful
(g) [vultus–us] [tristis–e] **dixit**
she spoke with a sad face
(h) **carmina** [gratus–a–um] **sed non** [utilis–e] **sunt**
songs are pleasing but not useful

3   Translate into Latin:

(a) The farmer is larger than the slave.
(b) Cicero was wiser than Catiline.
(c) Are girls more faithful than boys?
(d) I want to marry (**nubo–ere** + dat.) a better man than Tiberius.
(e) The poet is very pleasing, but lazier than all the slaves.

4   The word *tandem*, a bicycle for two people, was coined directly from the Latin **tandem** meaning *at last, at length*. The word *omnibus* has a less lateral derivation: how would you account for its ending?

5   What English words are at least partly derived from **ancilla**, **natus** and **optimus**?

6   Find Latin ancestors (in this chapter) of *digit* and *reverberate*.

10 LEISURE

Present, past and future participles

Compare these sentences:

1   *Jumping on the horse,*
    he disappeared from view.

2   *He disappeared from view*
    jumping on the horse.

In the first sentence, the man has jumped (participle) on the horse before he disappears (main verb); in the second, the jumping and disappearing are both happening at the same time. In Latin, a past participle generally describes an action which happens <u>before</u> that of the main verb (as in the first example above), while a present

101

participle describes something happening <u>at the same time</u> as the action of the main verb (see the second example). The future participle describes something which is <u>yet to happen</u>, e.g. *about to disappear, he jumped on the horse.*

The form of participles

The past participle is formed like the supine (the fourth principal part), has the same endings as **bonus–a–um**, and is usually passive:

> e.g. **vinum captum**   *the wine having been taken*

The present participle is active and has endings like **ingens**:

> e.g. **ille capiens vinum**   *he, (while) taking the wine*

The future participle is also active and has endings like **bonus–a–um**:

> e.g. **ille capturus vinum**   *he, about to take the wine*

Remember that participles, though formed from verbs, are adjectives. For a full list, see p. 157.

Ablative absolute

The participle is an adjective, and agrees with a noun (or pronoun). So the ending of the participle is determined by the noun's function in the sentence (subject, object, etc.)

> e.g. **<u>ille</u>, <u>capiens</u> vinum, senatori dicebat**
> *he, (while) taking the wine, spoke to the senator*

However, when the noun and participle have no grammatical relation to the main verb, together they form an independent clause in the ablative:

> e.g. **ille, <u>capto</u> <u>vino</u>, senatori dicebat**
> *he, with the wine having been taken, spoke to the senator*
>
> **<u>domino</u> <u>interfecto</u> servus effugit**
> *with the master having been killed, the slave fled away*
>
> **<u>magistro</u> <u>intrante</u> pueri tacuerunt**
> *with the master entering, the boys hushed*

Reading notes

Latin participles can be translated in different ways (see p. 50), e.g.:

Galli <u>capti</u> flebant
the Gauls, having been captured, wept
the captured Gauls wept
the Gauls were captured and began to weep
the Gauls wept because (when, after, etc.) they had been captured
the Gauls, who were captured, wept
the Gauls wept after their capture

imperator senatores <u>egredientes</u> conspexit
the emperor saw the departing senators
the emperor saw the senators while/as they were departing
the emperor saw the senators who were departing
the emperor saw the senators' departure

<u>attonitae</u> ridebant
the astonished (women) laughed

Practice

Identify the case, gender and number of each participle and translate:

1 **dominus servum vinum <u>bibentem</u> vidit.**

103

2 **dominus servum vino
capto dormientem vidit.**
[**dormio-ire:** *sleep*]

3 **dominus servum vinum
capturum vidit.**

Bread and circuses

By the time Italy had absorbed Greece's theatrical tradition, the fifth-century plays of Aeschylus, Sophocles and Euripides had become distant classics. These Athenian dramatists had staged tragedies which were intellectually and emotionally engaging, and yet which were appreciated by the whole community. In Italy their appeal was now limited to an erudite few. Even the comedies of Terence, adaptations of Greek plays that delighted the literati of both his day and later generations, were not broadly popular. A hundred years on, at the dawn of classical Rome, we find theatres serving up much frothier and more frivolous fare in the form of mimes, farces and pantomimes.

Serious works were not written for the stage. Romans of refinement preferred instead to be entertained by readings in the privacy of their own homes, far from the vulgarities of the common throng. This form of presentation had a bearing on the style of writing: Seneca's *Oedipus* has a richness of language that makes visual props and stage machinery almost superfluous. These educated audiences, however, appear to have retained a relish for the violence normally associated with the amphitheatre, in their case not in the arena itself, but on the page. Seneca's description of Oedipus putting out his eyes isn't the only bloodthirsty episode in the literature of the period.

The amphitheatre was perhaps the most unpleasant feature of ancient Rome. The infamous arenas were built all over the empire – primarily to entertain the soldiers – and here thousands of slaves, gladiators and social miscreants died horrible deaths in front of wildly applauding spectators. Derived from funeral rites, the shows presented displays of beasts eating humans, animals being slaughtered in 'hunts', the execution of criminals, duelling gladiators and even sea battles in flooded arenas. Vast numbers of lions, bears, bulls, elephants and other animals were rounded up from all corners of the empire and brought to Rome. Some combats would involve only animals, such as bulls pitted against bears.

The inhumanity of the amphitheatre seemed largely lost on the moralists of the time. Many thought such spectacles were distasteful, but very few had sympathy for the victims. One reason for this insensitivity may have been the long-standing practice of dramatic criticism to measure artistic quality solely in terms of its moral impact upon the audience. This had been central to Aristotle's criticism of drama, and remained influential long after him, with a wider application to shows and spectacles of all kinds.

Athletic contests, another import from Greece, were also popular; so too the racing of chariots and horses. Different teams were fiercely supported, and professional drivers achieved a status on a par with sporting celebrities of today. Racing was arguably the most popular of all forms of entertainment. Rome's largest amphitheatre, the Colosseum, had room for 50,000 spectators; the Circus Maximus, where the horses were raced, could entertain five times as many.

In the republican period, wealthy politicians might stage a show to encourage support in a forthcoming election or, if successful, as a gratuity afterwards. The emperors, though less concerned by the outcome of elections, were still sensitive to popular opinion, and their munificence might distract the people's attention from social problems.

The emperor Nero preferred singing and music to shows at the amphitheatre, for which he was later held in contempt. This was soft and unRoman, and worse, objected Tacitus and others, he even performed himself. Though Nero was undeniably cruel, it is ironic that his statue, the 'Colossus Neronis', was destroyed as a celebration of his passing, and gave its name to the Colosseum that was built in its place.

1 Catullus invited his friend Fabullus to dinner, but there were strings attached.

> **cenabis bene, mi Fabulle, apud me**
> **paucis, si tibi di favent, diebus,**
> **si tecum attuleris bonam atque magnam**
> **cenam, non sine candida puella**
> **et vino et sale et omnibus cachinnis.**
> **haec si, inquam, attuleris, venuste noster,**
> **cenabis bene: nam tui Catulli**
> **plenus sacculus est aranearum.**

Catullus, XIII, 1–8

apud mē *at my place*
arānea–ae *cobweb*
attuleris (afferō–erre) *you will have brought,*
  bring
cachinnus–ī *laugh*
candidus–a–um *fair, pretty*
cēna–ae *dinner*
cēnō–āre *dine*
dī *gods* (nom.pl. of **deus–ī**)
diēs–iēī *day*

faveō–ēre [+dat.] *be kind*
inquam *I say*
mī *my* (vocative of **meus–a–um**)
paucī–ae–a *few*
plēnus–a–um *full*
sacculus–ī [m.] *purse*
sāl–is *salt, wit*
sine [+abl.] *without*
venuste noster *my charming friend*

2 Few guests would have brought their dinner! One or two, however, might have tried to take home what they did not eat.

> quidquid ponitur hinc et inde verris.
> haec cum condita sunt madente mappa,
> traduntur puero domum ferenda:
> nos accumbimus otiosa turba.
> ullus si pudor est, repone cenam.

Martial, *Epigrams* 2, XXXVII, 1; 7–10

accumbō–ere *recline*
condita sunt (condō–ere) *have been hidden*
ferendus–a–um *to be carried*
hinc et inde *this way and that*
madente (madeō–ēre) *dripping*
mappa–ae *napkin*
ōtiōsus–a–um *inactive*
pōnitur (pōnō–ere) *is placed*

pudor–ōris *shame*
puer–ī *boy, slave*
quidquid *whatever*
repōne (repōnō–ere) *put back!*
trāduntur (trādō–ere) *are handed over*
turba–ae *crowd*
ūllus *any*
verrō–ere *sweep away*

3 In 160 BC, the playwright Terence experienced a miserable first night for his play *The Mother-in-law*. He produced it again five years later, adding a new prologue:

> Hecyram ad vos refero, quam mihi per silentium
> numquam agere licitumst: ita eam oppressit calamitas.
> eam calamitatem vostra intellegentia
> sedabit, si erit adiutrix nostrae industriae.

Terence, *Hecyra*, Second Prologue

adiūtrīx–cis *assistant*
agō–ere *produce, stage*
hecyra–ae *mother-in-law*
ita *in such a way*

licitum [e]st *it was allowed*
referō–erre *bring back*
sēdō–āre *calm, stop*
vostra = **vestra**

4 The theatre was not much liked by patricians, who considered it vulgar. They preferred to entertain their friends at home, after dinner, with recitals.

> **quid enim delectationis habent sescenti muli in Clytaemnestra? Aut in Equo Troiano craterarum tria milia?**

Cicero, Ad Familiares VII, 1, 2

Clytaemnēstra i.e. a play	**mūlus–ī** *mule*
crātēra–ae *bowl*	**sescentī** *six hundred*
dēlectātiō–nis *pleasure, enjoyment*	**tria mīlia** *three thousand*

5 The story of Oedipus, who unwittingly murdered his father and married his mother, is dramatised by the Greek playwright Sophocles, and again by Seneca. Once Oedipus discovers the dreadfulness of his predicament, he puts out his eyes, which in the Latin version is more gruesome than symbolic.

> **rigat ora foedus imber et lacerum caput**
> **largum revulsis sanguinem venis vomit.**

Seneca, Oedipus 978–979

foedus–a–um *foul*	**ōs, ōris** [n.] *facial feature*
imber–bris *shower*	**revulsīs ... vēnīs** *from the torn veins*
lacer–era–erum *mutilated*	**rigat** (**rigō–āre**) *soaks*
largus–a–um *abundant*	**vomit** (**vomō–ere**) *pours forth*

6 Like the theatre, the amphitheatre was thought to be distasteful. Moralists wondered what good could come from watching all this brutality – though concern for the victims was seldom an issue.

> **sed quae potest homini esse polito delectatio, cum aut homo imbecillus a valentissima bestia laniatur, aut praeclara bestia venabulo transverberatur?**

Cicero, Ad Familiares VII, 1, 3

bēstia–ae *beast*	**praeclārus–a–um** *magnificent*
homō–inis *man*	**trānsverberātur** *is transfixed*
imbēcillus–a–um *weak*	(**trānsverberō–āre**)
laniātur (**laniō–āre**) *is torn*	**valēns** *powerful*
polītus–a–um *refined*	**vēnābulum–ī** *hunting spear*

7   Little had changed by the middle of the first century AD.

> **nihil vero tam damnosum bonis moribus quam in aliquo spectaculo desidere. tunc enim per voluptatem facilius vitia subrepunt.**
>
> Seneca, *Epistulae Morales* VII, 2

damnōsus–a–um *harmful*
dēsideō–ēre *sit idly*
facilius *more easily*
mōs, mōris *custom, (pl.) character*
subrēpō–ere *advance slowly*

tam *so*
tunc *then*
vērō *indeed*
vitium–ī *vice*
voluptās–tātis *thrills*

8   There was no end to the slaughter.

> **victorem in aliam detinent caedem. exitus pugnantium mors est; ferro et igne res geritur. haec fiunt, dum vacat harena. 'sed latrocinium fecit aliquis, occidit hominem.' quid ergo? quia occidit ille, meruit ut hoc pateretur; tu quid meruisti miser, ut hoc spectes? 'occide, verbera, ure! quare tam timide incurrit in ferrum? quare parum audacter occidit? quare parum libenter moritur?' intermissum est spectaculum: 'interim iugulentur homines, ne nihil agatur.'**
>
> Seneca, *Epistulae Morales* VII, 4–5

agātur (agō–ere) *is being performed*
audācter *boldly*
caedēs–is *killing*
dētineō–ēre *keep*
exitus–ūs *end*
faciō–ere, fēcī, factum *do, make*
ferrum–ī *iron, sword*
fīō, fierī *happen*
gerō–ere *accomplish*
harēna–ae *sand*
ignis–is *fire*
incurrō–ere *run*
interim *meanwhile*
intermissum est *has an interval*
iugulentur (iugulō–āre) *let . . . have throats cut*
latrōcinium–ī *robbery*
libenter *willingly*
mereō–ēre–uī–itum *deserve*

miser–a–um *wretched*
moritur *he dies*
mors–tis *death*
nē nihil *that something*
occidō–ere, occidī *fall, die*
occīdō–ere, occīdī, occīsum *kill*
parum *not enough*
paterētur *he should suffer*
pugnantium *of those fighting*
pugnō–āre *fight*
quāre *why*
quid ergō? *what then?*
spectēs (spectō–āre) *you should watch*
tam *so*
timidē *timidly*
ūrō–ere *burn*
verberō–āre *whip*
victor–ōris *winner, survivor*

9   The more popular view is expressed by a character in Petronius' *Satyricon*. He complains about the poor quality of a show:

**quid ille nobis boni fecit? dedit gladiatores sestertiarios iam
decrepitos, quos si sufflasses, cecidissent; iam meliores bestiarios
vidi. ad summam, omnes postea secti sunt.**

Petronius, *Satyricon* 45

ad summam *in fact*
bēstiārius–ī *animal-fighter*
cecidissent (cadō–ere) *would have fallen over*
dēcrepitus–a–um *decrepit*
iam *now, already*
ille i.e. the producer

posteā *afterwards*
quid bonī *what good* (see p. 160)
secō–āre–uī, sectum *cut, lash*
sēstertiārius–a–um *worth twopence*
sufflāssēs (sufflō–āre) *you had blown
upon*

10 The emperor Nero staged these entertainments, and 'encouraged' senators and
their wives to participate in performances (to their horror).

**spectaculorum plurima et varia genera edidit: iuvenales, circenses,
scaenicos ludos, gladiatorium munus.**

Suetonius, *Nero* 11, 1

ēdō–ere–didī–ditum *put on*
genus–eris *type*
iuvenālēs *coming-of-age parties*

mūnus–eris *display*
plūrimus–a–um *very many*
spectāculum–ī *show*

Vocabulary

TEXT

tam	*so*
plānē	*clearly*
posteā	*afterwards*
sine [+abl.]	*without*
plēnus–a–um	*full*
turba–ae	*crowd*
mors–tis	*death*
pudor–ōris	*sense of shame*
ignis–is	*fire*
genus–eris	*race, origin, class, character*
agō–ere, ēgī, āctum	*do, manage, produce*

WORDS COMMONLY CONFUSED

anima–ae	*spirit, soul, life-breath*
animus–ī	*courage, mind, intention*

cadō, cadere, cecidī, cāsum	*fall, die*
caedō, caedere, cecīdī, caesum	*strike, kill*
concilium–ī	*council*
cōnsilium–ī	*plan, policy*
fugiō, fugere, fūgī, fugitum	*flee, run away*
fugō, fugāre, fugāvī, fugātum	*put to flight, rout*
genus, generis	*race, type, kind*
gēns, gentis	*family, tribe*
līber–a–um	*free*
liber, librī	*book*
līberī, līberōrum	*children*
occidō–ere, occidī	*fall, die*
occīdō–ere, occīdī, occīsum	*kill*
parō, parāre, parāvī, parātum	*prepare*
pāreō, pārēre, pāruī, pāritum	*obey*
quīdam, quaedam, quoddam	*a certain (adj.), someone (pron.)*
quondam	*formerly*
quidem	*even, indeed*
servō, servāre, servāvī, servātum	*save*
serviō, servīre, servīī, servītum	*serve*

Exercises

1 Identify the case of each participle and translate:

   (a) **spectatores Augustum in amphitheatrum venturum viderunt.**
   (b) **senatores praefecto audito Neronem laudaverunt.**
   (c) **ego poetam epistulam scribentem vidi.**
   (d) **Caesar Gallos captos Romam duxit.**
   (e) **hostes urbem captam incenderunt.**

2 Choose the correct participle and translate:

   (a) **senatores consilio Caesaris [auditi/audito] tristes erant.**
   (b) **Hannibal militem epistulam ex Romanorum castris [ferens/ferentem] vidit.**
   (c) **servus [fugitus/fugiturus] feminam audivit.**

3 Translate into Latin:

   (a) After Antonius was killed, Augustus was made princeps.
   (b) We were in the amphitheatre, about to see the gladiators.
   (c) After saying this (this: *use neuter plural of* **hic**) Caesar was quiet (**taceo–ere–ui–itum**).

(d) Intending to prepare the dinner (*say* have in mind *or use the future participle*), the slave came into the villa.

(e) The man saw his wife working in the fields.

4   Translate: **te morituri salutamus.**

5   Identify Latin words in this chapter which are ancestors of *ferrous*, *bestial*, *disturb* and *polite*.

6   What is a **sine qua non**?

7   What are the Latin ancestors of *voluntary* and *volatile*?

11 BRITAIN

Gerundives

A gerundive is an adjective formed from a verb:

e.g.	**paro–are**	*to prepare*
	parandus–a–um	*to-be-prepared*
	cena <u>paranda</u> est	*the dinner is <u>to-be-prepared</u>*

The gerundive often carries a sense of obligation, and always so in the nominative and accusative with no preposition:

e.g.	**cena <u>paranda</u> est**	*the dinner <u>must be prepared</u>*

The gerundive is passive, but is normally translated into English with an active expression:

e.g.	**vino <u>bibendo</u>**	*by <u>drinking</u> wine* (lit. *by wine <u>to-be-drunk</u>*)
	mater ad filium <u>inveniendum</u> venit	*the mother came <u>to find</u> her son* (lit. *for the son <u>to-be-found</u>*)

Practice

Match each sentence with its illustration and translate:

(a)	**liberi videndi non audiendi sunt.**	Illustration no. . . . . .
(b)	**vinum domini non bibendum est!**	Illustration no. . . . . .
(c)	**poeta militibus non laudandus est.**	Illustration no. . . . . .
(d)	**ludus in amphitheatro videndus est.**	Illustration no. . . . . .

Agent

With other passive forms, the agent is expressed by **a** (**ab** before a vowel) with the ablative:

    e.g. **Cicero <u>a</u> <u>te</u> videtur.**   *Cicero is seen by you.*

The agent of a gerundive is usually expressed by the dative:

    e.g. **Cicero <u>tibi</u> videndus est.**   *Cicero must be seen by you.*

The gerundive often carries a sense of obligation, but not always: the context will make it clear.

Deponent verbs

Deponent verbs are <u>passive</u> in form but have an <u>active</u> meaning:

> e.g. **conor–ari, conatus sum** *try*

Past participles in Latin are all passive, with the exception of deponent verbs:

> e.g. **conatus** *having tried*
> (but **missus** *having <u>been</u> sent*)

There is a full list of passive endings on p. 151. For other deponent verbs, see the vocabulary section of this chapter.

Conquest and civilisation

The Roman invasion of Britain was the first documented occupation of this island. At the time Britain was inhabited by different tribes with no national unity – a **natio** wasn't a 'nation' in our sense today, but a tribe. The tribes that attempted to join together and resist the invasion showed little common will and were poorly coordinated. Others welcomed the Romans, realising that the issue wasn't annexation or freedom but a choice of masters. The arrival from the continent of warlike people evading the advance of Rome had made life uncomfortable for many already living here.

Caesar had several reasons for his invasions of 55 and 54 BC: curiosity to see what was on the other side of the sea from Gaul; a desire to expand the empire (and his own prestige); and a concern that hostile Gauls were supported and sheltered by Britons. His invasions did not give Rome control of the island, for his attention was diverted back to the capital where political rivalries were fast evolving into civil war. Some decades later, when peace had been restored, Augustus expressed an interest in annexing Britain; but it was left to Claudius to accomplish the task. The south of Britain was finally in Roman hands in AD 48, more than a hundred years after Caesar first arrived. The north of the island was under Roman control some thirty years later, though some of Scotland remained outside the province.

Many provincials lived contentedly, enjoying the protection, scope for commerce and various other cultural attractions that Rome offered. From time to time, however, this authority was abused, and rebellions occurred. The most famous was that of Boudicca (or Boadicea), which took place in AD 61 following the death of Prasutagus, her husband and chieftain of the Iceni. He had left half of his inheritance to Rome, and the rest to his wife. The Romans decided to help themselves to all of it, and Boudicca soon found herself at the head of a large number of resentful Britons, many displaced by Roman settlers. Colchester and London were

Roman Britain

stormed and sacked, but the Britons came to grief at some point close to the modern A5 between London and Birmingham (the site is still unknown). Here they encountered the military commander, Suetonius, who was hastily returning from a successful campaign against the druids on the island of Anglesey. Overconfident and undisciplined, the Britons were annihilated by Suetonius' much smaller army, and Boudicca took her own life. Thereafter, the Romans took care not to be so provocative.

Traders were quick to realise the commercial potential of the new province. There were metals to be mined, especially tin; and the plentiful supply of cattle provided hides as well as meat. During the early period of conquest, the country was rich in 'human resources', and the flow of captives kept the slave-markets busy.

The local people absorbed Roman ideas, from town planning and heated houses to politics and religion. Conversely, it was perhaps the most enduring feature of

Rome's empire-building that Roman practices, habits and culture could be merged with indigenous ones. The success of this absorption and coexistence is amply illustrated by the length of time Roman authority prevailed: over four hundred years – or a fifth of the period of this island's documented history.

1 Caesar describes the people he finds in Britain.

ex his omnibus longe sunt humanissimi qui Cantium incolunt, quae regio est maritima omnis, neque multum a Gallica differunt consuetudine. interiores plerique frumenta non serunt, sed lacte et carne vivunt pellibusque sunt vestiti. omnes vero se Britanni vitro inficiunt, quod caeruleum efficit colorem, atque hoc horridiores sunt in pugna aspectu; capilloque sunt promisso atque omni parte corporis rasa praeter caput et labrum superius. uxores habent deni duodenique inter se communes et maxime fratres cum fratribus parentesque cum liberis; sed qui sunt ex his nati, eorum habentur liberi, quo primum virgo quaeque deducta est.

Caesar, *De Bello Gallico* V, 14

aspectus–ūs [m.] *appearance*
caeruleus–a–um *sky-blue*
Cantium–ī *Kent*
capillus–ī *hair*
caput, capitis *head*
carō, carnis *meat*
cōnsuētūdō–inis *custom*
corpus–oris *body*
dēducta est (dēdūcō–ere) *was escorted, married*
dēnī *in tens*
duodēnī *in twelves*
efficiō–ere *produce*
frūmentum–ī *corn*
habentur *are considered*
hūmānus–a–um *civilised*
incolō–ere *inhabit*
īnficiō–ere *stain*

labrum–ī *lip*
lac, lactis *milk*
longē *far*
maritimus–a–um *by the sea*
pars–tis [f.] *part*
pellis–is *skin*
plērīque *for the most part*
praeter [+acc.] *except*
prōmissus–a–um *grown long*
quaeque [fem. of **quisque**] *each*
quō *(to where) to whose home*
rāsus–a–um *shaved*
regiō–nis *region*
serō–ere *sow*
superior–ius *upper*
vitrum–ī *woad*

2 Cicero, whose brother was on Caesar's staff, passes on information to his friend Atticus.

neque argenti scripulum est ullum in illa insula neque ulla spes praedae nisi ex mancipiis.

Cicero, *Ad Atticum* IV, 17, 6

argentum–ī   *silver*
īnsula–ae [f.]   *island*
mancipium–ī   *slave*
praeda–ae   *plunder, loot*

scrīpulum–ī   *a small weight*
spēs–ēī [f.]   *hope*
ūllus–a–um   *any*

3 The Britons were proverbially unfriendly.

visam Britannos hospitibus feros.

Horace, Odes III, 4, 33

ferus–a–um   *savage*
hospes–itis   *guest*

vīsō–ere   *visit*

4 Horace predicts a successful conquest of Britain by Augustus.

... praesens divus habebitur
Augustus adiectis Britannis
imperio gravibusque Persis.

Horace, Odes III, 5, 2–4

adiectus–a–um (adiciō–ere)   *added*
dīvus–ī   *a god*
gravis–e   *threatening*

habēbitur (habeō–ēre)   *will be regarded as*
praesēns   *here and now*

5 In fact, Britain was ignored for many years after Caesar's exploratory visits.

primus omnium Romanorum divus Iulius cum exercitu Britanniam
ingressus, quamquam prospera pugna terruerit incolas ac litore
potitus sit, potest videri ostendisse posteris, non tradidisse; mox
bella civilia et in rem publicam versa principum arma, ac longa
oblivio Britanniae etiam in pace: consilium id divus Augustus
vocabat, Tiberius praeceptum.

Tacitus, Agricola 13

cōnsilium–ī   *plan, policy*
exercitus–ūs   *army*
incola–ae   *inhabitant*
ingredior–ī–gressus   *invade*
lītus–oris   *shore*
mox   *soon*
oblīviō–nis [f.]   *neglect*
ostendisse (ostendō–ere)   *to have revealed*

posterī–ae–a   *those after* (i.e. *posterity*)
potior–īrī–ītus [+abl.]   *take possession of*
praeceptum–ī   *maxim, precept*
prīnceps–ipis   *leader*
pugna–ae   *battle*
quamquam   *although*
terruerit (terreō–ēre)   *he intimidated*
trādidisse (trādō–ere)   *to have passed on*
vidērī (videō–ēre)   *to be seen*

6 Britain was finally annexed during the reign of Claudius, but not without resistance. The chieftain Caratacus was captured only after the treachery of Cartimandua, the queen of another tribe. Caratacus was taken to Rome, where he impressed his captors.

> **habui equos, viros, arma, opes: quid mirum, si haec invitus amisi? nam si vos omnibus imperitare vultis, sequitur ut omnes servitutem accipiant?**
>
> Tacitus, *Annals* XII, 37

accipiō–ere *welcome*
āmittō–ere, āmīsī *let go, lose*
habeō–ēre–uī *have*
imperitō–āre [+dat.] *rule over*
invitus–a–um *unwilling*
mīrus–a–um *extraordinary*

nam *for*
ops, opis *wealth*
quid *what*
sequor, sequī *follow*
servitūs–tūtis *slavery*
vultis (volō, velle) *you want*

7 Boudicca led a revolt against Rome.

> **femina duce (neque enim sexum in imperiis discernunt) sumpsere universi bellum.**
>
> Tacitus, *Agricola* 16

fēminā duce *under a woman's leadership*
sūmpsēre (sūmō, sūmere) *they took up*

ūniversus–a–um *all*

8 Britons were similar to their Gallic neighbours.

> **Gallos vicinam insulam occupasse credibile est. sermo haud multum diversus, in deposcendis periculis eadem audacia et, ubi advenere, in detrectandis eadem formido. plus tamen ferociae Britanni praeferunt, ut quos nondum longa pax emollierit. nam Gallos quoque in bellis floruisse accepimus; mox segnitia cum otio intravit, amissa virtute pariter ac libertate. quod Britannorum olim victis evenit: ceteri manent quales Galli fuerunt.**
>
> Tacitus, *Agricola* 11

accēpimus (accipiō–ere) *we have heard*
advēnēre *(the dangers) have arrived*
āmissus–a–um (āmittō–ere) *lost*
audācia–ae [f.] *boldness*
dīversus–a–um *different*
ēmollierit (ēmolliō–īre) *softened*
ēvēnit *(it) happened*

flōruisse (flōreō–ēre) *that ... were successful*
formīdō–inis *fear*
fuērunt (sum, esse) *were*
haud *not*
īdem, eadem, idem *the same*
in dēposcendīs *in challenging*

in dētrectandīs *in shirking them*
maneō–ēre *remain*
multum [adverb] *much*
nōndum *not yet*
occupāsse (occupō–āre) *to have occupied*
ōlim *some time ago*
ōtium–ī *peace*
pariter *equally*

praeferō–ferre *display*
quālēs *just as*
segnitia–ae *sluggishness*
sermō–nis [m.] *speech*
ubī *when*
ut quōs *because . . . them*
vīcīnus–a–um *neighbouring*
virtūs–tūtis [f.] *courage*

9 Our weather has not changed much over the last two thousand years.

caelum crebris imbribus ac nebulis foedum; asperitas frigorum abest.

Tacitus, *Agricola* 12

absum, abesse *be absent*
asperitās–tātis *harshness*
caelum–ī *sky*
crēber–bra–brum *frequent*

foedus–a–um *dirty*
frīgus–oris *cold, chill*
imber–bris *rain-cloud*
nebula–ae *mist*

10 British people readily absorbed Roman culture, and learnt to speak Latin – a sign of their moral collapse, says Tacitus.

qui modo linguam Romanam abnuebant, eloquentiam concupiscebant. paulatimque descensum ad delenimenta vitiorum, porticus et balinea et conviviorum elegantiam. idque apud imperitos humanitas vocabatur, cum pars servitutis esset.

Tacitus, *Agricola* 21

abnuō–ere *reject*
apud [+acc.] *among*
balineum–ī *bath*
concupīscō–ere *desire, aspire to*
convīvium–ī *dinner-party*
cum *although*
dēlēnīmentum–ī *allurement*
dēscēnsum (est) *there was a decline*

hūmānitās–tātis *civilisation*
imperītus–a–um *ignorant*
lingua–ae *language*
modo *recently*
paulātim *little by little*
porticus–ūs *colonnade*
vitium–ī *vice*

Vocabulary

TEXT

īnsula–ae *island*
pugna–ae *battle*
lingua–ae *tongue, language*
perīculum–ī *danger*
caelum–ī *sky, heaven*
ars, artis *art, skill*
hospes–itis *guest, host*
lītus–oris *shore*
caput–itis *head*

exercitus–ūs *army*
incolō–ere *inhabit*
pāreō–ēre [+dat.] *obey*
pugnō–āre *fight*
ōlim *once (upon a time)*
quamquam *although*
mox *soon*
apud [+acc.] *in the presence of*
praeter [+acc.] *except, beside*

DEPONENT VERBS

cōnfiteor, cōnfitērī, cōnfessus sum	*admit*
cōnor, cōnārī, cōnātus sum	*try*
fateor, fatērī, fassus sum	*admit*
hortor, hortārī, hortātus sum	*encourage*
ingredior, ingredī, ingressus sum	*go in, attack*
loquor, loquī, locūtus sum	*speak*
minor, minārī, minātus sum	*threaten*
mīrōr, mīrārī, mīrātus sum	*admire*
morior, morī, mortuus sum	*die*
moror, morārī, morātus sum	*delay*
patior, patī, passus sum	*suffer, allow*
proficīscor, proficīscī, profectus sum	*set out, depart*
progredior, progredī, progressus sum	*advance*
reor, rērī, ratus sum	*think*
sequor, sequī, secūtus sum	*follow*
ūtor, ūtī, ūsus sum [+abl.]	*use*

Exercises

1 Identify the ending of each gerundive and translate:

(a) **Cicero** [laudandus–a–um] **est.**
(b) **carmina post cenam** [audiendus–a–um] **sunt.**
(c) **Caesar in templum ad deos** [laudandus–a–um] **venit.**
(d) **vinum non servis** [bibendus–a–um] **est.**

2 Replace each infinitive with the gerundive and translate:

e.g. **nunc est** [bibere]

answer: **nunc est bibendum**   *now it is to be drunk*
                                      (*now is the time for drinking*)

(a)   **nunc est** [laborare]
(b)   **nunc est** [vivere]
(c)   **nunc est** [dormire]
(d)   **nunc est** [agere]

3   Translate into Latin:

(a)   I tried to encourage the soldiers.
(b)   We set out before midday.
(c)   The dinner must be prepared by the slaves.
(d)   Caesar encouraged the Gauls.
(e)   We set out from the city to Cicero's villa.

4   What is the etymology of

Amanda, Miranda, memorandum, referendum, addendum and *agenda*?

5   **Mutatis mutandis** is an ablative absolute comprising the gerundive and past participle of the verb **muto–are** (*to change*). What is the literal meaning?

6   What is the meaning of **quod erat demonstrandum**?

12 RELIGION

Infinitives

	Present	Future	Perfect
Active	**parāre** *to prepare*	**parātūrus esse** * *to be about to prepare*	**parāvisse** *to have prepared*
Passive	**parārī** *to be prepared*	**parātum īrī** *to be about to be prepared*	**parātus esse** * *to have been prepared*

* The forms **paraturus** and **paratus** are like **bonus–a–um** and agree with the infinitive's subject.

The infinitive is used with verbs like **volo** (*I want*) and **possum** (*I am able*):

> e.g. **Ciceronem <u>videre</u> volo**   *I want <u>to see</u> Cicero*
> **poetam <u>audire</u> non poteramus**   *we were unable <u>to hear</u> the poet*

Accusative and infinitive

The infinitive is also used to express a reported statement or thought:

> e.g. **Ciceronem in urbe**   *He said Cicero <u>to be</u> in the city*
> **<u>esse</u> dixit**   (*He said that Cicero was in the city*)

In this expression, the infinitive is used with an accusative (here: **Ciceronem**). This was what was actually said (the direct statement):

> **Cicero in urbe est**   *Cicero is in the city*

The tense of the infinitive in the indirect statement (**esse**) is in the same tense as the verb of the direct statement (**est**), i.e. present. Consider these different tenses:

Direct	Indirect
Cicero in urbe <u>fuit</u> *Cicero was in the city*	**Ciceronem in urbe <u>fuisse</u> dixit** *he said that Cicero had been in the city*
Cicero in urbe <u>erit</u> *Cicero will be in the city*	**Ciceronem in urbe <u>futurum esse</u> dixit** *he said that Cicero would be in the city*

In the last example, **futur<u>um</u> esse** agrees with its subject **Cicero<u>nem</u>** (see * above).

The accusative and infinitive is used to express an indirect thought as well as statement:

Direct	Indirect
Cicero in urbe est *Cicero is in the city*	**Ciceronem in urbe esse <u>putat</u>** *he <u>thinks</u> that Cicero is in the city*
Cicero in urbe est *Cicero is in the city*	**Ciceronem in urbe esse <u>credit</u>** *he <u>believes</u> that Cicero is in the city*

The reflexive pronoun **se** (*him, her, them*) is used when the person referred to is the same as the subject of the verb of speaking or thinking.

> e.g. **<u>puellae</u> dixerunt <u>se</u> in agris ambulare**
> *the <u>girls</u> said that <u>they</u> were walking in the fields*
>
> **<u>Hannibal</u> credidit <u>se</u> Romam victurum esse**
> *<u>Hannibal</u> believed that <u>he</u> would conquer Rome*

Practice

Complete each indirect statement:

	Direct	Indirect
e.g.	**Cicero est in urbe**	**dixit *Ciceronem in urbe esse***

123

1   **Brutus Ciceronem vidit**   **dixit . . . . .**
2   **servi cenam parabunt**   **dixit . . . . .**
3   **Marcus est civis Romanus**   **Marcus dixit . . . . .**

Reading notes

The accusative and infinitive gave Latin the facility to re-create what a character said or thought without the need for a phrase like 'he continued' or 'in her opinion' to be added to distinguish between the writer's own views and those of the characters, e.g. (p. 87):

> **Boudicca solitum Britannis (esse*) feminarum ductu bellare testa-batur; vincendum illa acie vel cadendum esse; id mulieri destinatum (esse*): viverent viri et servirent.**
> *Boudicca declared that it was customary for Britons to go to war under the leadership of women; in that battle it was a matter of victory or death; that, she said, was a woman's decision: the men might live and be slaves if they so wished.*

* Note that **esse** is often left out.

Beliefs and attitudes

At first sight it is tempting to assume that religion in ancient Rome wasn't taken very seriously. We read of gods behaving wantonly or trivially; there was no singular coherent religion; the empire embraced a variety of different cults and beliefs; and there were countless gods and spirits. Roman gods were often perceived as frivolous and fancy-free, but this had an underlying menace which subsequent Christian thinking has sometimes obscured.

Roman religion had its roots in animism. Spirits were identified in all things that could influence human life, and people prayed and sacrificed to these spirits in the hope that the activity or condition each spirit represented would turn out to their advantage. Belief in predestination was widespread, and the idea of fate or destiny appears throughout Roman literature. The relationship between fate and the gods is often vague, for sometimes the gods conform to fate, while elsewhere they shape it; a reflection, perhaps, of the tension felt by a people with both a strong sense of self-will and a belief in a determining influence.

Romans were superstitious, and would look for signs and portents that might reveal future events. The future could be predicted, they believed, by the study of animals' entrails, the flight of birds, the weather and dreams. The good will of the gods was elicited by sacrifices and festive days in their honour. Virgil's simile for the cries of the dying Laocoon (No. 10) is a bull escaping from an altar and shaking an axe from his neck, a clear and accessible image for the poet's contemporary audience. But the smells and noises of an abattoir are not things we later readers would readily associate with the solemnity of a cathedral.

From the earliest days of contact with Greece, Romans had been importing across the sea their stories, myths, poetic forms, literary conventions, and even their gods. These gods had personalities, which their own spirits lacked, and were irresistible to poets and storytellers. Roman deities quickly absorbed the characteristics and functions of their counterparts: Jupiter and Zeus, Juno and Hera, Minerva and Athene, Diana and Artemis, Mars and Ares, Venus and Aphrodite, Vulcan and Hephaestus, Mercury and Hermes, Neptune and Poseidon.

Every household had its own deity (**Lar**) and spirits of the cupboard (**Penates**). These spirits were responsible for food and family happiness, and would no doubt have received more sacrifices and prayers than the more celebrated Greek personality-gods enshrined in literature. State religion was similar to that practised by families but on a larger scale. Protection, prosperity and good fortune were prayed for in public as well as in the home. Vesta, the hearth-goddess, was worshipped in private and at public functions. Jupiter and Juno were the divine **paterfamilias** and **matrona** of Rome.

Greek philosophy was studied and respected, though with some reservations. For Greek intellectuals, philosophy was an inevitable part of a social occasion, where the activity of discussion and reasoning was itself a pleasure. Romans were more interested in the conclusion of an argument than in the rhetoric leading up to it, and discussions of ethical questions rarely lost sight of their practical value. Two Greek schools of philosophy had lasting influence in Rome: the Stoics and the Epicureans. The Stoics taught people to confront life's dangers and losses with equanimity, an attitude that was popular with military disciplinarians and with senators who suffered under bullying emperors. The Epicureans, on the other hand, encouraged people to steer clear of life's troubles: they cherished the Greek concept of *ataraxia* (freedom from stress), which in its extreme form meant no ambition, career, marriage, family or anything else that might upset the peace.

As Rome annexed lands in the east, new cults were discovered, and these found their way back to the capital. At the time of Augustus' rise to power, many different cults were being practised in Rome. He did not persecute them, but nevertheless encouraged traditional ones. He even introduced a new god to counter the wide variety of religious cults in the empire – himself. The cult of Divus Augustus was publicised to promote loyalty to the empire and his leadership. This wasn't meant to supplant existing cults, but to give greater coherence. The authorities were on the whole very tolerant of all the different cults and practices. They even allowed their own cults and spirits to be merged with provincial ones – for diplomatic gains. However, not all religions welcomed such conciliation: no doctrine could embrace both the Roman pantheon and Christianity.

1 Saint Augustine ridiculed the pagan belief in so many gods. Even a doorway had to have three spirits.

> **unum quisque domui suae ponit ostiarium, et quia homo est, omnino sufficit: tres deos isti posuerunt, Forculum foribus, Cardeam cardini, Limentinum limini. ita non poterat Forculus simul et cardinem limenque servare.**

Augustine, De Civitate Dei IV, 8

Cardea–ae *spirit (of the hinge)*
cardō–inis *hinge*
domus–ūs [f.] *house*
Forculus–ī *spirit (of the door)*
forēs–ium *gate*
homō–inis *man, human being*
istī (like **ille** in form and meaning) *those people* (i.e. pagans)
ita *thus*
līmen–inis *threshold*

Līmentīnus–ī *spirit (of the threshold)*
omnīnō *altogether*
ōstiārius–ī *doorkeeper*
pōnō–ere, posuī *place*
poterat [**possum**: see p. 153] *could*
quia *because*
quisque [nom.] *each man*
servō–āre *look after*
simul *at the same time*
sufficiō–ere *be enough*

2 On his visit to the underworld, Aeneas passed the home of some spirits.

> **vestibulum ante ipsum primis in faucibus Orci**
> **Luctus et ultrices posuere cubilia Curae;**
> **pallentes habitant Morbi tristisque Senectus,**
> **et Metus et malesuada Fames ac turpis Egestas,**
> **terribiles visu formae, Letumque Labosque.**

Virgil, Aeneid VI, 273–277

cubīle–is [n.] *couch*
cūra–ae *care, anxiety*
egestās, ātis *need, poverty*
famēs–is [f.] *hunger*
faux, faucis *jaw*
fōrma–ae *shape*
ipsum [acc.] *itself*
labōs–ōris *toil*
lētum–ī *death*
lūctus–ūs *grief*
malesuādus–a–um *evil-counselling*

metus–ūs *fear*
morbus–ī *disease*
Orcus–ī *Hades*
pallēns *pallid-making*
posuēre (**pōnō–ere**) *have placed*
senectūs–tūtis *old age*
terribilis–e *terrible*
turpis–e *disgraceful*
ultrīx–īcis *avenging*
vestibulum–ī *hall*
vīsū *to see*

3 Deities were responsible for stirring up Horace's amorous feelings.

> **mater saeva Cupidinum**
> **Thebanaeque iubet me Semelae puer**

et lasciva Licentia
   finitis animum reddere amoribus.

                              Horace, *Odes* I, XIX, 1–4

amor–ōris   *passion* (pl. for sing.)
animus–ī   *mind, heart*
fīnītus–a–um   *ended*
iubeō–ēre   *command*
lascīvus–a–um   *playful*
licentia–ae   *wantonness*

māter Cupīdinum   *mother of the Cupids*
   (i.e. Venus)
puer–ī   *boy, son*
reddō–ere   *restore, give again*
Semela–ae   i.e. Bacchus' mother
Thēbānus–a–um   *Theban*

4   Fortuna was the spirit of fate, and her favours were much courted (she was worshipped all over the empire).

Fortuna saevo laeta negotio et
ludum insolentem ludere pertinax
   transmutat incertos honores,
      nunc mihi, nunc alii benigna.

                              Horace, *Odes* III, XXIX, 49–52

aliī [dat.]   *other*
benignus–a–um   *kind*
honor–ōris [m.]   *honour, favour*
incertus–a–um   *uncertain, fickle*
īnsolēns–tis   *wanton*

lūdō–ere   *play*
lūdus–ī   *game*
negōtium–ī   *business, work*
pertināx–ācis   *determined*
trānsmūtō–āre   *transfer, switch*

5   Followers of the Epicurean school of philosophy believed that although the gods existed, they had no relevance to people.

                        nos te,
   nos facimus, Fortuna, deam caeloque locamus.

                              Juvenal, *Satire* X, 365–366

6   The Stoics, on the other hand, did believe in Fortuna, and sought to endure whatever she brought to them.

tolerabimus damna et dolores, ignominias, locorum commutationes,
orbitates, discidia, quae sapientem, etiam si universa circumveniant,
non mergunt.

                              Seneca, *De Constantia* 8, 3

commūtātiō–nis   *change*
damnum–ī   *loss*
discidium–ī   *divorce*

dolor–ōris   *grief*
ignōminia–ae   *disgrace*
mergō–ere   *overwhelm*

orbitās–tātis *bereavement*
sapiēns–tis *wise person*

tolerō–āre *endure*
ūniversus–a–um *all together*

7 The Greeks had enjoyed the intellectual arguments of philosophy. The Romans preferred practical benefits, and ridiculed Greek-inspired games with logic.

> **mus syllaba est. mus autem caseum rodit; syllaba ergo caseum rodit. verendum est ne, si neglegentior fuero, caseum liber comedat.**

> Seneca, *Epistulae Morales* 48, 6

cāseus–ī *cheese*
comedō–ere *gobble up*
fuerō *I shall have been, am*
liber, librī *book*
mūs, mūris *mouse*

nē *lest*
neglegentior *too careless*
rōdō–ere *nibble*
syllaba–ae *syllable*
verendum est *it is to be feared*

8 Horace, like many others of his day, was an eclectic. Echoes both of Stoicism and of Epicureanism appear in his poems. Below, his (imaginary?) girlfriend, Leuconoe, is advised not to worry about her future:

> **tu ne quaesieris – scire nefas – quem mihi, quem tibi**
> **finem di dederint, Leuconoe, nec Babylonios**
> **temptaris numeros ... / ... sapias, vina liques, et spatio brevi**
> **spem longam reseces. dum loquimur, fugerit invida**
> **aetas: carpe diem, quam minimum credula postero.**

> Horace, *Odes* I, XI, 1–3, 6–8

aetās–tātis *time*
carpe *pluck! enjoy!*
crēdulus–a–um [+ dat.] *trusting*
dederint (dō, dare) *have given*
deus–ī (dī: nom. pl.) *god*
fīnis–is *end, death*
invidus–a–um *hateful*
liquēs (liquō–āre) *strain!*
loquimur (loquor–ī) *we speak*

nē quaesierīs (quaerō–ere) *do not inquire*
numerus–ī *number* (astrologer's)
posterō (diēī) *tomorrow*
quam minimum *as little as possible*
resecēs (resecō–āre) *cut back!*
sapiās (sapiō–ere) *be wise!*
scīre nefās *not ours to know*
spatium–ī *space*
temptārīs (temptō–āre) *you should try*

9 Horace commemorates a sacrifice to the fountain of Bandusia, but his attention is drawn to the victim.

> **o Fons Bandusiae, splendidior vitro,**
> **dulci digne mero non sine floribus,**
> ** cras donaberis haedo,**
> **   cui frons turgida cornibus**

primis et venerem et proelia destinat.
frustra: nam gelidos inficiet tibi
  rubro sanguine rivos
    lascivi suboles gregis.

Horace, Odes III, XIII, 1–8

cornū–ūs *horn*
crās *tomorrow*
cui *whose*
dēstinat (dēstinō–āre) *foretells*
digne [+ abl.] *deserving* (agrees with **Fōns**)
dōnāberis (dōnō–āre) *you'll be presented*
dulcis–e *sweet*
frōns–tis [f.] *forehead*
frūstrā *in vain, not to be*
gelidus–a–um *cool*
grex–gis *flock*
haedus–ī *young goat, kid*
īnficiō–ere *stain*

lascīvus–a–um *playful*
merum–ī *wine*
proelium–ī *battle, joust*
rīvus–ī *stream*
ruber–bra–brum *red*
sanguis–inis *blood*
splendidus–a–um *bright*
subolēs–is *offspring*
tibi *your* (i.e. the fountain's)
turgidus–a–um *swollen*
venus–eris *love, mating*
vitrum–ī *glass*

10 Sacrifices were commonplace. Virgil described one which went awry as a simile for the death of Laocoon (see Chapter 3, No. 11). The story of Neptune sending a pair of serpents to kill him tells us something about the ancients' perception of divine justice. Poor Laocoon accurately foresaw the dangers of the Wooden Horse, but the grander scheme of things would not permit his comrades to believe him.

ille simul manibus tendit divellere nodos
perfusus sanie vittas atroque veneno,
clamoresque simul horrendos ad sidera tollit:
qualis mugitus, fugit cum saucius aram
taurus et incertam excussit cervice securim.

Virgil, Aeneid II, 220–4

āra–ae *altar*
āter–tra–trum *black*
cervīx–īcis *neck*
clāmor–ōris *shout, cry*
dīvellō–ere *tear apart*
excussit (excutiō–ere) *has shaken off*
fugiō–ere, fūgī *escape*
ille [nom.] *he*
incertus–a–um *ill-aimed*
manus–ūs *hand*
mūgītus–ūs *bellowing*

nōdus–ī *knot*
perfūsus vittās *his headband spattered*
  (see p. 160)
quālīs [acc. pl.] *just like*
saniēs–ēī *slaver*
saucius–a–um *wounded*
secūris–is [f.] *axe*
sīdus–eris *star*
simul *at the same time*
tendō–ere *struggle*
tollō–ere *raise*
venēnum–ī *poison*

11   Italian storytellers and poets invested their own gods with the personalities of the Greek Olympians. By the time Virgil was composing the *Aeneid*, Venus was synonymous with Aphrodite, the goddess of love. She persuades Vulcan, her husband, to forge new weapons for Aeneas, her son.

> **dixerat et niveis hinc atque hinc diva lacertis**
> **cunctantem amplexu molli fovet. ille repente**
> **accepit solitam flammam, notusque medullas**
> **intravit calor et labefacta per ossa cucurrit.**

Virgil, Aeneid VIII, 387–390

amplexus–ūs *embrace*	**lacertus–ī** *arm*
calor–ōris *glow*	**medullae–ārum** *marrow*
cūnctāns–tis *hesitating*	**mollis–e** *soft*
currō–ere, cucurrī *run*	**niveus–a–um** *snow-white*
dīxerat *(Venus) had spoken*	**nōtus–a–um** *well-known*
foveō–ēre *enfold*	**os, ossis** [n.] *bone*
hinc atque hinc *from one side then the other*	**repente** *suddenly*
intrō–āre–āvī *enter*	**solitus–a–um** *familiar*
labefactus–a–um *shaken, trembling*	

12   Virgil shows Augustus winning the battle of Actium with the help of all the gods of Rome.

> **hinc Augustus agens Italos in proelia Caesar**
> **cum patribus populoque, penatibus et magnis dis.**

Virgil, Aeneid VIII, 678–9

agēns *leading*	**hinc** *on this side*
Augustus . . . Caesar *Augustus Caesar*	**penātēs–ium** *spirits of the household*
deus–ī *god*	**proelium–ī** *battle*

13   Virgil and his friend Horace were encouraged by Augustus to promote traditional religious values.

> **delicta maiorum immeritus lues,**
> **Romane, donec templa refeceris**
> **aedesque labentes deorum et**
> **foeda nigro simulacra fumo.**

Horace, Odes III, VI, 1–4

aedēs–is *shrine*	**foedus–a–um** *soiled*
dēlictum–ī *sin*	**fūmus–ī** *smoke*
dōnec *until*	**immeritus–a–um** *undeserving*

lābēns–tis *collapsing*
luō–ere *atone for*
māiōrēs–um *ancestors*
niger–gra–grum *black*

refēceris (reficiō–ere) *you have rebuilt*
Rōmāne *you Roman(s)*
simulācrum–ī *statue*
templum–ī *temple*

14 Many of the emperors were given divine status after they died. The emperor Vespasian's dying words show that he did not take this too seriously.

'vae,' inquit, 'puto deus fio.'

Suetonius, *Life of Vespasian* 23

fīō-ierī *become*

vae *oh dear*

Vocabulary

TEXT

putō–āre, putāvī, putātum *think*
sciō–īre, scīvī, scītum *know*
doceō–ēre, docuī, doctum *teach*
crēdō–ere, crēdidī, crēditum *believe*
nūntiō–āre, nūntiāvī, nūntiātum *announce*
crās *tomorrow*
hodiē *today*
simul *at the same time*
repente *suddenly*

dīvus–a–um *divine*
niger–gra–grum *black*
invīsus–a–um *hateful, hated*
dulcis–e *sweet*
mollis–e *soft*

proelium–ī *battle*
negōtium–ī *business*
sanguis–inis *blood*
āra–ae *altar*
calor–ōris *heat*

Exercises

1 Change each sentence to express what was actually said or thought:

(a) **Caesar Romanos victuros esse dicit.**
(b) **Hannibal omnes Romanos inimicos esse credidit.**
(c) **Neronem omnium principum avarissimum fuisse dicunt.**
(d) **poeta sperabat hospites post cenam carmina sua audituros esse.**

131

(e) **Cicero milites nimium laudatos esse putavit.**

2   Change each sentence into a reported statement, beginning each sentence with **Cloelia dixit** (*Cloelia said that . . .*):

(a) **amici in Gallia habitant.**
(b) **imperator hodie in amphitheatrum veniet.**
(c) **Antonius epistulam ad Cleopatram misit.**
(d) **orationes validiores quam arma sunt.**
(e) **consilium a senatoribus audietur.**

3   Translate into Latin:

(a) She said that she wanted to go to Rome.
(b) Julius said that his mother would prepare the dinner.
(c) Clodius said he was a friend of Cicero.
(d) The slaves told the soldiers that Cicero was in Greece.
(e) The soldiers reported Cicero's absence to Antony (*say* . . . *that* Cicero was absent).

4   What are the initials **n.b.**, **e.g.** and **p.s.** short for?

5   Identify Latin words which are etymologically linked to: *library, computer, current, rodent* and *quality*.

13 CHRISTIANITY

Gerunds

An English gerund is a noun that is formed from a verb, and ends '-ing'. English participles are spelt the same, but they are adjectives:

> *I do not like <u>flying</u>* (gerund/noun)
> *<u>flying</u> into a rage, he broke the teapot* (participle/adjective)

The Latin gerund is a neuter singular noun formed from a verb, e.g. **parandum** (*preparing*), **videndum** (*seeing*). It is not used in the nominative – instead the Romans used the infinitive:

> e.g. **videre est credere**   *to see is to believe/seeing is believing*

In other cases, the gerund is used:

> e.g. **<u>videndo</u> credimus**   *by seeing we believe*
> **servus est ad <u>laborandum</u> aptus**   *the slave is fit for working*

The gerund is similar to the gerundive (see Chapter 11) except that the gerund is active, and not an adjective but a noun:

acc.	**videndum**	*seeing*
gen.	**videndī**	*of seeing*
dat.	**videndō**	*for seeing*
abl.	**videndō**	*by seeing*

A gerund is sometimes used in place of a gerundive:

> Gerundive: **Romae <u>videndae</u> causa venimus**
> *we came for the sake of Rome-to-be-seen*

Gerund: **Romam <u>videndi</u> causa venimus**
we came for the sake of seeing Rome

Note that a gerundive is <u>passive</u> and an <u>adjective</u>, while a gerund is <u>active</u> and a <u>noun</u>.

Practice

With the gerunds from **fugio–ere**, **laboro–are**, **pugno–are** and **bibo–ere**, complete each sentence and translate:

1 **servus est aptus ad . . . . .**

2 **servus est aptus ad . . . . .**

3 **miles est aptus ad . . . . .**

4 **miles est aptus ad . . . . .**

se, ipse

se is a <u>reflexive</u> pronoun (i.e. refers to the subject of the sentence, but is never the subject itself: **se** has no nominative). It can mean *him*(*self*), *her*(*self*), *it*(*self*) or *them*(*selves*). **ipse** is an emphatic form of **is, ea, id** and means *self*:

    e.g.   **Caesar <u>ipse</u> dixit**   *Caesar <u>himself</u> spoke*
          Caesar <u>sibi</u> dixit   *Caesar spoke <u>to himself</u>*

For the endings of **se** and **ipse**, see pp. 147–148.

A new age

Rome was tolerant of the many different religions practised in the empire, and persecution was rare. In Britain the druids were attacked because they encouraged rebellion and indulged in human sacrifices, often of Roman captives. If a religion was focal to rebellion, then worshippers could expect rough treatment. In the case of the Christians the perceived threat arose from their refusal to practise any rituals other than their own, which gave the impression that they were rejecting the authority of the state. Roman officials and priests were civic magistrates, and the public rituals they supervised were performed for the well-being of the state. Any reluctance to recognise this formal religion was seen by some to be bordering on insurrection, a resentment that wasn't eased by the cult's existence on the fringe of respectable society. The Christians' preference for the fellowship of sinners and no-hopers irritated many, and for some their ideological inflexibility was disturbing.

    Despite intermittent opposition and persecution, the Christian faith established itself in the capital and spread throughout the empire. The gospels were translated into Latin, and their message that hardship in this world would win a foothold in the next brought comfort to thousands of poorer people across Europe. Here was something they had seldom glimpsed – a sense of hope. Stoicism had attracted those who had something to lose, and reminded them that they might just lose it. The poor had too little to start with, and were consoled by the promise of salvation in the next world for those who suffered in this one. Christians even welcomed suffering, going out of their way to be poor, abstemious and in some cases martyred. Suffering was not divinely caused, but certainly increased the chances of salvation. This was bewildering to pagans, who believed that gods were responsible for human suffering, either to punish mortal error and disrespect, or merely to give vent to their whimsical and unpredictable natures – according to the ancients, the source of undeserved misfortune.

Christianity didn't remain for ever the religion of the poor. In due course, a number of rich and powerful people were converted, including, in the fourth century, emperors themselves; and differences – literary, intellectual and political – between Christians and pagans continued to surface throughout the later years of the empire. One such quarrel concerned the appropriateness of classical literature. Many Christians thought it shouldn't be read – most were unable to read it in any case. Even educated converts, like Augustine and Jerome, were conscious of their new loyalty, and joined in the rejection of the classics. The pleasure of reading these books gave educated Christians an opportunity for self-denial: Jerome felt guilty because he was tempted by the books of Cicero (p. 140). Poets such as Virgil and Ovid had always been held in high regard, but now the content of their stories were censured for the amoral – and immoral – antics of the gods. Polytheism was considered not only blasphemous but ridiculous: Augustine (p. 126) wondered why there had to be one spirit for the doorway, one for the door and yet another for its hinge. However, their quarrel wasn't really with the books, but with the pagans who upheld them, and after this opposition had receded, classical works became acceptable to churchmen as allegorical tales. Before long, the full circle had turned, with the early monasteries playing an important role in the survival of classical literature.

The new religion gave a fresh stimulus to intellectual life. In an era when the reworking of classical thought had grown ever more slavish, Christianity posed new questions for intellectuals to ponder, not least the concept and identity of God. A pagan divinity was identified with the phenomenon which it represented. Light, for example, was a mystery to pagans, and they explained it in terms of a sun-god. Christians now inverted the formula: God was the mystery, light the metaphorical representation. To frame this new and complex theology, intellectuals borrowed ideas from previous philosophers. Plato's theory of forms, which begins (or ends) with corporeal images and leads to the absolute form from which all things are derived, inspired a number of Christian intellectuals, who became known as the *Neoplatonists*.

The political momentum of Christianity overcame paganism and, some would say, the empire too. A distinctive characteristic of Roman administration was essentially a Greek idea which the Romans had put into wider practice: the partially autonomous municipality. In towns all over the empire local magistrates were elected to supervise local affairs, including a portion of the taxes. In later years corruption, mismanagement and insecurity in the face of barbarian immigration from the east prompted central government to replace local elections with magistrates of their own choosing, who were obliged to collect the taxes for central government to spend. The ensuing vacuum in popular representation was filled by the leaders of the Church, who soon earned more favour than the magistrates: bishops were infinitely preferable to bailiffs. In this way the church replaced the forum as the centre of local affairs, and the self-administered towns began to disappear. It wasn't very long, of course, before the bishop became the bailiff too, sharing power with a local lord in a manner that underpinned the political structure of the medieval era to follow.

The growth of Christianity was certainly a symptom of the fall of the empire. Whether or not it was one of the causes remains a bone of contention between humanists and the Church, neither of whom are consistently capable of a dispassionate view. In our attempts to trace the causes of decline, we sometimes overlook how long the empire survived before it finally submitted to old age. In any case, it is doubtful whether any single factor was solely responsible for an inevitable end, which occurred for a variety of internal and external reasons, arguably over some hundreds of years. Rome may not have been built in a day; she did not disappear in one either.

1 Christianity did not allow the worship of any other gods. Since the emperor himself had divine status, this was a difficulty which the enemies of Christ tried to exploit.

> (The chief priests) **miserunt insidiatores qui se iustos simularent, ut caperent eum in sermone, et traderent illum principatui et potestati praesidis. et interrogaverunt illum, dicentes: 'magister, scimus quia recte dicis et doces: licet nobis dare tributum Caesari, an non?' considerans autem dolum illorum, dixit ad eos: 'quid me temptatis? ostendite mihi denarium: cuius habet imaginem et inscriptionem?' respondentes dixerunt: 'Caesaris.' et ait illis: 'reddite ergo quae Caesaris sunt, Caesari: et quae Dei sunt, Deo.' et non potuerunt verbum eius reprehendere coram plebe: et mirati in responso eius, tacuerunt.**
>
> St Luke, *New Testament* 20, 20–26 (Trans. Jerome)

ait *he said*
caperent (capiō–ere) *they might catch*
cōram [+abl.] *in the presence of*
dolus–ī *trick*
īnsidiātor–ōris *trickster*
iūstus–a–um *proper, reasonable*
licet *it is allowed*
mīror–ārī–ātus *wonder at*

ostendō–ere *show*
potestās–tātis *power*
praeses–idis *governor*
prīncipātus–ūs *control*
quia *that* (classical Latin: *because*)
sciō–īre *know*
taceō–ēre–uī *be silent*
temptō–āre *test, tempt*

2   Christianity's message of salvation gave poor people a measure of hope, something to live (and die) for. The rich were actively discouraged:

> **et iterum dico vobis: facilius est camelum per foramen acus transire quam divitem intrare in regnum caelorum.**
>
> St Matthew, *New Testament* 19, 24 (Trans. Jerome)

dīves–itis *rich (man)*	**forāmen acūs** *the eye of a needle*
facilius (facilis) *more easily*	**iterum** *again*

3   Sinners were no less welcome to join than respectable citizens, which fostered hostile prejudices. Nero was able to use Christians as scapegoats for the fire of Rome (AD 64) following rumours that he himself had started it.

> **ergo abolendo rumori Nero subdidit reos et quaesitissimis poenis adfecit quos per flagitia invisos vulgus Christianos appellabat. auctor nominis eius Christus Tiberio imperitante per procuratorem Pontium Pilatum supplicio adfectus erat; repressaque in praesens exitiabilis superstitio rursum erumpebat, non modo per Iudaeam, originem eius mali, sed per urbem etiam quo cuncta undique atrocia aut pudenda confluunt celebranturque.**
>
> Tacitus, *Annals* 15, 44, 2–3

aboleō–ēre *destroy*	**per flāgitia (flāgitium–ī)** *for their crimes*
adficiō–ere–fēcī–fectum *afflict, inflict upon*	**poena–ae** *punishment*
auctor–ōris *founder*	**pudendus–a–um** *shameful*
celebrō–āre *practise*	**quaesītus–a–um** *far-fetched*
cōnfluō–ere *flow together*	**quō** *to where*
cūnctus–a–um *all*	**reus–ī** *defendant*
ergō *so*	**rūmor–ōris** [m.] *rumour*
ērumpō–ere *break out*	**rūrsum** *again*
exitiābilis–e *deadly*	**subdō–ere–didī** *introduce (falsely)*
imperitō–āre *rule*	**superstitiō–nis** *superstition*
in praesēns *for the time being*	**supplicium–ī** *death-penalty*
invīsus–a–um *hated*	**undique** *from all sides*
nōn modo *not only*	**vulgus–ī** *crowd*

4   As governor of Bithynia (c. AD 112), Pliny often wrote to the emperor Trajan for guidance on matters of administration. Pliny sought his advice on how to deal with the Christians, and until he heard from the emperor, he decided to treat them as follows:

> **interim in iis, qui ad me tamquam Christiani deferebantur, hunc sum secutus modum. interrogavi ipsos an essent Christiani. confitentes**

iterum ac tertio interrogavi supplicium minatus. perseverantes duci iussi. neque enim dubitabam pertinaciam certe et inflexibilem obstinationem debere puniri.

Pliny, Letters X, 96

an *whether*
certē *certainly*
cōnfiteor–ērī *admit*
dēbēre pūnīrī *ought to be punished*
dēferō–erre *accuse*
dubitō–āre *doubt*
dūcī (dūcō–ere) *to be led (to execution)*
essent (sum, esse) *they were*
īīs : abl. pl. of **is, ea, id** [see p. 148]

interim *meanwhile*
ipsōs (ipse–a–um) *them in person*
iterum ac tertiō *a second and third time*
iussī (iubeō–ēre) *I ordered*
minātus (minor–ārī) *threatening (them with)*
modus–ī [m.] *method, procedure*
pertinācia–ae *stubbornness*
secūtus sum (sequor) *I followed*
tamquam *on a charge of being*

5   Pliny reported that anonymous informers had produced lists of Christians.

propositus est libellus sine auctore multorum nomina continens. qui negabant se esse Christianos aut fuisse, cum praeeunte me deos appellarent, dimittendos esse putavi.

Pliny, Letters X, 96

appellārent (appellō–āre) *they called upon*
cum *when*
dīmittō–ere *release*
esse ... aut fuisse *that (they) were or had been*
libellus–ī *small book, list*

praeeunte (praeeō–īre) *with (me) going first*
prōpositus est (prōpōnō–ere) *was put before me*
putō–āre–āvī *think*

6   Pliny found the Christians to be secretive and superstitious, but not threatening any serious harm. He had to extract the information from adherents (the torture of slaves who gave evidence was conventional and commonplace).

necessarium credidi ex duabus ancillis, quae ministrae dicebantur, quid esset veri et per tormenta quaerere. sed nihil aliud inveni, quam superstitionem pravam, immodicam.

Pliny, Letters X, 96

ancilla–ae [f.] *maidservant*
et per tormenta *and that through torture*
immodicus–a–um *excessive*
inveniō–īre, invēnī *find*
ministra–ae *deaconess*

necessārius–a–um *indispensable*
prāvus–a–um *depraved*
quaerō–ere *investigate*
quam *than*
quid esset vērī *what was the truth*

139

7 The emperor Trajan's reply to Pliny:

conquirendi non sunt. si deferantur et arguantur, puniendi sunt.

Pliny, *Letters* X, 97

arguō–ere *convict*	**dēferō–erre** *charge*
conquīrō–ere *search for*	**pūniō–īre** *punish*

8 Jerome, the scholar and monk who translated the Bible into Latin (c. AD 400), wrote of a dream in which his loyalties were tested.

interrogatus condicionem, Christianum me esse respondi: et ille qui residebat, 'mentiris,' ait, 'Ciceronianus es, non Christianus; ubi thesaurus tuus, ibi et cor tuum.'

Jerome, *Letter* XXII, 30

cor–dis [n.] *heart, soul*	**mentīris (mentior–īrī)** *you lie*
ibī *there*	**respondeō–ēre, respondī** *reply*
ille quī residēbat i.e. the judge	**thēsaurus–ī** *treasure*

Vocabulary

TEXT

tamquam *as if, as it were*
rūrsum *again*
undique *from all sides*
iterum *again*
nihil, nīl *nothing*
taceō–ēre, tacuī, tacitum *be quiet*
iubeō–ēre, iussī, iussum *order*
trādō–ere, trādidī, trāditum *hand over*
accipiō–ere, accēpī, acceptum *receive*
inveniō–īre, invēnī, inventum *find*
cūnctus–a–um *all*
solitus–a–um *accustomed*
modus–ī *manner, method*
simulācrum–ī *image*
scelus–eris *crime*
lūx–cis *light*

PREPOSITIONS (AND PREFIXES)

WITH THE ACCUSATIVE:

ad   *to* (acc-, add-, aff-, agg-, all-, ann-, app-, ass-, att-)
adversus *against*
ante *before, in front of* (ante-)
in   *in, on, into* (ill-, imm-, inn-, irr-)
inter *among, between* (inter-)
per *through, thorough* (per-)
post *after, behind* (post-)
sub *underneath* (sub-, succ-, suff, sugg-, summ-, supp-, surr-)
trāns *across* (trans-)

WITH THE ABLATIVE:

ā, ab *away, from, by* (a-, ab-, au-)
cum *with, together* (cum-, coll-, com-, con-, corr-)
dē *concerning, down* (de-)
ē, ex *out, from* (e-, ex-)
in (as above)
prae *in front of, before* (prae-, pre-)
prō *before, in front of* (pro-)
sub (as above)

Remember the general distinction between prepositions with the accusative which imply motion and those with the ablative which describe a location only.

Exercises

1   Translate into Latin:

(a) Pliny (**Plinius**) himself spoke to the Christians.
(b) Marcus had soldiers with him in the amphitheatre.
(c) I saw the image of the emperor himself.
(d) Nero gave all the gifts to himself.
(e) The gladiator handed over his sword to the soldier.

2   What are the meanings of **modus vivendi**, **modus operandi** and **nil desperandum**?

3   Identify Latin words which are etymologically linked to *courage*, *trade*, *interrogation*, *sermon* and *contribution*.

4   What are the meanings of **per se**, **inter se** and **ipso facto**?

5 Make a list of English words that are derived directly or indirectly from a combination of any of the prepositions in the list above with either of these words:

fero (*I carry*)   **facio** (*I make, do*)

6 Match the English words with their ancestors:

fragilis	*count*
radius	*chattel*
dignitas	*frail*
caput	*dainty*
computo	*ray*

APPENDICES

GRAMMATICAL WORDS

Ablative	name of a case of nouns, pronouns and adjectives (see p. 161 for examples).
Accusative	name of a case of nouns, pronouns and adjectives (see p. 159 for examples).
Active	one of two 'voices' of verbs, the other being passive; it means that the subject is doing the action (e.g. *she writes the book* is active, *the book is written by her* is passive).
Adjective	words which qualify nouns: adjectives 'agree' with the nouns they qualify in case, number and gender.
Adverb	words which qualify verbs, adjectives or other adverbs (e.g. *he spoke so quickly*).
Agent	a noun or pronoun that is responsible for the action of a passive verb (and would become the subject if the verb were made active), e.g. *the book is written by her*.
Article	the definite article is 'the', the indefinite article 'a' ('an').
Case	form of the noun, pronoun or adjective which, by its ending, defines the function of the word in the sentence. The cases: nominative, accusative, genitive, dative and ablative. Also: the vocative (for a person being addressed) and the locative (*at* . . .).
Clause	a main clause contains a subject and a verb, and could serve as a sentence by itself. A subordinate clause also has a subject and a verb, but could not serve as a sentence. A subordinate clause is introduced by words such as *while, that, because, when, if, who,* or *though*.
Comparative	form of an adjective or adverb which indicates a comparison (e.g. *bigger, more quickly*).
Conjunction	words which have fixed endings and are used to link clauses and sentences (e.g. *and, but, however, when, if, though, because, since*).
Dative	name of a case of nouns, pronouns and adjectives (see p. 160 for examples).
Declension	traditional word for categories of nouns with similar case-endings: five declensions in all, e.g. **femina, servus, civis, gradus, res.** To decline a noun is to list its different case-endings.

Deponent	verbs which have a passive form but an active meaning (e.g. **loquor** *I speak*).
Future	the tense of a verb describing action yet to happen (e.g. *I shall . . . , he will . . .*).
Future perfect	the tense of a verb describing action yet to happen but projecting forward to a moment when the action is completed (e.g. *he will have eaten supper . . .*).
Gender	there are three genders: masculine, feminine and neuter. A 'common' noun has one form for both male and female (e.g. **bos, bovis**: *an ox*).
Genitive	name of a case of nouns, pronouns and adjectives (see p. 160 for examples).
Imperative	the form of a verb which expresses a command.
Imperfect	the tense of a verb describing past action which was continuous or repeated.
Indicative	the form of a verb denoting a fact rather than a possibility (subjunctive) or a command (imperative).
Indirect object	name of a noun when used as a secondary object (e.g. *he gave the book <u>to me</u>*), usually expressed by the dative in Latin.
Indirect speech	describes a person's statement or thoughts when reported (e.g. *he said that he was hungry*; the direct speech was *I am hungry*).
Infinitive	form of a verb which is usually expressed in English with 'to' placed in front (e.g. *to be or not to be*).
Interrogative	asks a question: distinguish between *who is the man?* (where *who* is an interrogative pronoun) and *he is the man who . . .* (where *who* is a relative pronoun).
Intransitive	a verb which has no object (e.g. *she waits*).
Locative	name of a case (rarely used) to describe where something is.
Mood	the mood of a verb may be indicative, subjunctive or imperative.
Nominative	name of a case of nouns, pronouns and adjectives which indicates the subject (see p. 159 for examples).
Noun	name of a person, place, thing or abstract idea.
Object	the noun or pronoun affected by the verb (e.g. *he kicks the <u>ball</u>, she sees the <u>mountain</u>*).
Participle	a form of a verb with the function of an adjective (e.g. *the <u>finished</u> chapter, the <u>moving</u> play*), often functioning as the equivalent of a subordinate clause (e.g. *I saw the man <u>sitting</u> (as he sat) on the bench; I knew the lady (who was) <u>struck</u> by lightning*). A participle is the only kind of adjective which can have a direct object (e.g. *John, saying these words, . . .*).
Passive	see <u>active</u>.
Perfect	the tense of a verb describing a completed, as distinct from a continuous or repeated, action in the past.

Person	the persons of a verb are expressed by the pronouns *I . . . , you . . . , he . . . , she . . . , it . . . , we . . . , they . . . .*
Plural	more than one (as opposed to <u>singular</u>).
Prefix	an addition to the front of a word (e.g. *pre-, in-, per-*).
Preposition	a word placed before a noun or pronoun (e.g. *in, with, by, from, to*), and determining its case.
Present	the tense of a verb describing action which is happening now or during the current period.
Principal parts	the four parts of a verb from which all the other parts are formed (e.g. **paro, parare, paravi, paratum**).
Pronoun	a word used in place of a noun (e.g. *he, she, them*).
Singular	describes only <u>one</u> (as opposed to <u>plural</u>).
Subject	the active subject is the <u>doer</u> of the action of the verb, the passive subject is on the receiving end of the verb's action.
Subjunctive	the mood of a verb to describe potential action (as opposed to <u>indicative</u>).
Suffix	an addition to the end of a word (e.g. *suffer-<u>ance</u>, laugh-<u>able</u>.*
Superlative	the form of an adjective or adverb which expresses the maximum meaning (e.g. *most, biggest, most unusual*).
Supine	fourth principal part: translated by 'to . . .', conveying purpose.
Tense	the time of the action of a verb (present, future, imperfect, perfect, future perfect, pluperfect).
Transitive	a verb which takes a direct object.
Verb	a word describing an action or a state: every sentence must have (or imply) one.
Vocative	name of a case of nouns and adjectives where a person is addressed.
Voice	a verb has two voices: active and passive.

GRAMMATICAL TABLES

Nouns

FIVE DECLENSIONS

	First	Second			
	woman	*slave*	*master*	*boy*	*wine*

Singular

	woman	*slave*	*master*	*boy*	*wine*
nom.	fēmina	servus	magister	puer	vīnum [n.]
acc.	fēminam	servum	magistrum	puerum	vīnum
gen.	fēminae	servī	magistrī	puerī	vīnī
dat.	fēminae	servō	magistrō	puerō	vīnō
abl.	fēminā	servō	magistrō	puerō	vīnō

Plural

	woman	*slave*	*master*	*boy*	*wine*
nom.	fēminae	servī	magistrī	puerī	vīna
acc.	fēminās	servōs	magistrōs	puerōs	vīna
gen.	fēminārum	servōrum	magistrōrum	puerōrum	vīnōrum
dat.	fēminīs	servīs	magistrīs	puerīs	vīnīs
abl.	fēminīs	servīs	magistrīs	puerīs	vīnīs

	Third					
	father	*citizen*	*leader*	*tribe, nation*	*elegance*	*time*

Singular

	father	*citizen*	*leader*	*tribe, nation*	*elegance*	*time*
nom.	pater	cīvis	dux	nātiō	suāvitās	tempus [n.]
acc.	patrem	cīvem	ducem	nātiōnem	suāvitātem	tempus
gen.	patris	cīvis	ducis	nātiōnis	suāvitātis	temporis
dat.	patrī	cīvī	ducī	nātiōnī	suāvitātī	temporī
abl.	patre	cīve (-ī)	duce	nātiōne	suāvitāte	tempore

	father	citizen	leader	tribe, nation	elegance	time
Plural						
nom.	patrēs	cīvēs	ducēs	nātiōnēs	–	tempora
acc.	patrēs	cīvēs (-īs)	ducēs	nātiōnēs	–	tempora
gen.	patrum	cīvium	ducum	nātiōnum	–	temporum
dat.	patribus	cīvibus	ducibus	nātiōnibus	–	temporibus
abl.	patribus	cīvibus	ducibus	nātiōnibus	–	temporibus

	Fourth			Fifth
	step	*horn*		*thing*
Singular				
nom.	gradus	cornū [n.]		rēs
acc.	gradum	cornū		rem
gen.	gradūs	cornūs		reī
dat.	graduī	cornū		reī
abl.	gradū	cornū		rē
Plural				
nom.	gradūs	cornua		rēs
acc.	gradūs	cornua		rēs
gen.	graduum	cornuum		rērum
dat.	gradibus	cornibus		rēbus
abl.	gradibus	cornibus		rēbus

Pronouns

	I/me	*you (s.)*	*we/us*	*you (pl.)*	*himself, herself, themselves*
nom.	ego	tū	nōs	vōs	—
acc.	mē	tē	nōs	vōs	sē
gen.	meī	tuī	nostrī/nostrum	vestrī/vestrum	suī
dat.	mihi	tibi	nōbīs	vōbīs	sibi
abl.	mē	tē	nōbīs	vōbīs	sē

147

	Singular			*Plural*		
	masculine	*feminine*	*neuter*	*masculine*	*feminine*	*neuter*
	this, he, she, it			*these, they, them*		
nom.	hic	haec	hoc	hī	hae	haec
acc.	hunc	hanc	hoc	hōs	hās	haec
gen.	hūius	hūius	hūius	hōrum	hārum	hōrum
dat.	huic	huic	huic	hīs	hīs	hīs
abl.	hōc	hāc	hōc	hīs	hīs	hīs
	that, he, she, it			*those, they, them*		
nom.	ille	illa	illud	illī	illae	illa
acc.	illum	illam	illud	illōs	illās	illa
gen.	illīus	illīus	illīus	illōrum	illārum	illōrum
dat.	illī	illī	illī	illīs	illīs	illīs
abl.	illō	illā	illō	illīs	illīs	illīs
	that, he, she, it			*those, they, them*		
nom.	is	ea	id	eī (iī)	eae	ea
acc.	eum	eam	id	eōs	eās	ea
gen.	ēius	ēius	ēius	eōrum	eārum	eōrum
dat.	eī	eī	eī	eīs (iīs)	eīs (iīs)	eīs (iīs)
abl.	eō	eā	eō	eīs (iīs)	eīs (iīs)	eīs (iīs)
	who, which					
nom.	quī	quae	quod	quī	quae	quae
acc.	quem	quam	quod	quōs	quās	quae
gen.	cūius	cūius	cūius	quōrum	quārum	quōrum
dat.	cui	cui	cui	quibus	quibus	quibus
abl.	quō	quā	quō	quibus	quibus	quibus
	he himself, she herself, itself			*they themselves*		
nom.	ipse	ipsa	ipsum	ipsī	ipsae	ipsa
acc.	ipsum	ipsam	ipsum	ipsōs	ipsās	ipsa
gen.	ipsīus	ipsīus	ipsīus	ipsōrum	ipsārum	ipsōrum
dat.	ipsī	ipsī	ipsī	ipsīs	ipsīs	ipsīs
abl.	ipsō	ipsā	ipsō	ipsīs	ipsīs	ipsīs

Adjectives

bonus–a–um: *good*

	masc.	fem.	neut.	masc.	fem.	neut.
	Singular			*Plural*		
nom.	**bonus**	**bona**	**bonum**	**bonī**	**bonae**	**bona**
acc.	**bonum**	**bonam**	**bonum**	**bonōs**	**bonās**	**bona**
gen.	**bonī**	**bonae**	**bonī**	**bonōrum**	**bonārum**	**bonōrum**
dat.	**bonō**	**bonae**	**bonō**	**bonīs**	**bonīs**	**bonīs**
abl.	**bonō**	**bonā**	**bonō**	**bonīs**	**bonīs**	**bonīs**

	omnis: *all, every*		**ingēns**: *huge*		**māior**: *greater*	
	MF	N	MF	N	MF	N
	Singular					
nom.	**omnis**	**omne**	**ingēns**	**ingēns**	**māior**	**māius**
acc.	**omnem**	**omne**	**ingentem**	**ingēns**	**māiōrem**	**māius**
gen.	**omnis**		**ingentis**		**māiōris**	
dat.	**omnī**		**ingentī**		**māiōrī**	
abl.	**omnī**		**ingentī**		**māiōre**	
	Plural					
nom.	**omnēs**	**omnia**	**ingentēs**	**ingentia**	**māiōrēs**	**māiōra**
acc.	**omnēs (-īs)**	**omnia**	**ingentēs (-īs)**	**ingentia**	**māiōrēs**	**māiōra**
gen.	**omnium**		**ingentium**		**māiōrum**	
dat.	**omnibus**		**ingentibus**		**māiōribus**	
abl.	**omnibus**		**ingentibus**		**māiōribus**	

Comparison of adjectives

REGULAR:

		comparative	*superlative*
cruel	**saevus**	**saevior**	**saevissimus**
sad	**trīstis**	**trīstior**	**trīstissimus**
easy	**facilis**	**facilior**	**facillimus**
quick	**celer**	**celerior**	**celerrimus**

IRREGULAR:

good	**bonus**	**melior**	**optimus**
bad	**malus**	**pēior**	**pessimus**
much, many	**multus**	**plūs***	**plūrimus**

plūs in the singular is used as a neuter noun.

149

Verbs

ACTIVE INDICATIVE

	parāre	monēre	mittere	audīre
	to prepare	*to warn*	*to send*	*to hear*
Stem:	**para-**	**mone-**	**mitt-**	**audi-**

	Present			
1	parō	moneō	mittō	audiō
2	parās	monēs	mittis	audīs
3	parat	monet	mittit	audit
4	parāmus	monēmus	mittimus	audīmus
5	parātis	monētis	mittitis	audītis
6	parant	monent	mittunt	audiunt

	Future			
1	parābō	monēbō	mittam	audiam
2	parābis	monēbis	mittēs	audiēs
3	parābit	monēbit	mittet	audiet
4	parābimus	monēbimus	mittēmus	audiēmus
5	parābitis	monēbitis	mittētis	audiētis
6	parābunt	monēbunt	mittent	audient

	Imperfect			
1	parābam	monēbam	mittēbam	audiēbam
2	parābās	monēbās	mittēbās	audiēbās
3	parābat	monēbat	mittēbat	audiēbat
4	parābāmus	monēbāmus	mittēbāmus	audiēbāmus
5	parābātis	monēbātis	mittēbātis	audiēbātis
6	parābant	monēbant	mittēbant	audiēbant

	Perfect			
1	parāvī	monuī	mīsī	audīvī
2	parāvistī	monuistī	mīsistī	audīvistī
3	parāvit	monuit	mīsit	audīvit
4	parāvimus	monuimus	mīsimus	audīvimus
5	parāvistis	monuistis	mīsistis	audīvistis
6	parāvērunt (-vēre)	monuērunt (-uēre)	mīsērunt (-sēre)	audīvērunt (-vēre)

Future perfect

1	parāverō	monuerō	mīserō	audīverō
2	parāveris	monueris	mīseris	audīveris
3	parāverit	monuerit	mīserit	audīverit
4	parāverimus	monuerimus	mīserimus	audīverimus
5	parāveritis	monueritis	mīseritis	audīveritis
6	parāverint	monuerint	mīserint	audīverint

Pluperfect

1	parāveram	monueram	mīseram	audīveram
2	parāverās	monuerās	mīserās	audīverās
3	parāverat	monuerat	mīserat	audīverat
4	parāverāmus	monuerāmus	mīserāmus	audīverāmus
5	parāverātis	monuerātis	mīserātis	audīverātis
6	parāverant	monuerant	mīserant	audīverant

PASSIVE INDICATIVE

Present

1	paror	moneor	mittor	audior
2	parāris	monēris	mitteris	audīris
3	parātur	monētur	mittitur	audītur
4	parāmur	monēmur	mittimur	audīmur
5	parāminī	monēminī	mittiminī	audīminī
6	parantur	monentur	mittuntur	audiuntur

Future

1	parābor	monēbor	mittar	audiar
2	parāberis	monēberis	mittēris	audiēris
3	parābitur	monēbitur	mittētur	audiētur
4	parābimur	monēbimur	mittēmur	audiēmur
5	parābiminī	monēbiminī	mittēminī	audiēminī
6	parābuntur	monēbuntur	mittentur	audientur

Imperfect

1	parābar	monēbar	mittēbar	audiēbar
2	parābāris	monēbāris	mittēbāris	audiēbāris
3	parābātur	monēbātur	mittēbātur	audiēbātur
4	parābāmur	monēbāmur	mittēbāmur	audiēbāmur
5	parābāminī	monēbāminī	mittēbāminī	audiēbāminī
6	parābantur	monēbantur	mittēbantur	audiēbantur

Perfect

1	parātus sum	monitus sum	missus sum	audītus sum
2	parātus es	monitus es	missus es	audītus es
3	parātus est	monitus est	missus est	audītus est
4	parātī sumus	monitī sumus	missī sumus	audītī sumus
5	parātī estis	monitī estis	missī estis	audītī estis
6	parātī sunt	monitī sunt	missī sunt	audītī sunt

Future perfect

1	parātus erō	monitus erō	missus erō	audītus erō
2	parātus eris	monitus eris	missus eris	audītus eris
3	parātus erit	monitus erit	missus erit	audītus erit
4	parātī erimus	monitī erimus	missī erimus	audītī erimus
5	parātī eritis	monitī eritis	missī eritis	audītī eritis
6	parātī erunt	monitī erunt	missī erunt	audītī erunt

Pluperfect

1	parātus eram	monitus eram	missus eram	audītus eram
2	parātus erās	monitus erās	missus erās	audītus erās
3	parātus erat	monitus erat	missus erat	audītus erat
4	parātī erāmus	monitī erāmus	missī erāmus	audītī erāmus
5	parātī erātis	monitī erātis	missī erātis	audītī erātis
6	parātī erant	monitī erant	missī erant	audītī erant

SUBJUNCTIVE

Present active

1	parem	moneam	mittam	audiam	sim (sum/esse)
2	parēs	moneās	mittās	audiās	sīs
3	paret	moneat	mittat	audiat	sit
4	parēmus	moneāmus	mittāmus	audiāmus	sīmus
5	parētis	moneātis	mittātis	audiātis	sītis
6	parent	moneant	mittant	audiant	sint

Imperfect active

1	parārem	monērem	mitterem	audīrem	essem
2	parārēs	monērēs	mitterēs	audīrēs	essēs
3	parāret	monēret	mitteret	audīret	esset
4	parārēmus	monērēmus	mitterēmus	audīrēmus	essēmus
5	parārētis	monērētis	mitterētis	audīrētis	essētis
6	parārent	monērent	mitterent	audīrent	essent

Perfect active

1	**parāverim**	**monuerim**	**mīserim**	**audīverim**
2	**parāverīs**	**monuerīs**	**mīserīs**	**audīverīs**
3	**parāverit**	**monuerit**	**mīserit**	**audīverit**
4	**parāverīmus**	**monuerīmus**	**mīserīmus**	**audīverīmus**
5	**parāverītis**	**monuerītis**	**mīserītis**	**audīverītis**
6	**parāverint**	**monuerint**	**mīserint**	**audīverint**

Pluperfect active

1	**parāvissem**	**monuissem**	**mīsissem**	**audīvissem**
2	**parāvissēs**	**monuissēs**	**mīsissēs**	**audīvissēs**
3	**parāvisset**	**monuisset**	**mīsisset**	**audīvisset**
4	**parāvissēmus**	**monuissēmus**	**mīsissēmus**	**audīvissēmus**
5	**parāvissētis**	**monuissētis**	**mīsissētis**	**audīvissētis**
6	**parāvissent**	**monuissent**	**mīsissent**	**audīvissent**

Present passive

1	**parer**	**monear**	**mittar**	**audiar**
2	**parēris**	**moneāris**	**mittāris**	**audiāris**
3	**parētur**	**moneātur**	**mittātur**	**audiātur**
4	**parēmur**	**moneāmur**	**mittāmur**	**audiāmur**
5	**parēminī**	**moneāminī**	**mittāminī**	**audiāminī**
6	**parentur**	**moneantur**	**mittantur**	**audiantur**

Imperfect passive

1	**parārer**	**monērer**	**mitterer**	**audīrer**
2	**parārēris**	**monērēris**	**mitterēris**	**audīrēris**
3	**parārētur**	**monērētur**	**mitterētur**	**audīrētur**
4	**parārēmur**	**monērēmur**	**mitterēmur**	**audīrēmur**
5	**parārēminī**	**monērēminī**	**mitterēminī**	**audīrēminī**
6	**parārentur**	**monērentur**	**mitterentur**	**audīrentur**

Perfect passive:	**parātus sim,**	**monitus sim,**	etc.
Pluperfect passive:	**parātus essem,**	**monitus essem,**	etc.

IRREGULAR VERBS

	esse	posse	velle	ferre	īre
	to be	*to be able*	*to wish*	*to carry*	*to go*

Present

1	**sum**	**possum**	**volō**	**ferō**	**eō**
2	**es**	**potes**	**vīs**	**fers**	**īs**
3	**est**	**potest**	**vult**	**fert**	**it**
4	**sumus**	**possumus**	**volumus**	**ferimus**	**īmus**
5	**estis**	**potestis**	**vultis**	**fertis**	**ītis**
6	**sunt**	**possunt**	**volunt**	**ferunt**	**eunt**

Future

1	erō	poterō	volam	feram	ībō
2	eris	poteris	volēs	ferēs	ībis
3	erit	poterit	volet	feret	ībit
4	erimus	poterimus	volēmus	ferēmus	ībimus
5	eritis	poteritis	volētis	ferētis	ībitis
6	erunt	poterunt	volent	ferent	ībunt

Imperfect

1	eram	poteram	volēbam	ferēbam	ībam
2	erās	poterās	volēbās	ferēbās	ībās
3	erat	poterat	volēbat	ferēbat	ībat
4	erāmus	poterāmus	volēbāmus	ferēbāmus	ībāmus
5	erātis	poterātis	volēbātis	ferēbātis	ībātis
6	erant	poterant	volēbant	ferēbant	ībant

Perfect

1	fuī	potuī	voluī	tulī	īī
2	fuistī	potuistī	voluistī	tulistī	īstī
3	fuit	potuit	voluit	tulit	iit
4	fuimus	potuimus	voluimus	tulimus	iimus
5	fuistis	potuistis	voluistis	tulistis	īstis
6	fuērunt	potuērunt	voluērunt	tulērunt	iērunt

Future perfect

1	fuerō	potuerō	voluerō	tulerō	ierō
2	fueris	potueris	volueris	tuleris	ieris
3	fuerit	potuerit	voluerit	tulerit	ierit
4	fuerimus	potuerimus	voluerimus	tulerimus	ierimus
5	fueritis	potueritis	volueritis	tuleritis	ieritis
6	fuerint	potuerint	voluerint	tulerint	ierint

Pluperfect

1	fueram	potueram	volueram	tuleram	ieram
2	fuerās	potuerās	voluerās	tulerās	ierās
3	fuerat	potuerat	voluerat	tulerat	ierat
4	fuerāmus	potuerāmus	voluerāmus	tulerāmus	ierāmus
5	fuerātis	potuerātis	voluerātis	tulerātis	ierātis
6	fuerant	potuerant	voluerant	tulerant	ierant

For the subjunctive of **sum**, **esse**, see p. 152.

PRINCIPAL PARTS

	Present	Infinitive	Perfect	Supine
	First conjugation			
love	amō	amāre	amāvī	amātum
give	dō	dare	dedī	datum
praise	laudō	laudāre	laudāvī	laudātum
beg	ōrō	ōrāre	ōrāvī	ōrātum
prepare	parō	parāre	parāvī	parātum
	Second conjugation			
teach	doceō	docēre	docuī	doctum
have	habeō	habēre	habuī	habitum
order	iubeō	iubēre	iussī	iussum
warn	moneō	monēre	monuī	monitum
laugh	rīdeō	rīdēre	rīsī	rīsum
sit	sedeō	sedēre	sēdī	sessum
hold	teneō	tenēre	tenuī	tentum
fear	timeō	timēre	timuī	–
see	videō	vidēre	vīdī	vīsum
	Third conjugation			
do, drive	agō	agere	ēgī	āctum
drink	bibō	bibere	bibī	–
fall	cadō	cadere	cecidī	cāsum
beat, kill	caedō	caedere	cecīdī	caesum
discover	cognōscō	cognōscere	cognōvī	cognitum
run	currō	currere	cucurrī	cursum
say	dīcō	dīcere	dīxī	dictum
learn	discō	discere	didicī	–
lead	dūcō	dūcere	dūxī	ductum
carry on	gerō	gerere	gessī	gestum
read, choose	legō	legere	lēgī	lēctum
send	mittō	mittere	mīsī	missum
chase, seek	petō	petere	petīvī	petītum
place, put	pōnō	pōnere	posuī	positum
rule	regō	regere	rēxī	rēctum
write	scrībō	scrībere	scrīpsī	scrīptum
conquer	vincō	vincere	vīcī	victum
live	vīvō	vīvere	vīxī	victum

	Present	Infinitive	Perfect	Supine
	Mixed conjugation			
capture, take	**capiō**	**capere**	**cēpī**	**captum**
make, do	**faciō**	**facere**	**fēcī**	**factum**
throw	**iaciō**	**iacere**	**iēcī**	**iactum**
	Fourth conjugation			
hear	**audiō**	**audīre**	**audīvī**	**audītum**
open	**aperiō**	**aperīre**	**aperuī**	**apertum**
feel	**sentiō**	**sentīre**	**sēnsī**	**sēnsum**
come	**veniō**	**venīre**	**vēnī**	**ventum**
know	**sciō**	**scīre**	**scīvī**	**scītum**
	Irregular verbs			
be	**sum**	**esse**	**fuī**	–
be able	**possum**	**posse**	**potuī**	–
carry	**ferō**	**ferre**	**tulī**	**lātum**
go	**eō**	**īre**	**iī**	**itum**
wish	**volō**	**velle**	**voluī**	–

Imperatives

	Active				*Passive*		
	Singular	*Plural*			*Singular*	*Plural*	
parō-āre	**parā**	**parāte**	*prepare!*		**parāre**	**parāminī**	*be prepared!*
videō-ēre	**vidē**	**vidēte**	*see!*		**monēre**	**monēminī**	*be warned!*
mittō-ere	**mitte**	**mittite**	*send!*		**mittere**	**mittiminī**	*be sent!*
audiō-īre	**audī**	**audīte**	*hear!*		**audīre**	**audīminī**	*be heard!*

Some commonly used imperatives have lost the final vowel from the singular form:

faciō-ere	**fac**	*do!*
dīcō-ere	**dīc**	*say!*
ferō, ferre	**fer**	*bring!*
dūcō-ere	**dūc**	*lead!*

Gerundives (adjectives)

parandus-a-um	*(ought)-to-be-prepared*
agendus-a-um	*(ought)-to-be-done*
etc.	

156

Gerunds (nouns)

acc.	**parandum**	*preparing*
gen.	**parandī**	*of preparing*
dat.	**parandō**	*for preparing*
abl.	**parandō**	*by preparing*

Participles

Infinitive		Present	Future	Past
parāre	*prepare*	**parāns**	**parātūrus**	**parātus**
amāre	*love*	**amāns**	**amātūrus**	**amātus**
monēre	*warn*	**monēns**	**monitūrus**	**monitus**
vidēre	*see*	**vidēns**	**vīsūrus**	**vīsus**
mittere	*send*	**mittēns**	**missūrus**	**missus**
dīcere	*say*	**dīcēns**	**dictūrus**	**dictus**
audīre	*hear*	**audiēns**	**audītūrus**	**audītus**
venīre	*come*	**veniēns**	**ventūrus**	**ventum ***

***veniō** is intransitive and does not govern a direct object, so the passive cannot be used in the usual way (although there is the impersonal passive: **ventum est** *it was come*). Several compounds of **veniō–īre** are transitive and so do have a straightforward passive (e.g. **circum-ventus–a–um** *surrounded*, **inventus–a–um** *found*).

Infinitives

Stem	Present Active	Present Passive	Past Active
para-	**parāre**	**parārī**	**parāvisse (parāsse)**
	to prepare	*to be prepared*	*to have prepared*
mone-	**monēre**	**monērī**	**monuisse**
	to advise	*to be advised*	*to have advised*
mitt-	**mittere**	**mittī**	**mīsisse**
	to send	*to be sent*	*to have sent*
audi-	**audīre**	**audīrī**	**audīvisse (audīsse)**
	to hear	*to be heard*	*to have heard*

Note:
a future active infinitive is supplied by the <u>future participle</u> + **esse**,

> e.g. **parātūrus esse**   *to be about to prepare*

and a past passive infinitive is supplied by the <u>past participle</u> + **esse**,

    e.g. **parātus esse**   *to have been prepared*

The **esse**, like other parts of **sum**, is often left out,

    e.g. **dīxit sē cēnam parātūrum**   *he said he was going to prepare the dinner*

The future passive infinitive is formed with the verb's supine + **īrī** (the present infinitive passive of **eō**),

    e.g. **dīxit cēnam parātum īrī**   *he said that dinner would be prepared*

EXAMPLES OF THE CASES

Nominative

Subject	**Cloelia Tiberim tranavit** (p. 11) *Cloelia swam across the Tiber*
As a complement to the subject	**patres appellati sunt** (p. 9) *they were called fathers*
	id apud imperitos humanitas vocabatur (p. 119) *that was called civilisation by the foolish*
	puto deus fio (p. 131) *I think I am becoming a god*

Accusative

Object	**timeo Danaos** (p. 31) *I fear Greeks*
Object of motion	**in senatum venit** (p. 40) *he comes into the senate*
	Italiam fato profugus . . . venit (p. 55) *by destiny he came, a fugitive, to Italy*
With an infinitive: indirect speech	**Pompeius confirmat eum nihil esse facturum contra me** (p. 41) *Pompey assures me that he will do nothing against me*
Length of time	**Tarquinius Superbus regnavit annos quinque et viginti** (p. 10) *Tarquinius Superbus ruled for twenty-five years*
Exclamation	**tristem et acerbum casum Helvidiarum sororum!** (p. 86) *Oh sorrowful and bitter misfortune of the Helvidia sisters!*

Adverbial **neque <u>multum</u> a Gallica differunt consuetudine** (p. 116)
they do not differ <u>much</u> from Gallic custom

With a passive verb **perfusus sanie <u>vittas</u> atroque veneno** (p. 129)
(accusative of *he was spattered (with respect to his) <u>headband</u> with slaver and*
'respect') *black poison (i.e. his headband was spattered . . .)*

Two objects **<u>te</u> <u>haec</u> docet** (p. 97)
he teaches <u>you</u> <u>these things</u>

Genitive

Possession **<u>cuius</u> habet imaginem et inscriptionem? – <u>Caesaris</u>** (p. 137)
<u>whose</u> likeness and inscription does it have? – <u>Caesar's</u>

Part of something **<u>familiarium</u> quidam** (p. 64)
or measure of *one <u>of the attendants</u>*
quantity
**quid enim <u>delectationis</u> habent sescenti muli in
Clytaemnestra?** (p. 107)
what <u>pleasure</u> do six hundred mules in Clytaemnestra bring?

quid ille nobis <u>boni</u> fecit? (p. 109)
what <u>good</u> has that man done for us?

Object of feeling **primo <u>pecuniae</u>, deinde <u>imperii</u>, cupido crevit** (p. 38)
at first there grew a desire <u>for money</u>, then <u>for power</u>

cura <u>placendi</u> (p. 87)
a concern <u>to please</u>

<u>novarum rerum</u> studio (p. 39)
with an eagerness <u>for political innovations</u>

Value **<u>unius</u> aestimemus <u>assis</u>** (p. 38)
let us value <u>at one penny</u>

Dative

Indirect object **Hannibal <u>militibus</u> Italiam ostentat** (p. 19)
Hannibal shows Italy <u>to the soldiers</u>

vereor ne <u>nobis</u> Idus Martiae nihil dederint praeter laetitiam
(p. 43)
*I fear that the Ides of March have given <u>(to) us</u> nothing but
a moment of joy*

Possession	**at <u>populo Romano</u> numquam scriptorum copia fuit** (p. 29) *the <u>Roman people</u> never had a great number of writers*
	Augustus . . . crura <u>ei</u> fregit (p. 54) *Augustus . . . broke <u>his</u> legs (another person's)*
Object of (dis)pleasing	**si <u>tibi</u> di favent** (p. 105) *if the gods are kind <u>to you</u>*
	<u>viro</u> ut morem geras (p. 85) *that you should humour your <u>husband</u>*
	Clodius inimicus <u>nobis</u> (p. 41) *Clodius is hostile <u>to me</u>*
Disadvantage	**centum quadrantes abstulit illa <u>mihi</u>** (p. 67) *that has taken a hundred coins away <u>from me</u>*
	ea <u>nobis</u> erepta sunt (p. 65) *those things have been taken <u>from us</u>*
	<u>Ascanio</u>-ne pater Romanas invidet arces? (p. 20) *does his father begrudge <u>Ascanius</u> the Roman citadels?*
Object of believing, trusting or forgiving	**carpe diem, quam minimum credula <u>postero</u>** (p. 128) *enjoy the moment, and trust as little as possible <u>in tomorrow</u>*
	<u>facinori</u> plerique hominum ignoscebant (p. 65) *most people forgave the <u>crime</u>*
Agent	**discite . . . quo sit <u>vobis</u> forma tuenda modo** (p. 87) *learn . . . in what way your beauty is to be preserved <u>by you</u>*
With adjectives	**nec <u>cuiquam serio ministerio</u> adcommodatus** (p. 95) *unsuited <u>to any serious task</u>*

Ablative

Separation	**citiusque e <u>mundo</u> genus hominum quam Cicero cedet** (p. 44) *sooner will the human race fade <u>from the world</u> than will Cicero*
	Hannibal <u>patria</u> profugus (p. 28) *Hannibal, a fugitive <u>from his own country</u>*
Agent	**homo imbecillus a <u>valentissima bestia</u> laniatur** (p. 107) *a feeble man is torn to pieces <u>by a very powerful beast</u>*
Accompaniment	**cum <u>patribus populoque</u>** (p. 130) *<u>with the senators and the people</u>*

Instrument	**nunc <u>pede libero</u>/pulsanda tellus** (p. 53) *now let us dance upon the earth <u>with unfettered feet</u>*
	Hylan <u>flagellis</u> verberavit (p. 55) *he beat Hylas <u>with whips</u>*
Cause	**aedes sacras <u>vetustate</u> conlapsas aut <u>incendio</u> absumptas refecit** (p. 53) *he restored sacred shrines that had collapsed <u>with age</u> or been destroyed <u>by fire</u>*
	adficior <u>dolore</u> (p. 86) *I am afflicted <u>by grief</u>*
Ablative absolute	**<u>hac pugna pugnata</u>, Romam profectus est, <u>nullo resistente</u>** (p. 19) *<u>after fighting this battle</u> (lit. with this battle fought) he set out for Rome and <u>met no resistance</u> (lit. with no one resisting)*
Comparison	**nihil est agri <u>cultura</u> melius** (p. 74) *nothing is better <u>than agriculture</u>*
Description	**<u>capillo</u> sunt <u>promisso</u>** (p. 116) *they are <u>with hair grown long</u>*
	puer <u>facie liberali</u> (p. 56) *a boy <u>with a noble face</u>*
Manner	**<u>amplexu molli</u> fovet** (p. 130) *(she) wraps (him) up <u>in a soft embrace</u>*
A point of time	**<u>hoc tempore</u> Catilinam defendere cogitamus** (p. 39) *<u>at this time</u> we are (i.e. I am) contemplating defending Catiline*
	<u>nono die</u> in iugum Alpium perventum est (p. 18) *<u>on the ninth day</u> they reached the summit of the Alps*
After prepositions	**pro <u>epistula</u>** (p. 54) *in return for <u>a letter</u>*
Measure of difference	**primum <u>multo</u> obstinatior adversus lacrimas muliebres erat** (p. 64) *he was at first <u>much</u> more stubborn against their female tears*
Price	**<u>magno</u> tibi constat** (p. 77) *it costs you <u>much</u>*
With adjectives	**nihil homine <u>libero</u> dignius** (p. 74) *nothing more worthy <u>of a free man</u>*

solutus <u>omni faenore</u> (p. 73)
free <u>from all interest repayment</u>

With certain verbs **<u>victoria</u> uti nescis** (p. 19)
you do not know how to make use of <u>victory</u>

KEY TO GRAMMATICAL ENDINGS

The endings are in alphabetical order, with the last letters first:

Line 1:   NOUNS declensions numbered [1–5]
Line 2:   ADJECTIVES   [i] like **bonus** or **pulcher**,
                                 [ii] like **tristis**, **celer** or **ingens**
Line 3:   VERBS all conjugations, unless numbered [I-IV]

Endings are singular unless marked 'pl.', and genders are abbreviated to 'm.', 'f.', and 'n.'. Verbs are active unless marked 'passive', and indicative unless marked otherwise.

-a   NOUNS   nom./abl. [1], n. nom./acc. pl. [2, 3, 4]
          ADJS   nom./abl. f. [i], n. nom./acc. pl.
          VERBS   imperative [I]

-e   NOUNS   abl. [3,5], vocative [2]
          ADJS   n. nom./acc. [ii], m. vocative [i]
          VERBS   imperative: [II,III]
                      present infinitive
                      they . . . occasional perfect (always **-ere**)
                      you . . . occasional passive: future, imperfect, present subjunctive, imperfect subjunctive (always **-re**)

-ae   NOUNS   gen./dat., nom. pl. [1]
           ADJS   f. gen./dat., f. nom. pl. [i]

-(i)sse   VERBS   perfect infinitive

-i   NOUNS   gen. [2,5], nom. pl. [2], dat. [3,4,5], occasional abl. [3]
          ADJS   m. n. gen. [i], m. nom. pl. [i], dat./abl. [ii]
          VERBS   *I* . . . perfect
                      you . . . perfect (always **-sti**)
                      imperative [IV]
                      present passive infinitive

-mini   NOUNS   a few nouns like **nomen** (**nomini**: dat.) and **homo** (**homini**)

            VERBS   *you* ... pl. passive: present, future, imperfect, present subjunctive, imperfect subjunctive

                     imperative passive pl.

-am   NOUNS   acc. [1]

        ADJS   f. acc. [i]

        VERBS   *I* ... future [III,IV], imperfect, pluperfect, present subjunctive [II,III,IV]

-em   NOUNS   acc. [3,5]

        ADJS   acc. [ii]

        VERBS   *I* ... present subjunctive [I], imperfect subjunctive, pluperfect subjunctive

-um   NOUNS   acc. [2,4], n. nom. [2], gen. pl. [all]

        ADJS   m. n. acc., n. nom. [i], gen. pl. [all]

-o   NOUNS   dat./abl. [2], occasional nom. [3]

        ADJS   dat./abl. [i]

        VERBS   *I* ... present, future [I,II], future perfect

                     imperative (rare) *let him/her, let them*

-ar   NOUNS   occasional nom. [3] (e.g. **nectar**)

        VERBS   *I* ... imperfect passive, present subjunctive passive [II,III,IV], future passive [III,IV]

-er   NOUNS   occasional nom. [2,3]

        ADJS   nom. [i,ii]

        VERBS   *I* ... imperfect subjunctive passive, present subjunctive passive [I], (occasional) present passive infinitive (**-ier**)

-or   NOUNS   nom. [3]

        ADJS   nom. [comparative form of all adjectives: **-ior**]

        VERBS   *I* ... present passive, future passive (I, II)

                     imperative passive (rare) *let him/her, let them*

-mur   VERBS   *we* ... passive: present, future, imperfect, present subjunctive, imperfect subjunctive

-tur   VERBS   *he/she/they* ... passive: present, future, imperfect, present subjunctive, imperfect subjunctive

-as   NOUNS   acc. pl. [1], nom. [3] (abstract nouns e.g. **suavitas**)

        ADJS   f. acc. pl. [i]

        VERBS   *you* ... present [I], imperfect, pluperfect, present subjunctive [II,III,IV]

-es   NOUNS   nom./nom. pl./acc. pl. [3,5]

        ADJS   nom. pl./acc. pl. [ii]

	VERBS	*you* ... present [II], future [III,IV], present subjunctive [I], imperfect subjunctive, pluperfect subjunctive
-is	NOUNS	dat./abl. pl. [1,2], gen. [3], occasional acc. pl. [3]
	ADJS	dat/abl. pl. [i], gen. [ii], nom. [ii], occasional acc. pl. [ii]
	VERBS	*you* ... **-is** present [III,IV], future [I,II]

-tis <u>plural</u> all active tenses

-ris active: future perfect, perfect subjunctive

passive: present, future, imperfect, present subjunctive, imperfect subjunctive

-os	NOUNS	acc. pl. [2], occasional nom. [3]
	ADJS	m. acc. pl. [i]
-us	NOUNS	nom. [2,4], gen. [4], nom./acc. pl. [4], n. nom./acc. [3]
	ADJS	m. nom. [i], n. nom./acc. of comparative form (also: comparative adverb)
	VERBS	*we* ... all active tenses (always **-mus**)
-bus	NOUNS	dat./abl. pl. [3,4,5]
	ADJS	dat./abl. pl. [ii]
-at	VERBS	*he/she* ... present [I], imperfect, pluperfect, present subjunctive [II,III,IV]
-et	VERBS	*he/she* ... present [II], future [III,IV], present subjunctive [I], imperfect subjunctive, pluperfect subjunctive
-it	VERBS	*he/she* ... present [III,IV], future [I,II], perfect, future perfect, perfect subjunctive
-nt	VERBS	*they* ... all active tenses
-u	NOUNS	abl. [4], n. nom./acc. [4], occasional dat. [4]
	VERBS	supine (rare)

ANSWERS TO EXERCISES

1

Practice A

1	**puella equum fugat.**	*The girl chases the horse.*
2	**servum dominus fugat.**	*The master chases the slave.*
3	**nautam femina fugat.**	*The woman chases the sailor.*
4	**deus** (*or* **dea**) **poetam fugat.**	*The god* (or *goddess*) *chases the poet.*

Practice B

1	**agricola cum tauro ambulat.**	*The farmer walks with the bull.*
2	**equus in villa est.**	*The horse is in the villa.*
3	**puella tauri faenum equo dat.**	*The girl gives the hay of the bull to the horse.*
4	**poeta agricolae taurum deo dat.**	*The poet gives the bull of the farmer to the god.*

Exercises

1. (a) Accusative.   *The farmer chases the slave.*
   (b) Nominative.   *Augustus has a bull.*
   (c) Accusative.   *Tiberius sees the woman.*
   (d) Ablative.   *Julius is in Britain.*
   (e) Ablative.   *The poet walks with the sailor.*
   (f) Genitive.   *Tiberius' villa is in Italy.*
   (g) Accusative.   *Julius chases Tiberius into Britain.*
   (h) Dative.   *The sailor gives the bull to the god.*
2. (a) **agricolam:** *the daughter walks towards the farmer.*
   (b) **equum:** *the master gives the horse to the slave.*

167

(c) **Britannia:** *the sailor sees Augustus in Britain.*

(d) **amico:** *Julius walks with a friend.*

(e) **Augusti:** *Augustus' daughter has a horse in Italy.*

3   In memory; for ever.

4   Duet, dual, etc.

5   Annual, urban, omnibus, initial, unit, ligament, etc.

2

Practice

1   **agricolae taurum vident.**   *The farmers see the bull.*

2   **agricolas taurus videt.**   *The bull sees the farmers.*

3   **amici poetae taurum non vident.** *The friends of the poet do not see the bull.*

4   **nauta deam videt.**   *The sailor sees the goddess.*

Exercises

1   (a) Accusative.   *Julius comes into the forum.*

    (b) Ablative.   *The son is in the villa.*

    (c) Ablative.   *The woman is with the girls.*

    (d) Ablative.   *Tiberius walks out of the villa.*

    (e) Genitive.   *Augustus' son is in Italy.*

    (f) Accusative.   *The slave is drinking wine!*

2   (a) **dat:** *the girl gives water to the horse.*

    (b) **audit:** *the goddess hears the poet.*

    (c) **bibunt:** *the slaves do not drink the wine.*

    (d) **laudat:** *the master praises the daughter.*

    (e) **ducit:** *the slave leads the bull to water.*

    (f) **vident:** *the sailors see the poet in the forum.*

3   (a) **servus feminam videt.**

    (b) **agricola filios laudat.**

    (c) **filia Iulium audit.**

    (d) **Hannibal Italiam capit.**

    (e) **servus dominum orat.**

    (f) **puellae poetam amant.**

    (g) **Augustus imperium habet.**

4   **exit** is singular and **exeunt** plural.

5   **loco:** ablative (*in the place of a parent*). **domini:** genitive (*in the year of the Lord*). **toto:** ablative (*in all*). **via:** ablative (*by way of*). **infinitum:** accusative (*for ever*). **annum:** accusative (*each year*).

6   **videt, urbs, mittit, bellum, facit, bibit.**

3

Practice

1 **bonus:** *the good man does not drink the wine.*
2 **bonis:** *the girl gives hay to the good horses.*
3 **bonum:** *the slave sees the good wine.*
4 **bonas:** *Augustus praises the good women.*

Exercises

1 (a) Nom. Neut. Sing.   *Wine is pleasing.*
 (b) Acc. Fem. Sing.   *The poet sees a beautiful woman.*
 (c) Gen. Masc. Sing.   *The slave does not love the master's*
            cowardly son.
 (d) Abl. Masc. Pl.   *The farmer walks with the slaves.*
 (e) Abl. Fem. Sing.   *There are many men in the villa.*
2 (a) **femina donum filiis dat.** *The woman gives a gift to her sons.*
 (b) **nautae laeti amicum vident.** *The happy sailors see their friend.*
 (c) **puella equos habet.** *The girl has horses.*
 (d) **vir aquam cum servis bibit.** *The man drinks water with the slaves.*
 (e) **tauri in villam agricolam fugant.** *The bulls chase the farmer into the villa.*
 (f) **Augustus filios pios audit.** *Augustus listens to his dutiful sons.*
3 (a) **Marcus est filius pius.**
 (b) **Iulia poetam gratum audit.**
 (c) **multi servi in foro ambulant.**
 (d) **multa dona sunt Augusto.**
 (e) **domini servos ignavos non laudant.**
 (f) **agricola taurum iratum non fugat.**
4 All are neuter plural.
5 <u>Alexander</u> the Great.
6 Magnanimous, magnify, magnate, etc. Multiply, multiple, multilingual, etc. Avarice, avaricious, etc.

4

Practice

1 **vos non video.**
2 **te amo.**
3 **faenum est meum.**
4 **nostrum vinum bibis!**

Exercises

1   *Would throw*: imperfect; *stood*: imperfect; *opened*: perfect; *was trying*: imperfect; *going to give*: future; *said*: perfect.
2   (a) Nominative.   *Augustus was the first princeps.*
    (b) Dative.   *Julius was my father.*
    (c) Nominative.   *We slaves are pleasing to Augustus.*
    (d) Accusative   *The poet does not love me but the beautiful woman.*
    (e) Nominative.   *Augustus is a friend to (of) the fatherland.*
    (f) Accusative.   *Cleopatra is drinking your wine.*
3   (a) **magister noster te non videt.**
    (b) **o amici, femina non aquam nostram sed vestrum vinum bibit.**
    (c) **vos avari (estis), nos irati sumus.**
    (d) **o Iulia, filius tuus nos fugat.**
    (e) **non mihi erunt servi superbi.**
4   **ambitio:** *ambition;* **avaritia:** *avarice;* **vitia:** *vice,* etc.
5   **ante meridiem:** *before midday;* **post meridiem:** *after midday;* **inter alia:** *among other things;* **curriculum vitae:** *the course (record) of life.*
6   The seventh, eighth, ninth and tenth months (before the addition of July and August).

5

Practice A

(a) *We prepare;* (b) *we shall send;* (c) *you* (pl.) *advise;* (d) *he/she sends;* (e) *he/she (has) heard;* (f) *you* (s.) *(have) advised;* (g) *you* (pl.) *were preparing;* (h) *you* (pl.) *will hear.*

Practice B

1   **audiebant:** *the boys were not listening to the teacher.*
2   **misit:** *the man sent the slave into the amphitheatre.*
3   **mittet:** *the angry mistress will send the master.*
4   **monebit:** *the slave will warn Nero.*

Exercises

1   (a) **agricolae taurum viderunt.**   *The farmers saw the bull.*
    (b) **dona sunt puellae.**   *They are the gifts of the girl,* or *The girl has gifts.*

     (c) **saeva nobis est fortuna.**   *Fortune is cruel to us.*

     (d) **Augustum-ne vos audivistis?**   *Did you hear Augustus?*

     (e) **filias Augusti laudabam.**   *I was praising the daughters of Augustus.*

     (f) **magistri in forum pueros ducent.**   *The teachers will lead the boys into the forum.*

2 (a) **sedebit:** *the slave will sit in the kitchen.*

    (b) **spectabant:** *the boys were watching the games in the amphitheatre.*

    (c) **dicet:** *Augustus will speak to us in the forum.*

    (d) **vidit:** *the woman saw (has seen) the girls in the garden.*

    (e) **audiverunt:** *the farmers (have) heard the plan of Augustus.*

    (f) **erat:** *the poet was not pleasing to Julia.*

3 (a) **spectabant**; (b) **ducet**; (c) **scripsit**; (d) **docebat**; (e) **monebit**; (f) **veniebat**.

4 (a) **feminae consilium audivimus.**

    (b) **Augustus ad amphitheatrum venit.**

    (c) **dominus avarus, servi ignavi sunt.**

    (d) **dei vinum acerbum non bibent.**

    (e) **agricola in agro femina in horto laborat, sed servus in culina vinum bibit.**

5 Pram.

6 Tilling/tending.

7 Culinary (**culina**): of the kitchen, cooking.

   Puerile (**puer**): childish.

8 Preparation; oration; spectator; data; navigation; exculpate; laudatory; admonition; vision; habit; doctor; retention; session; mission; petition; reduction; diction; direction; inscription; audition; convention, etc.

9 Original: execution of one in every ten soldiers; modern: almost complete destruction.

6

Practice A

(a) Third; (b) fourth; (c) third; (d) fifth.

Practice B

(a) **loci**; (b) **temporis**; (c) **meridiei**; (d) **anni**.

Practice C

1 **patris:** *the horse is in father's villa.*
2 **cives:** *the leader sends the citizens to the fields.*
3 **manibus:** *the girl saw the gift in the hands of the boy.*
4 **ducem:** *the citizens do not fear the leader.*

Exercises

1 (a) **servi canes** [acc.] **fugant.**   *The slaves chase the dogs.*
   (b) **cives ducem** [acc.] **laudabant.**   *The citizens were praising the leader.*
   (c) **pater matrem** [acc.] **culpat.**   *The father blames the mother.*
   (d) **gladiator ducem gemitu** [abl.] **audiebat.**   *The gladiator listened to the leader with a groan.*
   (e) **dux hostium** [gen.] **ad Africam navigabat.**   *The leader of the enemy sailed towards Africa.*
2 (a) Nominative.   *The soldiers chased the boys from the camp.*
   (b) Nominative.   *The crimes of the slave were great.*
   (c) Accusative.   *The slave saw the gift of Cicero.*
   (d) Accusative.   *Marcus heard the groans of the enemy.*
   (e) Nominative.   *The sisters of Julius live in Gaul.*
3 (a) **pueri cum patre ambulant.**
   (b) **corpora gladiatorum vidimus.**
   (c) **canes cenam Marci spectabant.**
   (d) **fratres epistulam ad senatum mittent.**
   (e) **magna sunt munera deorum.**
   (f) **vos, o senatores, rem publicam amabatis!**
4 They are all related to: **pendo, pendere, pependi, pensum** (*weigh, hang*).

7

Practice A

1 **pueri a matre monentur.**   *The boys are warned by their mother.*
2 **canis ab Augusto in villam fugatur.**   *The dog is chased by Augustus into the villa.*
3 **gladiatores a femina laudantur.**   *The gladiators are praised by the woman.*
4 **senator a civibus auditur.**   *The senator is heard by the citizens.*

Practice B

1 **victi:** *the enemy were conquered by Caesar.*
2 **doctus:** *the boy was taught by Seneca.*
3 **missa:** *a letter was sent by the mother.*
4 **datum:** *the wine was given to Britannicus by a slave.*

Practice C

1 **missae:** *the girls, <u>who were sent</u> into the fields, did not see their mother* (lit. *the girls <u>having been sent</u> into the fields did not see their mother*).
2 **visum:** *the bull <u>saw</u> the soldier in the field, and chased him* (lit. *the bull chased the soldier <u>having been seen</u> in the field*).
3 **laudato:** *the teacher <u>praised</u> the boy and gave him a gift* (lit. *the teacher gave a gift to the boy <u>having been praised</u>*).

Exercises

1 (a) **laudati:** *the boys were praised by the teacher.*
   (b) **amata:** *the girl was loved by the poet.*
   (c) **audita:** *the songs (poems) were heard by the emperor.*
   (d) **ducti:** *the gladiators were led into the amphitheatre.*
   (e) **monitus:** *Caesar was warned by a woman.*
   (f) **visum:** *the wine was seen by the slave.*

2 (a) **cena a servo paratur.**   *The dinner is prepared by the slave.*
   (b) **gladiatores in amphitheatrum a milite ducuntur.**   *The gladiators are led into the amphitheatre by the soldier.*
   (c) **epistula a senatore scribitur.**   *The letter is written by the senator.*
   (d) **canes a femina culpantur.**   *The dogs are blamed by the woman.*
   (e) **gladiator a pueris spectatur.**   *The gladiator is watched by the boys.*
   (f) **munera matri a Iulio dantur.**   *Gifts are given by Julius to his mother.*

3 (a) **cena in culina parata est.**
   (b) **Roma numquam capta est.**
   (c) **hostes a Caesare victi sunt.**
   (d) **puellae a matre laudatae sunt.**
   (e) **epistula a senatore scripta est.**
   (f) **taurus in horto visus est.**

4 **dictus:** addict, predict, edict, contradict, etc.
   factus: effect, defect, infect, etc.
   latus: translate, prelate, relate, collate, etc.
   missus: submission, permission, etc.

5 Relinquish, relic; computer, reputation, etc.

8

Practice

(a) *If I were a horse, I would eat hay.* [3]
(b) *The citizens come to the amphitheatre to watch the games.* [4]
(c) *The teacher asks where Marcus is.* [2]
(d) *The slaves should come to the fields at once.* [1]

Exercises

1   (a) **huius:** *Fulvia is his (this man's) wife.*
    (b) **hoc:** *Caesar walks with him (this man).*
    (c) **haec:** *she (this woman) is the sister of Clodius.*
    (d) **hi:** *they (these men) were led into the amphitheatre.*
    (e) **haec:** *the poet gave these (things) to the woman.*
2   (a) **ille:** *he (that man) will come into Italy with an army.*
    (b) **illam:** *Cicero did not love her (that woman).*
    (c) **illos:** *we saw them (those men) in the amphitheatre.*
    (d) **illorum:** *we can hear their (those men's) groans.*
    (e) **illum:** *do you want to see him (that man)?*
3   (a) **eos:** *the bull chased them.*
    (b) **ei:** *Pliny used to give books to her.*
    (c) **eis:** *Hannibal was seen by them.*
    (d) **id:** *that is cruel.*
    (e) **eius** *have you heard his brother?*
4   (a) **quis:** *who sent the letter?*
    (b) **cuius:** *whose dog is in the amphitheatre?*
    (c) **quibus** or **quo:** *by whom were the Romans captured?*
    (d) **quem:** *the boy whom you used to love is here now.*
    (e) **cui:** *the lady to whom the poet gave the gifts was sitting in the garden.*
5   (a) *The women, when they saw the men, were laughing.*
    (b) *The Greeks, as they say, are impudent.*
    (c) *I am not so idle as to do that.*
    (d) *The emperor orders us to watch the games.*
    (e) *I am coming to see you.*
    (f) *When Caesar had reached Rome, he read Cicero's letter.*
    (g) *When you see, you will know.*
    (h) *Although these men are slaves, they are friends of Rome.*
6   **veho-ere** (*carry*); **volo, velle** (*want*); **simul** (*at the same time*).
7   French: le, la, les (*the*); il, elle (*he/she*); ils, elles (*they*).
    Spanish: el, la, los, las (*the*); él, ella (*he/she*); ellos, ellas (*they*), etc.
8   **id est**: *that is*; **ad hoc**: *for this (special purpose).*

9

Practice A

1   **laetior.**
2   **gratior.**
3   **ignavior.**

Practice B

1   **bibe:** *drink the water!*
2   **da:** *give me the wine!*

Exercises

1   (a) **tristi:** dat. or abl. singular (any gender).
    (b) **magni:** gen. singular, (masc. or neut.); nom. plural (masc.).
    (c) **multa:** nom. or abl. singular (fem.); nom. or acc. plural (neut.).
    (d) **breve:** nom. or acc. singular (neut.).
    (e) **facilium:** gen. plural (any gender).
    (f) **mollis:** nom. singular (masc. or fem.); gen. singular (any gender).
    (g) **saevis:** dat. or abl. plural (any gender).
    (h) **avidum:** acc. singular (masc. or neut.); nom. singular (neut.).
2   (a) **vinum acerbum.**
    (b) **gravis res.**
    (c) **digna.**
    (d) **opus difficile.**
    (e) **praemia humilibus ... superbis.**
    (f) **imperatores ... laeti.**
    (g) **vultu tristi.**
    (h) **grata ... utilia.**
3   (a) **agricola est maior {quam servus.**
                                    {servo.
    (b) **Cicero erat sapientior {quam Catilina.**
                                           {Catilina.
    (c) **puellae-ne sunt fideliores {quam pueri?**
                                             {pueris?
    (d) **viro meliori {quam Tiberio} nubere volo.**
                              {Tiberio}
    (e) **poeta gratissimus sed ignavior {quam omnes servi} est.**
                                                {omnibus servis}

4   **omnibus** (dative plural): for everyone.
5   Ancillary; native; optimist.
6   Digit: **digitus–i** (*finger*); reverberate: **verber–is** (*blow, beating*).

10

Practice

1   Acc. masc. sing.: *the master saw the slave as he was drinking the wine.*
2   Abl. neut. sing.; acc. masc. sing.: *the master saw the slave sleeping after the wine had been taken.*
3   Acc. masc. sing.: *the master saw the slave on the point of taking the wine.*

Exercises

1   (a) Accusative: *the spectators saw Augustus as he was about to come into the amphitheatre.*
     (b) Ablative (absolute): *upon hearing the prefect the senators praised Nero.*
     (c) Accusative: *I saw the poet as he was writing a letter.*
     (d) Accusative: *Caesar captured the Gauls and brought them to Rome.*
     (e) Accusative: *the enemy captured and burnt the city.*
2   (a) **audito:** *the senators were gloomy after listening to the advice of Caesar.*
     (b) **ferentem:** *Hannibal saw the soldier as he was bringing the letter from the camp of the Romans.*
     (c) **fugiturus:** *the slave heard the woman as he was about to run away.*
3   (a) **Augustus Antonio occiso princeps creatus/factus est.**
     (b) **nos visuri/visurae (spectaturi/spectaturae) gladiatores in amphi-theatro eramus.**
     (c) **his dictis Caesar tacitus erat/tacebat.**
     (d) **servus {in animo cenam parare habens} in villam venit.**
              {cenam paraturus}
     (e) **vir feminam in agris laborantem vidit.**
4   We who are about to die salute you.
5   Ferrous: **ferrum–i** (*iron*); bestial: **bestia–ae** (*beast*); disturb: **turba–ae** (*crowd*); polite: **politus–a–um** (*refined*).
6   An essential condition (lit. *without which not* ...).
7   **volo, velle** (*want, wish*); **volo–are** (*fly*).

11

Practice

(a) *Children should be seen and not heard.* [3]
(b) *The wine of the master should not be drunk.* [4]
(c) *The poet should not to be praised by soldiers.* [1]
(d) *The show in the amphitheatre ought to be seen.* [2]

Exercises

1   (a) **laudandus:** *Cicero ought to be praised.*
    (b) **audienda:** *the songs should be heard after dinner.*
    (c) **laudandos:** *Caesar came (comes) into the temple to praise the gods* (lit. *for the gods to-be-praised*).
    (d) **bibendum:** *wine should not be drunk by slaves.*
2   (a) **laborandum:** *now is the time for working.*
    (b) **vivendum:** *now is the time for living.*
    (c) **dormiendum:** *now is the time for sleeping.*
    (d) **agendum:** *now is the time for doing.*
3   (a) **hortari milites conatus/conata sum**.
    (b) **ante meridiem profecti/profectae sumus.**
    (c) **cena servis paranda est.**
    (d) **Caesar Gallos hortatus est.**
    (e) **ex urbe ad Ciceronis villam profecti/profectae sumus.**
4   **amanda:** fem. sing. of **amandus–a–um** (*to-be-loved*).
    miranda: fem. sing. of **mirandus–a–um** (*to-be-admired*).
    memorandum: neut. sing. of **memorandus–a–um** (*to-be-related*).
    referendum: neut. sing. of **referendus–a–um** (*to-be-referred*).
    addendum: neut. sing. of **addendus–a–um** (*to-be-added*).
    agenda: neut. pl. of **agendus–a–um** (*to-be-done*).
5   *When the things that ought to be changed* **(mutandis)** *have been changed* **(mutatis)**.
6   *That which had to be shown.*

12

Practice

1   **dixit Brutum Ciceronem vidisse.**
2   **dixit servos cenam paraturos esse.**

3   **Marcus dixit se esse civem Romanum.**

Exercises

1   (a) **Romani vincent.**
    (b) **omnes Romani inimici sunt.**
    (c) **Nero omnium principum avarissimus erat.**
    (d) **hospites post cenam carmina (mea) audient.**
    (e) **milites nimium laudati sunt.**
2   (a) **Cloelia dixit amicos in Gallia habitare.**
    (b) **Cloelia dixit imperatorem hodie/illo die in amphitheatrum venturum esse.**
    (c) **Cloelia dixit Antonium epistulam ad Cleopatram misisse.**
    (d) **Cloelia dixit orationes validiores quam arma esse.**
    (e) **Cloelia dixit consilium a senatoribus auditum iri.**
3   (a) **(ea/illa/haec) dixit se Romam ire velle.**
    (b) **Iulius dixit matrem cenam paraturam esse.**
    (c) **Clodius dixit se Ciceronis amicum esse.**
    (d) **servi militibus dixerunt Ciceronem in Graecia esse.**
    (e) **milites Antonio dixerunt Ciceronem abesse.**
4   **nota bene** (*note well*); **exempli gratia** (*by way of an example*); **post scriptum** (*postscript*).
5   Library: **liber** (*book*); computer: **cum** + **puto–are** (*calculate* or *consider things taken together*); current: **curro–ere** (*run*); rodent: **rodo–ere** (*gnaw*); quality: **qualis** (*just like*).

13

Practice

1   **laborandum:** *the slave is fit for working.*
2   **bibendum:** *the slave is fit for drinking.*
3   **pugnandum:** *the soldier is fit for fighting.*
4   **fugiendum:** *the soldier is fit for running away.*

Exercises

1   (a) **Plinius ipse Christianis dixit.**
    (b) **Marcus milites secum in amphitheatro habebat.**
    (c) **simulacrum ipsius imperatoris vidi.**
    (d) **Nero sibi dona omnia dedit.**

(e) **gladiator gladium militi tradidit.**

2   *Manner of living*; *manner of working*; *do not give up* (lit. *nothing to-be-despaired*).

3   Courage: **cor, cordis** (*heart*); trade: **trado–ere** (*hand over*); interrogation: **interrogo–are** (*interrogate*); sermon: **sermo–nis** (*conversation*); contribution: **tributum–i** (*payment*).

4   **per se**: *by itself/themselves*; **inter se**: *among themselves*; **ipso facto**: *by the deed itself*.

5   Prefer, infer, suffer, offer, differ (dis-), confer, refer, defer, transfer, interfere, etc.

Affect, defect, infect, effect, perfect, prefect, etc.

6   **fragilis**: *frail*; **radius**: *ray*; **dignitas**: *dainty*; **caput**: *chattel*; **computo**: *count*.

ENGLISH TRANSLATIONS

1 Early Rome

1 *In the beginning the Trojans founded and held the city of Rome.*
2 *Lavinia the daughter of Latinus was given in marriage to Aeneas.*
3 *The city was called by the name of its founder.*
4 *He appoints one hundred senators. They were called fathers.*
5 *From the beginning kings held the city of Rome.*
6 *Tarquinius Superbus ruled for twenty-five years.*
7 *Two consuls were then appointed, Lucius Iunius Brutus and Lucius Tarquinius Collatinus.*
8 *The children of the consul stood bound to a stake.*
9 *The bridge almost gave a passage to the enemy, had it not been for one man, Horatius Cocles.*
10 *Cloelia swam across the Tiber and restored them all safely to their relatives.*

2 Carthage

1 *The war was the most memorable of all.*
2 *On the ninth day they reached the summit of the Alps.*
3 *Hannibal shows Italy to the soldiers.*
4 *In Rome there was a stampede of people into the forum amid much panic and din.*
5 *After fighting this battle he set out for Rome and met no resistance; he stopped in mountains near the city.*
6 *You know how to conquer, Hannibal, but you do not know how to make use of victory.*
7 *Dido and the Trojan leader come to the same cave.*
8 *Does his father begrudge Ascanius the Roman citadels?*
9 *I do not make for Italy of my own free will.*
10 *Go, chase Italy with the winds [i.e. sail], seek the lands across the waves.*
11 *Phoenician Dido, fresh from her wounding, was wandering in a large wood.*
12 *At last she hurried away and fled back in an unfriendly manner.*

180

3   Greece

1   *The Macedonian war took the place of the Carthaginian peace.*

2   *After the herald's voice had been heard, there was joy.*

3   *Hannibal, a fugitive from his own country, had come to Antiochus.*

4   *Greece, though captured, herself captivated her wild conqueror and brought the arts to rustic Latium.*

5   *Civilisation, literature and even crops are believed to have been discovered first of all in Greece.*

6   *These days I hear too many people praising and admiring the ornaments of Corinth and Athens.*

7   *The Roman people never had a great number of writers, because all the best people preferred action to talking.*

8   *Others will more delicately fashion bronze statues – as if they were breathing – (Oh yes, I believe it) and they will bring to life faces from marble.*

9   *You, Roman, remember to rule the nations with your power (these will be your skills), and to impose your way of life on a foundation of peace, to spare the conquered and subdue the proud.*

10 *There are in that number many good, learned and scrupulous men, and also unscrupulous, uneducated and superficial ones. I make this point about the whole race of Greeks: I concede to them their literature, I grant them their knowledge of the many arts. But those people have never cultivated the sanctity and dependability of evidence given in court.*

11 *Laocoon in a rage ran down from the very top of the citadel and cried from afar, 'O wretched citizens, why such madness? Whatever that is, I fear Greeks even when bearing gifts.'*

12 *Teacher, professor, surveyor, painter, masseur, soothsayer, tight-rope artist, doctor, sorcerer – the hungry Greek chappie is a proper know-all.*

13 *The whole country is given to acting. You smile, and he [i.e. a Greek] roars with laughter; then he weeps if he has seen a friend's tears, but he does not grieve . . . If you say 'I am hot', he sweats.*

4   Cicero

1   *At first ambition rather than greed exercised the minds of men.*
    At first there grew a love of money, then of power. Greed ruined trust, honesty and other good qualities.
    We can bear neither our vices nor the remedies.

2   *Let us live, my Lesbia, and let us love, and let us value all the chatter of censorious old men at one penny.*

3   *At this time we are contemplating defending Catiline, our fellow-candidate. We have the judges we wanted, thanks to the utmost good will of the prosecutor.*

4 *All the ordinary people, with their eagerness for political innovations, approved of Catiline's initiative.*

5 *In the meantime he was not quiet, but prepared to ambush Cicero by all methods.*

6 *What times! What moral standards! The senate understands these things, the consul sees them; and still this man lives. Lives? Why, he even comes into the senate.*

7 *Here, they are here in our midst, senators.*

8 *How many times have you tried to kill me, the consul!*

9 *I saved the life of every citizen by the punishment of five crazed and desperate men.*

10 *I expected some thanks in your letter.*

11 *Clodius is hostile to me. Pompey assures me that he [i.e. Clodius] will do nothing against me. It is dangerous for me to believe it, and I am preparing myself for resistance.*

12 *Pompey tells us not to worry about Clodius.*

13 *If only I might see that day when I may give thanks to you because you compelled me to live!*

14 *Gentlemen of the jury, the whole matter in this case of ours rests with Clodia, a woman not only noble but also notorious.*

15 *First and foremost I seek from you an opportunity to see you.*

16 *My dear Atticus, I fear that the Ides of March have given us nothing but a moment of joy.*

17 *I certainly want to keep my friendship with Antony, and I shall write to him, but not before I see you.*

18 *In my youth I defended the republic, and now, an old man, I'll not abandon it. I scorned the swords of Catiline: I shall not fear yours.*

19 *The boy Caesar is outstanding.*

20 *Although Octavian may call Cicero his father, refer everything to him, and praise and thank him, it will however become apparent that his words are at odds with his actions.*

21 *All posterity will admire what Cicero has written about you, and will curse your action against him; sooner will the human race fade from the world than will Cicero.*

5 Augustus

1 *The armed forces of Lepidus and Antony passed into the hands of Augustus, who under the title of 'princeps' took charge of all things that had been exhausted by the civil wars.*

2 *I did not accept the dictatorship, which was offered to me both by the people and by the senate.*

3 *I banished into exile those men who murdered my parent.*

4 *Some write that on the Ides of March three hundred men were slaughtered in the manner of sacrificial victims at an altar built in honour of Divine Julius [i.e. Caesar].*

5 *I reintroduced many precedents of our ancestors.*

6 *He restored sacred shrines that had collapsed with age or been destroyed by fire; these and the other temples he decorated with the most lavish gifts.*

7 *Now let there be drinking, now let us dance upon the earth with unfettered feet.*

8 *Indeed, not even his friends deny that he practised acts of adultery.*

9 *He discovered the plans of opponents through the wives of each one.*

10 *He himself administered justice assiduously, sometimes into the night.*

11 *The cohorts, if any had given ground in battle, he decimated and fed with barley.*

12 *A decree went out from Caesar Augustus that the whole world should be registered.*

13 *Augustus broke Thallus' legs for receiving five hundred denarii to leak a letter.*

14 *He beat Hylas, a pantomime artist, in the hall of his own house with whips.*

15 *Here is the man whom you often hear being promised to you, here is Augustus Caesar, offspring of a god, who will found a golden age.*

16 *I sing of arms and a man, who, by fate a fugitive from the shores of Troy, first came to Italy and the Latin shores.*

17 *It was now almost the day on which Caesar had ordered my departure from the territories of outermost Italy.*

18 *Marcus Cicero was by chance recounting a dream of the night before to some friends: a boy with a noble face was lowered from heaven on a golden chain and he stood at the doors of the Capitol, and to him Jupiter handed a rod; then, on suddenly seeing Augustus, Cicero declared that this was the very boy.*

6 The Family

1 *I am hurrying to my daughter. I believe she does not know me.*

2 *Nero was adopted by Claudius in his eleventh year.*

3 *In his early youth Agricola would have drunk too deeply from philosophy's cup – beyond what was acceptable for a Roman senator – had not the good sense of his mother restrained his inflamed and burning spirit.*

4 *Veturia, the mother of Coriolanus, and Volumnia, carrying two small sons, were going into the camp of the enemy. When they reached the camp and it was brought to Coriolanus' attention that a large number of women were present, he was at first much more stubborn against their female tears. Then one of his attendants happened to recognise Veturia in the midst of the other women: 'Unless my eyes deceive me,' he said, 'your mother, wife and children are here.'*

5 *And yet he knew what the barbarian torturer was preparing for him. Nevertheless he removed relatives blocking his path and members of the public delaying his return, as if he were leaving behind the lengthy business of clients, with a case resolved, and making his way towards the Venafran fields or Spartan Tarentum.*

6 *Why does your personal grief disturb you so? Look at what has been taken from us – things which ought to be no less dear to people than their children – the state, our honour, prestige and all our public offices. But it is bad to lose children. Bad, yes; except that suffering and enduring these other losses is worse.*

7 *The poison pervaded all his limbs in such a way that his voice and breath were taken at the same time. Most people were inclined to forgive the crime, putting it down to long-standing feuds of the brothers and a kingdom that could not be shared.*

8 *The mother revives the ash and sleeping embers, extending her chores into the night, and puts the maids to work by lamplight with the time-consuming portion of wool [i.e. to keep them occupied], so that she can keep the bed of her husband chaste and bring up her small sons.*

9 *Someone was reprimanding his son for spending a little too much on horses and dogs. I said to this fellow after the boy had gone, 'Hey, did you never do anything that could be criticised by your father? Did you, do I say? Do you not sometimes do things that your son, if he suddenly became your father – and you his son – would scold with similar sternness?'*

10 *This morning I accidentally greeted you by your real name, Caecilianus, and did not say 'Sir'. Do you want to know how much such licence is costing me? That has taken a hundred coins [i.e. the price of a sandwich] away from me.*

11 *No one visits you out of any interest in you yourself, but in the hope of some acquisition from you. Once friendship was sought, now it's your loot; if lonely old men change their wills, the visitor will take his compliments to another threshold.*

7 Society

1 *In those days senators were in the fields.*

2 *'Raising livestock well.' What second? 'Raising livestock well enough.' What third? 'Raising livestock badly.' What fourth? 'Ploughing.' And when he who had asked had said 'What of moneylending?', then Cato replied, 'What about murdering someone?'*

3 *Happy is he who, like the ancient race of mortals, is far from the world of business and works his father's land with his oxen, free from all interest repayment; it pleases him to lie down, now under an old oak tree, now on the clinging grass.*

4 *For neither old men nor boys easily endure the difficulty of footpaths and the steepness and unevenness of mountains.*

5 *If an enterprise is small it should be considered demeaning; but if large and profitable, it is not to be disparaged. Of all things, however, from which a living is made, nothing is better than agriculture, nothing more fruitful, nothing sweeter, nothing more worthy of a free man.*

6 *This slave causes canes to break, that one is red from the whip, this one from the strap.*

7 *In this animal, the Roman knight Vedius Pollio found ways of showing his cruelty, plunging condemned slaves into pools of them.*

8 *Nothing arouses and stimulates affection as much as the fear of loss.*

9 *It is more profitable to cultivate difficult places with hired hands than with slaves.*

10   *'What are you up to?' he said, 'Do you think I am a pack-animal or a ship that transports stone? I have contracted the duties of a man, not a horse. I am no less a free man than yourselves, even if my father did leave me a pauper.' And not content with his abuse he then lifted one foot higher and simultaneously filled the road with an obscene noise and smell.*

11   *You have assets of 100,000. I offer you the sum of 300,000 sesterces to make up the knights' property qualification.*

12   *He who was reclining next to me noticed, and asked whether I approved. I said no. 'So what custom do you follow?' he said. 'I serve the same to everyone; for I am inviting them for dinner, not for their status branding, and I regard as equal in all things those whom I have made equal at the table and couch.' 'Even freedmen?' 'Even they; for at that time I consider them table-companions, not freedmen.' And he said: 'It must cost you a lot.' 'Not at all.' 'How can it be?' 'Because, of course, my freedmen do not drink the same as I do, but I drink the same as the freedmen.'*

8   Women

1   *I want to hear the reason why women have got themselves all worked up and have charged out into the open, barely keeping themselves from the forum and assembly. Once they start to be our equals, in no time they'll be our superiors.*

2   *Do you want to impose this competition on your wives, Romans, that rich women want to have what no other can have; and that poor women, so as not to be despised for this very reason, are stretched beyond their means?*

3   *You do not allow the lady of your household to have a purple cloak, and your horse will be clothed more lavishly than your wife is dressed.*

4   Wife: *I am an object of scorn.*

     Old man: *Who from?*

     Wife: *He to whom you entrusted me, my husband.*

     Old man: *Oh, more bickering! How many times, pray, have I made it clear to you that you should take care that neither of you come to me with your grumbling?*

     Wife: *How can I see to that, father?*

     Old man: *Are you asking me?*

     Wife: *If you don't mind.*

     Old man: *How many times have I pointed out to you that you should humour your husband, not observe what he does, where he goes or what he gets up to.*

     Wife: *But you see, he is making love to a prostitute here next door.*

     Old man: *He has good sense, and I'll warrant he will love her even more because of your interference.*

     Wife: *And he drinks there.*

Old man: *Will he drink any less on your account? Since he keeps you in gold and fine clothes and furnishes you properly with maids and provisions, it is better, woman, to adopt a sensible outlook.*

5 *You ask that I should watch out for a husband for the daughter of your brother.*

6 *More troublesome is that woman who as soon as she reclines at table volunteers a literary appreciation of Virgil. The teachers duck, the professors are seen off, and not one of the lot of them can get a word in.*

7 *She has my books, reads them repeatedly, and even learns them by heart.*

8 *Look at the sorrowful and bitter misfortune of the Helvidia sisters! Both have died in childbirth, both having given birth to daughters. I am afflicted by grief, but I do not grieve beyond measure; it seems sorrowful to me that fruitfulness has taken away most honourable girls in their first flowering.*

9 *Boudicca, carrying her daughters before her in the chariot, declared that it was indeed customary for Britons to go to war under the leadership of women; in that battle it was a matter of victory or death; that was a woman's decision: the men might live and be slaves if they so wished.*

10 *Learn what kind of attention improves the face, girls. And in what way your beauty is to be preserved. But it is not unworthy: you should have a concern to please, since our age has well-groomed men.*

9 Education

1 *These days once a baby is born it is entrusted to some little Greek maid, and one or other from any of the slaves is recruited to assist her, very often one who is quite worthless and unsuited to any serious task. Immediately, tender and impressionable minds are tainted by the fanciful stories and misconceptions of these people; and no one in the entire household cares a jot what he says or does in the presence of the little master.*

2 *Let there be another student, whom he may envy; from time to time let there be competition, and more often than not let him think himself successful; he should also be encouraged with rewards, which that age-group welcomes.*

3 *Why do you have it in for us, you miserable schoolmaster, hateful creature to boys and girls? Not yet have the crested cocks broken the silence, and already you are disturbing the peace with your harsh growling and wallopings. We neighbours do not ask for sleep all night long: you know, to be awake is neither here nor there, but to lie awake the whole night is no joke. Dismiss your students. Tell me, you chatterbox, will you accept as much as you earn to make this din – to shut up?*

4 *He who teaches you these things is a mutton-head, not a master. For our teacher used to say, 'Are your things safe? Go straight home; be sure not to look around; see that you don't cheek your elders.'*

5 *Seldom does one's salary not need a court order from the tribune. But you [i.e. parents] impose harsh conditions: that the standards of correct speech be met by*

the teacher, that he read the histories, that he know all the authors like the back of his hand.

6 *'You should attend to these matters,' he says, 'and when the year has turned its circle, accept the gold which the people demand for a champion.'*

7 *He did not want to send me to Flavius' school, where great boys born from great centurions went, but dared to take his son to Rome.*

8 *I have, moreover, begun to declaim Greek with Cassius; however, I wish to have my Latin training with Bruttius.*

9 *I seek from you that a clerk may be sent to me as quickly as possible, preferably a Greek; much of the work in writing out my notes will then be taken from me.*

10   Leisure

1 *You will dine well, Fabullus, at my place in a few days if the gods are kind to you and if you bring with you a tasty and large dinner, not forgetting a pretty girl, wine, wit and all your jokes. Bring these and I tell you, dear boy, you'll have a great dinner: your old Catullus' wallet is full – of cobwebs.*

2 *Whatever is put there you sweep away this way and that. When these things are hidden in your dripping napkin they are handed over to a slave to be taken home, while the whole lot of us do nothing but lie there. If you have any decency, put back the dinner!*

3 *I am putting on the* Mother-in-law *again for you, which I was never permitted to present to a silent house: thus did calamity overtake it. Your good sense, if it is supportive to our efforts, will put an end to that mischief.*

4 *What pleasure do six hundred mules in* Clytaemnestra *bring, or three thousand bowls in the* Trojan Horse?

5 *A foul shower soaks his face, and streams of blood spurt from the torn veins of his mutilated head.*

6 *What pleasure can there be for a person of refinement when a feeble man is torn to pieces by a very powerful beast or a magnificent animal skewered with a spear?*

7 *Indeed, nothing is so damaging to good behaviour as sitting idly at some show. For that is when vices make their stealthy advance more easily, through enjoyment.*

8 *The winner is kept for another killing. The way out for the combatants is death; the killing is done with sword and fire. These things happen while the arena is empty. 'But some person has committed a robbery, has killed a person.' So what? Because he has committed murder, he has deserved to suffer this; but what have you done, poor man, to deserve to watch it? 'Kill, flog, burn! Why does he run on to the blade so timidly? Why doesn't he go under more positively? Why doesn't he die more willingly?' The show has an interval: 'In the meantime let some men have their throats cut, so that at least something is happening.'*

9 *What good has that man done for us? He produced gladiators worth tuppence, already decrepit, who, had you blown on them, would have collapsed; I have seen better animal-fighters before now. In fact, afterwards they were all flogged.*

10 *He produced many shows of various kinds: coming-of-age parties, races, theatrical performances, and an exhibition of gladiators.*

11 Britain

1 *Of all these [i.e. tribes] by far the most civilised are those that inhabit Kent. This region is entirely by the sea, and they do not differ much from Gallic custom. Those who live inland for the most part do not sow corn, but live off milk and meat, and are clothed in skins. All Britons stain themselves with woad, which produces a sky-blue colour, and with this appearance are more frightening in battle; their hair is grown long and they shave all parts of their body except their head and upper lip. They share their wives with each other, in groups of ten or twelve, especially brothers with brothers and parents with offspring; but those who are born from these groups are considered to be the children of those to whom each girl was first given.*

2 *On that island there is neither the smallest piece of silver nor any prospect of loot except from slaves.*

3 *I shall visit the Britons, who are savage to guests.*

4 *Augustus will be considered a god here and now, once the Britons and threatening Persians have been added to the empire.*

5 *Divine Julius was first of all the Romans to invade Britain with an army, and although he intimidated the natives with a military victory and occupied the coast, he can be thought of as having revealed Britain to later generations without having passed it on as a province. Soon there were civil wars, and the forces of the leaders were turned against the republic. A long neglect of Britain followed, even in peacetime: Divine Augustus called this a policy, Tiberius a maxim.*

6 *I had horses, men, weapons and wealth: why is it extraordinary if I have let go of these things unwillingly? Just because you wish to rule over all, does it follow that all should welcome their subjection?*

7 *Under a woman's leadership (you see they do not discriminate between the sexes in matters of authority) they all took up arms.*

8 *It is believable that the Gauls occupied the neighbouring island. The language is not much different, there is the same boldness in facing dangers and, when these dangers have arrived, the same fear in avoiding them. However, the Britons display more ferocity, because a lengthy peace has not yet made them soft. For we have heard that the Gauls were also successful in war; but in due course idleness arrived with peace, and their courage disappeared along with their liberty. This happened to those of the Britons who were conquered some time ago: the others remain as the Gauls were.*

9 *The sky [i.e. in Britain] is dirty with frequent rain-clouds and mists; there are no severely cold spells.*

10 *Those who recently rejected the Roman language now wanted to be fluent. There was a gradual decline to the allurements of vices, of colonnades, baths and the*

sophistication of dinner-parties. That was called civilisation by the foolish, although in fact it was a part of their slavery.

12   Religion

1   *Each man puts one doorkeeper at his door, and because he is a human being he is quite sufficient: those people [i.e. pagans] have placed three gods, Forculus for the gate, Cardea for the hinge and Limentinus for the threshold. So Forculus was unable to look after the hinge and the threshold at the same time.*

2   *There is a hallway right at the mouth of the entrance to Hades. Here have Grief and vengeful Worries placed their beds; here are Diseases that make you pale, and gloomy Old Age, and Fear and evil-counselling Hunger and disgraceful Need, shapes terrible to see, and Death and Toil.*

3   *The harsh mother of the Cupids and the son of Theban Semele and playful Wantonness insist I revive my inclination for feelings that were finished.*

4   *Fortuna, who delights in her savage work and persistently plays her wanton game, switches her fickle favours, now kind to me, now to another.*

5   *Fortuna, we make you a goddess and place you in heaven.*

6   *We will endure losses, distress, humiliations, overseas postings, bereavements and divorces – things that do not overwhelm a wise man even if they all come together.*

7   *Mouse is a syllable. A mouse, however, nibbles cheese; a syllable, therefore, nibbles cheese. There is cause for concern that, if I am too careless, a book may gobble up the cheese.*

8   *You should not inquire – it's not ours to know – what end the gods have in store for yourself or for me, Leuconoë, nor should you dabble in Babylonian charts . . . Be wise, decant the wine and trim your long-term plans to a brief span. Even as we speak, the unkind hour will have slipped away: enjoy the moment, and trust as little as possible in tomorrow.*

9   *O Spring of Bandusia, brighter than crystal, deserving sweet wine and flowers, tomorrow you will be offered a young kid, whose forehead reveals the first swellings of horns and foretells mating and jousts – in vain. This offspring of the playful flock is to colour your cool streams with its red blood.*

10 *He struggles to tear open the knots with his hands, his headband spattered with slaver and black poison, and in the same moment he raises horrendous cries to the stars: just like the bellowing of a wounded bull when it has fled the altar and shaken off the ill-aimed axe from its neck.*

11 *She finished speaking, and slipping her snow-white arms this way and that she wraps him up in a cuddle. He hesitates. Then suddenly he felt the familiar spark, and the well-known warmth penetrated his innermost core and darted through his trembling bones.*

12 *On this side Augustus Caesar is leading the Italians into battle, with the senators and the people, with the household gods and the great gods.*

189

13 *You, Roman, though not to blame, will atone for the sins of your ancestors, until you have rebuilt the temples, the collapsing shrines of the gods and the statues soiled with black smoke.*

14 *'Oh dear!' he said. 'I think I am becoming a god.'*

13 Christianity

1 *The chief priests sent tricksters to pretend that they were fair-minded, so that they might catch him out in conversation and hand him over to the power and authority of the governor. And they interrogated him, saying, 'Master, we know that you speak and teach rightly: is it permitted for us to give tribute to Caesar or not?' But he was aware of their trick and said to them: 'Why do you tempt me? Show me a denarius: whose likeness and inscription does it have?' Answering him, they said: 'Caesar's.' And he said to them: 'So give to Caesar what is Caesar's: and what is God's to God.' And they, in the presence of the people, were unable to find fault with his argument: and amazed at his response, they fell silent.*

2 *And again I say to you: it is easier for a camel to go through the eye of a needle than for a rich man to enter the kingdom of heaven.*

3 *So to get rid of the rumour, Nero created scapegoats, and with very far-fetched punishments afflicted those whom, hated for their crimes, people called Christians. Christ, the founder of that name, had been put to death when Tiberius was emperor, on the orders of Pontius Pilate, the procurator. For a while the deadly superstition was checked, but then broke out again, not only in Judaea, the source of this evil, but also in Rome where from every corner all things sleaze-ridden and shameful ooze together and come into vogue.*

4 *As for those brought before me on the charge of being Christians, I followed this procedure: I asked them in person whether they were Christians. Those who freely admitted it I asked a second and third time, and threatened them with the death-penalty. If they persisted I had them taken away and executed. For I was in no doubt that at least their stubbornness and inflexible obstinacy ought to be punished.*

5 *An anonymous leaflet was put in front of me containing the names of many people. Those who denied that they were or had been Christians, and who, with me reciting first, called upon the gods, I thought should be released.*

6 *I believed it necessary to extract the truth from two maidservants who were called deaconesses – and that through torture. But I found nothing other than a depraved and excessive superstition.*

7 *They are not to be sought out; but if they are charged and convicted, they are to be punished.*

8 *When interrogated as to where I stood I replied that I was a Christian, and he who sat in judgement said, 'You are lying, you are a Ciceronian, not a Christian; where your treasure is, there too is your soul.'*

TIME CHART

Romulus founds Rome (traditional date: 753)
Tarquin expelled from Rome: beginning of the republic (510)   Aeschylus
Athens is governed by democracy   Sophocles, Euripides
The Parthenon is completed (432)   Thucydides
Gauls sack Rome (390)   Plato
Philip of Macedon subdues Greek cities   Aristotle
Alexander the Great dies (323)
First war with Carthage starts (264)
Romans make Sicily their first overseas province (241)
Hannibal invades Italy (218)   Plautus
Carthage defeated (201)   Cato
Romans take control of Greece with victory over Macedonians (168)   Terence
Spartacus leads slave revolt in Italy (73–71)
Cicero is consul and suppresses Catiline's conspiracy (63)   Varro
First triumvirate: Caesar, Pompey and Crassus (60)   Cicero
Caesar begins campaign in Gaul (58); crosses to Britain (55 and 54)   Catullus
Caesar is dictator (48) and assassinated (44)   Sallust
Second triumvirate: Antony, Octavian and Lepidus; Cicero is killed (43)
Antony and Cleopatra are defeated by Octavian at Actium (31)   Virgil, Horace
Octavian takes the title 'Augustus' (27)   Livy
Ovid

Augustus dies, succeeded by Tiberius (14)
Pontius Pilate is procurator of Judaea (26–36)
Invasion of Britain, under Claudius (43)   Seneca
Boudicca revolts in Britain (61)   Martial
Nero's fire in Rome (64)   Quintilian
Building of the Colosseum   Tacitus, Pliny
Vespasian dies; eruption of Vesuvius (79)   Juvenal, Suetonius
Trajan's Column and Forum completed (114)
Hadrian's Wall built in northern Britain (122–128)
Jewish uprising in Palestine suppressed (131–135)
Roman citizenship extended to all free people in the empire (212)
Incursions of Goths and other barbarians begin (251)
Constantine becomes first Christian emperor (306)
Empire divided into two halves: east and west (395)   Jerome, Augustine
Alaric and Visigoths sack Rome (410)
Romans defeat Attila the Hun (451)
Vandals sack Rome (455)

191

THE AUTHORS

Aurelius Augustinus (ST AUGUSTINE)

b. AD 354 in Numidia, north Africa; scholar and rhetorician; was converted to Christianity in 386; his surviving works are in bulk six times those of Cicero, and include *Confessiones*, *De Trinitate* and *De Civitate Dei*.

Gaius Octavius (AUGUSTUS)

b. 63 BC, great-nephew of Julius Caesar; emerged from civil wars during the first century BC as the sole source of authority; on the pretext of restoring the republic, he in fact established the imperial dynasty; his work *Res Gestae* is a subjective account of his achievements; d. AD 14.

Gaius Valerius CATULLUS

b. Verona, Italy, c. 84 BC into a wealthy family; extant works include erotic and satirical lyrics, hymns and an 'epyllion' (short epic); d. c. 54 BC.

Gaius Julius CAESAR

b. c. 102 BC into a wealthy family; successful general, politician and diplomat, who became dictator; extant works are *De Bello Gallico* and *De Bello Civili*; assassinated in 44 BC.

Marcus Tullius CICERO

b. Arpinum, Italy, 106 BC, into an equestrian family; extant work includes political and legal speeches, letters, treatises on rhetoric and on political and ethical philosophy; his style became the model for subsequent writers of Latin prose; d. 43 BC.

Quintus Horatius Flaccus (HORACE)

b. Venusia, Italy, 65 BC; son of a freedman; enjoyed Augustus' patronage; extant work includes *Odes*, *Epistles* and *Satires*; d. 8 BC.

JEROME

b. Dalmatia, c. AD 345; ordained priest in 379; commissioned by the pope to revise the Latin version of the New Testament; settled in Palestine where he learnt Hebrew and translated the whole Bible into Latin; d. c. AD 420.

Decimus Junius Juvenalis (JUVENAL)

b. c. AD 60; his sixteen *Satires* survive, of which the last is incomplete; d. after AD 130.

Titus Livius (LIVY)

b. Padua, Italy, 59 BC; his major work *Ab Urbe Condita Libri* comprised 142 volumes, of which 35 survive; d. AD 17.

Marcus Valerius Martialis (MARTIAL)

b. Bilbilis, Spain, c. AD 40; extant are 14 books of epigrams, containing over 1500 poems; d. c. AD 104.

Cornelius NEPOS

b. c. 99 BC; biographer of generals, kings, historians, poets and orators; his work *De Viris Illustribus* survives.

Publius Ovidius Naso (OVID)

b. Sulmo, Italy, 43 BC into an equestrian family; his erotic poetry provoked the anger of Augustus and he was banished to the Black Sea; extant are amatory poems, the *Metamorphoses*, the *Fasti*, and poetical letters; d. c. AD 17.

PETRONIUS

First century AD; a member of Nero's literary circle; extant are fragments of his comic novel the *Satyricon*.

Titus Maccius PLAUTUS

b. Sarsina, Italy, c. 254 BC; a writer of comedies; 20 plays survive him; he used Greek New Comedy as a model for his work, and in turn influenced later writers including Shakespeare; d. 184 BC.

Gaius Plinius Secundus (PLINY the Elder)

b. Como, Italy, AD 23/24; devoted much of his life to studies and writing; his sole extant work is the *Naturalis Historia*; uncle of Pliny the Younger; killed by eruption of Vesuvius, AD 79.

Gaius Plinius Caecilius Secundus (PLINY)

b. Como, Italy, c. AD 61; provincial governor, lawyer; his published letters offer a unique picture of upper-class life in the early imperial period; d. c. AD 113.

Marcus Fabius Quintilianus (QUINTILIAN)

b. Calagurris, Spain, c. AD 40; a teacher of rhetoric and oratory; his book *The Elements of Oratory* survives; d. c. AD 100.

Gaius Sallustius Crispus (SALLUST)

b. Amiternum, Italy, 86 BC; a supporter of Julius Caesar; two works are extant: *Bellum Catilinae* and *Bellum Jugurthinum*; d. c. 34 BC.

Lucius Annaeus SENECA

b. Cordoba, Spain, c. 4 BC; philosopher and political adviser to Nero; committed suicide (AD 65) after being accused of complicity in a plot against Nero's life; his prolific output included moral essays, letters, and adaptations of several Greek tragedies.

Gaius SUETONIUS Tranquillus

b. c. AD 69; biographer of Julius Caesar and the first eleven emperors of Rome.

Cornelius TACITUS

b. c. AD 55. Orator and historian; he married the daughter of Agricola, a governor of Britain; extant works include: *Dialogus de Oratoribus*, *Historiae*, *De Vita Agricolae*, and *Annales*; d. c. AD 118.

Publius Terentius Afer (TERENCE)

b. Carthage, Africa, c. 195 BC; brought to Rome as a slave, but his literary skill quickly found him freedom and patronage; six of his comedies survive; his Latinity was much respected by medieval scholars; d. c. 159 BC.

Marcus Terentius VARRO

b. Reate, Italy, 116 BC; scholar and antiquarian; two of his books survive: *On Agriculture* and *On The Latin Language*; d. 27 BC.

Gaius VELLEIUS PATERCULUS

b. Campania, Italy, c. 19 BC; his *History of Rome* covers the period from legendary beginnings to the first century AD; d. post AD 30.

Publius Vergilius Maro (VIRGIL)

b. Mantua, Italy, 70 BC; member of Augustus' literary circle; extant works are the *Eclogues*, the *Georgics* and the *Aeneid*; d. 19 BC.

FURTHER READING

Almost all classical Latin texts are available from Oxford University Press. Most texts are also published in the Loeb Classical Library: these include translations. Penguin and Oxford World's Classics (OUP) offer the longest lists of available translations:

Caesar	*The Conquest of Gaul*, S. A. Handford (Penguin).
Catullus	*The Poems of Catullus*, G. Lee (Oxford World's Classics).
Cicero	*Selected Political Speeches* and *Selected Works*, M. Grant (Penguin); *Selected Letters*, D. R. Shackleton-Bailey (Penguin).
Horace	*The Complete Odes and Epodes*, W. G. Shepherd; *The Satires*, N. Rudd (Penguin).
Juvenal	*The Satires*, N. Rudd (Oxford World's Classics).
Livy	*The Early History of Rome,* and *The War with Hannibal*, A. de Selincourt (Penguin).
Pliny	*The Letters of the Younger Pliny*, B. Radice (Penguin).
Ovid	*The Metamorphoses* (prose), M. Innes (Penguin); *The Metamorphoses* (verse), A. D. Melville (Oxford World's Classics).
Sallust	*The Jugurthine War and the Conspiracy of Catiline*, S. A. Handford (Penguin).
Seneca	*Letters from a Stoic*, R. Campbell; *Four Tragedies and Octavia*, E. Watling (Penguin).
Suetonius	*The Twelve Caesars*, R. Graves (Penguin).
Tacitus	*The Annals of Imperial Rome*, M. Grant (Penguin); *The Agricola and the Germania*, H. Mattingly, rev. S. A. Handford (Penguin).
Virgil	*The Aeneid*, C. Day Lewis (Oxford World's Classics).

Latin on the internet

www.lingua.co.uk (LATIN QVARTER)

195

A GLOSSARY OF CHARACTERS

(For the authors, see pp. 192–4)

Aeneas Legendary ancestor of Romans; a prince who escaped the destruction of Troy and settled in Italy.

Agricola AD 40–93, governor of Britain; father-in-law of the historian, Tacitus, who wrote his biography.

Agrippina AD 15–59, wife of Claudius; mother of Nero; murdered on Nero's instructions.

Alexander 356–323 BC, king of Macedonia who conquered territories as far east as India.

Antony 82–30 BC, lieutenant of Caesar; triumvir with Octavian and Lepidus (43 BC); with Cleopatra was defeated at Actium (31 BC) by Octavian.

Aphrodite Greek goddess of love; equivalent of Roman Venus.

Apollo God of sun, archery, healing and prophecy (same name in Greek and Latin).

Ares Greek god of war; equivalent of Roman Mars.

Ariadne Helped Theseus slay the Minotaur and eloped with him, only to be abandoned on the island of Naxos.

Aristotle 384–322 BC, influential philosopher and literary critic; Plato's pupil and Alexander the Great's tutor.

Artemis Greek goddess of hunting and childbirth; equivalent of Roman Diana.

Ascanius Son of Aeneas; otherwise known as Iulus.

Athene Greek goddess of protection, warfare, skill and wisdom; equivalent of Roman Minerva.

Atticus 109–32 BC, close friend and correspondent of Cicero.

Bacchus Roman god of wine; identified with Greek Dionysus.

Boudicca Queen of the Iceni tribe (East Anglia) whose rebellion was crushed by Suetonius; d. AD 61.

Britannicus AD 41–55, son of the emperor Claudius; poisoned, probably on Nero's orders.

Brutus (**Lucius Iunius**)	Helped to expel the Tarquins; founded the republic and was one of the first two consuls.
Brutus (**Marcus Iunius**)	85–42 BC, Caesar's assassin; raised an army but was defeated by Antony and Octavian at Philippi, where he committed suicide.
Caratacus (**Caractacus**)	Leader of the south-eastern Britons against the Roman invasion during the reign of Claudius; retreated to the west, then to the north, where the local queen handed him over to the Romans.
Cassius	Supporter of Pompey in the civil war against Caesar; later pardoned, but played a leading part in the assassination of Caesar (44 BC); fought against Antony and Octavian at Philippi, where he took his own life (42 BC).
Catiline	d. 62 BC, aristocratic reformer whose unscrupulous methods were unsuccessful; his conspiracy against the government was crushed during Cicero's consulship.
Cato	234–149 BC, tried to retain traditional Roman values of simplicity and austerity in the face of Greek and eastern influences; orator and writer.
Claudius	10 BC–AD 54, Roman emperor who succeeded Caligula (AD 41) and preceded Nero; Britain was annexed as a province during his reign.
Cleopatra	Queen of Egypt, mistress of Caesar; later, wife of Antony; after Antony's death, she took her own life.
Clodia	Sister of Publius Clodius (below); probably the 'Lesbia' of Catullus' poems; like Catullus, Caelius became infatuated with her, but the relationship soured and ended in the famous court case with Cicero speaking for Caelius (*Pro Caelio*).
Clodius	Caused a political scandal by appearing in women's clothes at the festival of Bona Dea, held in the house of Caesar; although he was finally acquitted, his alibi was destroyed by Cicero; killed by Milo, whom Cicero subsequently defended (*Pro Milone*). d. 52 BC.
Cloelia	A Roman girl given as hostage to Porsenna, king of the Etruscans; she escaped by swimming the Tiber, but was handed back to Porsenna, who released her out of admiration for her bravery.
Clytemnestra	Wife of Agamemnon; she killed him on his return from Troy, to avenge his sacrifice of their daughter Iphigenia.
Coriolanus	Early republican figure, who withdrew from Rome after being accused of tyranny; as leader of the Volscians, he would have defeated Rome, had not the entreaties of his mother and wife prevailed (491 BC).
Cupid	Love god; child of Venus.
Diana	Goddess of hunting and childbirth; identified with Greek Artemis.

Dido	Founder and queen of Carthage; received Aeneas when he was washed up on the shores of north Africa, and fell in love with him; took her own life when he left her.
Elissa	i.e. Dido.
Epicureans	Philosophical sect which originated in Greece, and became popular in Rome; encouraged adherents to avoid life's problems and potential sources of stress.
Fulvia	Married Clodius and later Mark Antony; enemy of Cicero; d. 40 BC.
Hannibal	247–c. 182 BC, Carthaginian general who all but defeated Rome; recognised by later Romans as the greatest of their enemies.
Hephaestus	Greek god of the forge; equivalent of Roman Vulcan.
Hera	Greek goddess and wife of Zeus; equivalent of Roman Juno.
Hermes	Greek messenger god; equivalent of Roman Mercury.
Homer	Composer of the Greek epic poems, the *Iliad* and the *Odyssey*, the earliest known Greek literature; was deliberately echoed and imitated by subsequent Greek and Roman poets.
Horatius Cocles	Legendary Roman who defended a bridge under attack from the Etruscans, while his comrades destroyed the bridge behind him; despite his wounds and armour, he swam to safety.
Jason	Leader of the Argonauts who sailed to Colchis to find the Golden Fleece; Medea, daughter of the king, helped him steal it, but he deserted her after his return to Greece.
Julia	39 BC–AD 14, daughter of Augustus; her third husband was Tiberius (11 BC); she was banished by her father (2 BC) for licentious conduct.
Juno	Goddess and wife of Jupiter; identified with Greek Hera.
Jupiter	Father of the gods; identified with Greek Zeus.
Laocoon	Trojan prince and priest; he protested against the proposal to drag the Wooden Horse (which concealed Greeks) into Troy; killed by two serpents immediately after his objections had been heard.
Lares	Spirits of farmland and dwelling-places.
Lavinia	Daughter of Latinus, an Italian king; married to Aeneas.
Lepidus	Triumvir with Antony and Octavian; d. c. 13 BC.
Lesbia	See Clodia.
Livia	58 BC–AD 29, wife of Augustus; mother of Tiberius.
Maharbal	Carthaginian general under Hannibal; in command of the cavalry.
Marius	157–86 BC, Marius acquired a good military reputation in Africa; the bitter enmity between him and Sulla began the civil conflicts which recurred during the first century BC.
Mars	God of war; identified with Greek Ares.
Medea	Daughter of the king of Colchis, who helped Jason steal the Golden Fleece, but was deserted by him after she accompanied him back to Greece.

Menander	342–291 BC, Greek comic playwright.
Mercury	Messenger god; identified with Greek Hermes.
Minerva	Goddess of handicrafts; identified with Greek Athene.
Minicius Macrinus	Contemporary of Pliny the Younger.
Narcissus	Freedman who became secretary to Claudius.
Neptune	God of the sea; identified with Greek Poseidon.
Nero	AD 37–68, Roman emperor (54–68) famed for his persecution of Christians; executed many senators in fear of conspiracies, but was popular with poorer people, whose taste for the theatre and horse-racing he shared.
Oedipus	King of Thebes, who killed his father and married his mother; his story was dramatised by Sophocles and later by Seneca.
Pallas	Highly influential freedman; secretary to Claudius, then to Nero.
Paris	Son of King Priam of Troy; while a guest of Menelaus, king of Sparta, Paris abducted his wife, Helen, which caused the Trojan War; traditionally an unheroic and cowardly figure.
Penates	Spirits of the store-cupboard.
Philip	King of Macedonia 359–336 BC; father of Alexander the Great; overran Athens and the other Greek states, bringing them under Macedonian control, where they remained until the arrival of the Romans at the end of the third century BC.
Plato	c. 429–347 BC, Greek philosopher, disciple of Socrates and teacher of Aristotle; his theory of forms had a profound influence on subsequent philosophy and Christian theology.
Pompey	106–48 BC, general and politician; his successes brought first a share in power (triumvirate) and then rivalry with Caesar; after losing the battle of Pharsalus to Caesar he fled to Egypt where he was killed.
Pontius Pilate	Procurator of Judea AD 26–36, during whose administration Jesus Christ was crucified.
Poseidon	Greek god of the sea; equivalent of Roman Neptune.
Prasutagus	King of the Iceni, husband of Boudicca; d. AD 61.
Romulus	Brother of Remus; legendary founder of Rome.
Semele	Daughter of Theban king, Cadmus, who bore Dionysus from a union with Zeus.
Sophocles	c. 496–406 BC, Greek writer, producer and actor of tragedies, including *Oedipus Tyrannus* and *Antigone*.
Stoics	Philosophical sect which originated in Greece, and became popular in Rome; encouraged adherents to confront life's problems without fear.
Sulla	138–78 BC, first of the military dictators in the first century BC; his regime was harsh and cruel to those who opposed him, and in Italy sowed the seeds of civil hostility which remained until the rise of Augustus.

Tarquinius Collatinus	Consul during the early days of the republic.
Tarquinius Superbus	Tarquin was the last of the kings of Rome (trad. date of removal: 510 BC); he enlisted the support of the Etruscans, but failed to return to power.
Thallus	A scribe working under the emperor Augustus.
Theseus	Athenian hero who killed the Cretan minotaur and escaped with Ariadne, the daughter of the king of Crete; he abandoned her on Naxos.
Thucydides	c. 460–400 BC, Athenian general and historian of the conflict between Athens and Sparta (*The Peloponnesian War*).
Tiberius	42 BC–AD 37, Roman emperor; stepson and successor to Augustus; a reclusive figure, who is much criticised by the historian Tacitus.
Tiro	Personal secretary and librarian to Cicero.
Venus	Goddess of love; identified with Greek Aphrodite.
Vespasian	AD 9–79, Roman emperor; a realist and pragmatic ruler of Rome.
Vesta	Hearth goddess; identified with Greek Hestia.
Vulcan	God of the forge; identified with Greek Hephaestus.
Zeus	Father of the Greek gods; equivalent of Roman Jupiter.

GENERAL VOCABULARY

Verbs like **parō–āre** are marked [1], like **moneō–ēre** [2], and like **audiō–īre** [4]. Verbs with principal parts that do not conform to these patterns are shown in full. Verbs belonging to the third conjugation, like **mittō–ere**, have various forms and these also are shown in full.

Nouns are shown with their nominative and genitive endings. Adjectives are shown in the nominative singular masculine, feminine and neuter; or, where the masculine and feminine are the same, in the masc./fem. and neuter. The few adjectives that have the same nominative form for all three genders will be shown in the nominative and genitive.

ā, ab [+abl.] *by, from*
abnuō–ere–nuī *reject*
aboleō–ēre–olēvī–olitum *destroy*
abstineō–ēre–stinuī–stentum *restrain*
absum, abesse, āfuī *be absent*
absūmō–ere–sūmpsī–sūmptum *consume*
ac *and*
accēdō–ere–cessī–cessum *approach*
accendō–ere–cendī–cēnsum *stimulate, inflame*
accipiō–ere–cēpī–ceptum *take possession of, receive*
accumbō–ere–cubuī–cubitum *recline, lay oneself down*
accūsātor–ōris [m.] *prosecutor*
ācer–cris–cre *keen, sharp*
acerbus–a–um *bitter*
aciēs–ēī [f.] *battle-line, sight*
acquīrō–ere–quīsīvī–quīsītum *acquire*
acus–ūs [f.] *needle, pin*
ad [+acc.] *to, towards*
adcommodātus–a–um *suited*
addō–ere–didī–ditum *add*
adeō *very much, to such an extent*
adficiō–ere–fēcī–fectum *afflict, inflict upon*

adhibeō [2] *apply*
adicio–ere–iēcī–iectum *add*
adiungō–ere–iūnxī–iūnctum *attach*
adiūtrīx–īcis [f.] *assistant*
adōrnō [1] *decorate*
adsum–esse–fuī *be present*
adulēscēns–ntis [m.] *young man*
adulterium–ī [n.] *adultery*
adveniō–īre–vēnī–ventum *arrive*
adversārius–ī [m.] *opponent*
adversus [+acc.] *against*
aedēs–is [f.] *shrine*
aequē *as much, equally*
aequō [1] *make equal*
aes, aeris [n.] *bronze*
aestimō [1] *value, estimate*
aestuō [1] *be hot*
aetās, aetātis [f.] *age, time*
afferō–ferre, attulī, allātum *bring*
affirmō [1] *declare*
ager, agrī [m.] *field, land*
agmen–inis [n.] *crowd, column*
agō–ere, ēgī, āctum *do, act, perform, lead*
agrestis–e *rustic*
agricola–ae [m.] *farmer*

201

ESSENTIAL LATIN

ait *he/she said*
alīptēs–ae [m.] *masseur*
aliquis–quid *someone, something*
aliter *otherwise*
alius–a–ud *other*
alter–era–erum *other (of two)*
altus–a–um *high, deep*
ambitiō–nis [f.] *ambition*
ambulō [1] *walk*
āmēns, gen. āmentis *crazed*
amīca–ae [f.] *friend (female)*
amīcitia–ae [f.] *friendship*
amiculum–ī [n.] *cloak*
amīcus–ī [m.] *friend (male)*
āmittō–ere–mīsī–missum *let go, lose*
amō [1] *love, like*
amor–ōris [m.] *love, affection*
amphitheātrum–ī [n.] *amphitheatre*
amplexus–ūs [m.] *embrace*
amplius *more*
an *whether, or*
ancilla–ae [f.] *maidservant*
anima–ae [f.] *soul, life-breath*
animadvertō–ere–vertī–versum *observe*
animal–is [n.] *animal*
animus–ī [m.] *mind, will*
annus–ī [m.] *year*
ante [+acc.] *before*
antequam *before*
antīquus–a–um *former, ancient*
aperiō–īre–uī, apertum *open, reveal*
appāreō [2] *be apparent, appear*
appellō [1] *call*
aptus–a–um *suited, fit*
apud [+acc.] *among, with*
aqua–ae [f.] *water*
āra–ae [f.] *altar*
arānea–ae [f.] *cobweb*
ārdeō–ēre, ārsī *burn, rage*
arduitās–tātis [f.] *steepness*
argentum–ī [n.] *silver*
arguō–ere–uī–ūtum *show, prove*
arma–ōrum [n. pl.] *weapons*
arō [1] *plough*
ars, artis [f.] *art, skill*
artus–ūs [m.] *limb*
arx, arcis [f.] *citadel*
as, assis [m.] *as (small coin)*
aspectus–ūs [m.] *appearance*
asperitās–tātis [f.] *harshness*
assiduē *assiduously*
at *but*

āter–tra–trum *black*
atque *and*
atquī *and yet*
ātrium–ī [n.] *hall*
atrōx, gen. atrōcis *atrocious*
auctor–ōris [m.] *author, founder*
audācia–ae [f.] *boldness*
audācter *boldly*
audeō–ēre, ausus sum *dare*
audiō [4] *hear*
auferō–ferre, abstulī, ablātum *take away, carry off*
augur–is [m.] *soothsayer*
aurātus–a–um *adorned in gold*
aureus–a–um *golden*
aurum–ī [n.] *gold*
aut, aut . . . aut *or, either . . . or*
autem *however, but*
avāritia–ae [f.] *greed*
avārus–a–um *greedy*
avidus–a–um *greedy*
balineum–ī [n.] *bath*
barbarus–a–um *barbarian*
beātus–a–um *happy*
bellō [1] *go to war*
bellum–ī [n.] *war*
bene *well*
benignus–a–um *kind*
bēstia–ae [f.] *beast*
bēstiārius–ī [m.] *animal-fighter*
bibō–ere, bibī *drink*
bonus–a–um *good*
bōs, bovis [m. & f.] *ox, cow*
brevis–e *short*
caballus–ī [m.] *horse*
cachinnus–ī [m.] *laugh*
cadō–ere, cecidī, cāsum *fall*
caedēs–is [f.] *killing*
caedō–ere, cecīdī, caesum *beat, kill*
caelum–ī [n.] *sky, heaven*
caeruleus–a–um *sky-blue*
calamitās–tātis [f.] *disaster*
callis–is [m.] *footpath*
calor–ōris [m.] *warmth, heat*
camēlus–ī [m.] *camel*
candidus–a–um *bright*
canis–is [c.] *dog*
canō–ere, cecinī, cantum *sing*
capillus–ī [m.] *hair*
capiō–ere, cēpī, captum *take, capture*
captīvus–ī [m.] *captive*
caput, capitis [n.] *head*

cardō–inis [m.] *hinge*

careō [+abl.] [2] *lose, lack*

carmen-inis [n.] *poem, song*

carō, carnis [f.] *flesh*

carpō–ere, carpsī, carptum *reap*

cārus–a–um *dear*

cāseus–ī [m.] *cheese*

castīgō [1] *punish*

castra–ōrum [n. pl.] *camp*

castus–a–um *chaste*

cāsus–ūs [m.] *fortune, chance*

catēna–ae [f.] *chain*

causa–ae [f.] *cause, case*

caveō–ēre, cāvī, cautum *look out (for)*

cēdō–ere, cessī, cessum *yield, give way*

celebrō [1] *practise*

celer, celeris, celere *quick*

cēna–ae [f.] *dinner*

cēnō [1] *dine*

cēnsus–ūs [m.] *assets*

centum *hundred*

certāmen–inis [n.] *competition*

certē *certainly, at least*

cervīx–īcis [f.] *neck*

cēterus–a–um [rarely used in sing.] *the other*

cinis–eris [m.] *ash*

circumspiciō–ere–spexī–spectum *look around*

citius *more quickly*

cīvīlis–e *civil*

cīvis–is [c.] *citizen*

clāmō [1] *shout*

clāmor–ōris [m.] *shout, cry*

cliēns–ntis [m.] *client*

coepī, coepisse, coeptum *begin*

coerceō [2] *restrain*

cōgitō [1] *think, contemplate*

cognitiō–nis [f.] *inquiry*

cognōscō–ere–nōvī–nitum *discover*

cōgō–ere, coēgī, coāctum *compel*

cohors–tis [f.] *troop*

colō–ere–uī, cultum *cultivate*

comedō–esse–ēdī–ēsum *consume, gobble up*

commendō [1] *improve, enhance*

commoveō–ēre–mōvī–mōtum *disturb*

commūnis–e *common, shared*

commūtātiō–nis [f.] *change*

cōmoedus–a–um *given to acting*

competītor–ōris [m.] *competitor*

cōmptus–a–um *well-groomed*

computō [1] *count*

concēdō–ere–cessī–cessum *concede*

concupīscō–ere–pīvī–pītum *desire, aspire to*

concursus–ūs [m.] *rushing together*

concutiō–ere–cussī–cussum *strike, shake*

condiciō–nis [f.] *circumstances, condition*

conditor–ōris [m.] *founder*

condō–ere–didī–ditum *found*

cōnfirmō [1] *confirm, assure*

cōnfiteor–ērī, cōnfessus sum *admit*

cōnfluō–ere–fluxī *flow together*

coniūnx–iugis [m. & f.] *spouse*

conlābor (coll–), collāpsus sum *fall in*

cōnor [1] *try*

conquīrō–ere–quīsīvī–quīsītum *search for*

cōnsīderō [1] *consider*

cōnsilium–ī [n.] *plan, policy, advice*

cōnsistō–ere–stitī *stand*

cōnspiciō–ere–spexī–spectum *catch sight of*

cōnsternātus–a–um *agitated*

cōnstō–āre–stitī *stand together, agree with, cost*

cōnsuētūdō–inis [f.] *custom, habit*

cōnsul–is [m.] *consul*

contemnō–ere–tempsī–temptum *despise*

contendō–ere–tendī–tentum *compete*

contentus–a–um *contented*

contiō–nis [f.] *assembly*

contrā [+acc.] *against*

contrārius–a–um *opposite*

convīctor–ōris [m.] *table-companion*

convīvium–ī [n.] *dinner-party*

cōpia–ae [f.] *abundance*

cōpiōsus–a–um *abundant*

cor–dis [n.] *heart, soul*

cōram [+abl.] *in the presence of*

cornū–ūs [n.] *horn*

corpus–oris [n.] *body*

corripiō–ere–ripuī–reptum *seize, hurry*

crās *tomorrow*

crātēra–ae [f.] *bowl*

crēber–bra–brum *frequent*

crēdibilis–e *credible*

crēdō–ere–didī–ditum [+dat.] *trust, believe*

crēdulus–a–um [+dat.] *trusting*

creō [1] *appoint*

crēscō–ere, crēvī, crētum *grow*

cristātus–a–um *crested*

crūs–ūris [n.] *leg*

cubīle–is [n.] *couch, bed*
culīna–ae [f.] *kitchen*
culpō [1] *blame*
cultūra–ae [f.] *tilling*
cum *with* [+abl.]; *when, since, although*
cum ... tum *when ... then, both ... and*
cūnctor [1] *hesitate*
cūnctus–a–um *all, whole*
cupīdō–inis [f.] *desire*
cūra–ae [f.] *care, anxiety, attention*
cūrō [1] *attend, see to*
curriculum–ī [n.] *course*
currō–ere, cucurrī, cursum *run*
currus–ūs [m.] *chariot*
damnō [1] *harm, condemn*
damnōsus–a–um *harmful*
damnum–ī [n.] *loss*
dē [+abl.] *from, about*
dea–ae [f.] *goddess*
dēbellō [1] *fight against, subdue*
dēbeō [2] *ought, owe*
dēcēdō–ere–cessī–cessum *withdraw, die*
decem *ten*
decimō [1] *select by lot every tenth man for
    execution*
dēclāmitō [1] *declaim*
dēcrepitus–a–um *decrepit*
dēcurrō–ere–currī–cursum *run down*
dēdūcō–ere–dūxī–ductum *bring*
dēfendō–ere–dī–sum *defend*
dēferō–erre, dētulī, dēlātum *bring down,
    offer, report, accuse*
deinde *then, next*
dēlectātiō–nis [f.] *pleasure*
dēlēgō [1] *assign*
dēlēnīmentum–ī [n.] *allurement*
dēligō [1] *tie*
dēlinquō–ere–līquī–lictum *make a mistake*
dēmittō–ere–mīsī–missum *lower, send
    down*
dēmōnstrō [1] *show*
dēnārius–ī [m.] *denarius*
dēnī *in tens*
dēposcō–ere–poposcī *demand, challenge*
dēscendō–ere–scendī–scēnsum *come
    down, fall*
dēscrībō–ere–scrīpsī–scrīptum *register,
    describe*
dēserō–ere–seruī–sertum *leave, abandon*
dēsideō [2] *sit idly*
dēspērō [1] *despair of*
dēstinō [1] *determine, destine*

dēstitūtus–a–um *abandoned, lonely*
dētineō [2] *keep*
dētrectō [1] *refuse, shirk*
deus–ī [m.] *god*
dēveniō–īre–vēnī–ventum *come down*
dīcō–ere, dīxī, dictum *say, speak*
dictātūra–ae [f.] *dictatorship*
diēs–ēī [m. & f.] *day*
differō–ferre, distulī, dīlātum *differ*
difficultās–tātis [f.] *difficulty*
digitus–ī [m.] *finger, toe*
dignitās–tātis [f.] *authority*
dignus–a–um [+abl.] *worthy of, deserving*
dīgredior–ī–gressus sum *depart*
dīmittō–ere–mīsī–missum *release*
dīmoveō–ēre–mōvī–mōtum *remove*
discēdō–ere–cessī–cessum *depart*
discernō–ere–crēvī–crētum *divide,
    separate*
discidium–ī [n.] *divorce*
disciplīna–ae [f.] *knowledge*
discipulus–ī [m.] *student*
discō–ere, didicī *learn*
discordia–ae [f.] *disagreement*
discumbō–ere–cubuī–cubitum *recline*
dīva–ae [f.] *goddess*
dīvellō–ere–vellī–vulsum *tear apart*
dīversus–a–um *different*
dīves, gen. dīvitis *rich*
dīvus–a–um *divine*
dō, dare, dedī, datum *give*
doceō–ēre–uī, doctum *teach*
documentum–ī [n.] *example*
doleō [2] *grieve*
dolor–ōris [m.] *grief*
dolus–ī [m.] *trick*
dominus–ī [m.] *master*
domus–ūs [f.] *home*
dōnec *until*
dōnō [1] *donate*
dōnum–ī [n.] *gift*
dormiō [4] *sleep*
dubitō [1] *doubt, hesitate*
dūcō–ere, dūxī, ductum *lead, bring*
ductus–ūs [m.] *leadership*
dulcis–e *sweet*
duo *two*
duodēnī *in twelves*
dux, ducis [m.] *leader*
ē, ex [+abl.] *out of, from*
ecce *oh! look!*
ēdīcō–ere–dīxī–dictum *make clear*

ēdīctum–ī [n.] *decree*
ēdiscō–ere–didicī *learn by heart*
ēdō–ere–didī–ditum *put forth*
ēdūcō–ere–dūxī–ductum *bring up, out*
efficiō–ere–fēcī–fectum *produce*
egeō–ēre–uī [+abl.] *need, want*
egestās–ātis [f.] *need, shortage*
ēgregius–a–um *outstanding*
emō–ere, ēmī, ēmptum *buy*
ēmolliō [4] *soften, mollify*
enim *for, you see*
ēnītor, ēnītī, ēnīxus sum *give birth to*
eō, īre, iī, itum *go*
epistula–ae [f.] *letter*
eques–itis [m.] *knight*
equester–tris–tre *belonging to a knight*
equidem *indeed*
equus–ī [m.] *horse*
ergō *so, therefore*
ēripiō–ere–ripuī–reptum *take away*
errō [1] *wander, make a mistake*
error–ōris [m.] *mistake*
ērumpō–ere–rūpī–ruptum *break out*
ēsuriēns, gen. ēsurientis *hungry*
et *and, also, even*
et . . . et *both . . . and*
etiam *also, even*
ēveniō–īre–vēnī–ventum *happen, turn out*
ēvocō [1] *encourage*
exaequō [1] *regard as equal*
excipiō–ere–cēpī–ceptum *take, follow after*
excūdō–ere–cūdī–cūsum *hammer out*
excutiō–ere–cussī–cussum *shake off*
exemplum–ī [n.] *example, precedent*
exeō–īre–iī–itum *go out*
exerceō [2] *exercise, employ*
exercitus–ūs [m.] *army*
exilium–ī [n.] *exile*
exitiābilis–e *deadly*
exitus–ūs [m.] *end*
expellō–ere–pulī–pulsum *banish*
exquīrō–ere–quīsīvī–quīsītum *discover*
exsecror [1] *curse*
exspectō [1] *expect, wait for*
exstruō–ere–struxī–structum *construct, build*
extemplō *immediately*
extendō–ere–tendī–tentum *stretch out*
extrēmus–a–um *furthest, outermost*
fābula–ae [f.] *myth, story*
faciēs–ēī [f.] *face*

facilis–e *easy*
facinus–oris [n.] *crime*
faciō–ere, fēcī, factum *make, do*
factum–ī [n.] *deed*
facultās–tātis [f.] *capability, opportunity*
faeneror [1] *lend money*
faenum–ī [n.] *hay*
faenus–oris [n.] *interest payment*
famēs–is [f.] *hunger, famine*
familia–ae [f.] *household*
familiāris–is [m.] *friend, attendant*
famula–ae [f.] *maidservant*
fātum–ī [n.] *fate*
faucēs–ium [f. pl.] *jaws, throat, entrance*
faveō–ēre, fāvī, fautum [+dat.] *be kind*
fēcunditās–tātis [f.] *fruitfulness*
fēlīx, gen. fēlīcis *happy, fortunate*
fēmina–ae [f.] *woman*
ferō, ferre, tulī, lātum *carry, bear*
ferōcia–ae [f.] *fierceness*
ferrum–ī [n.] *iron, sword*
ferula–ae [f.] *cane*
ferus–a–um *wild, savage*
fidēlis–e *loyal, faithful*
fidēs–ēī [f.] *trust, trustworthiness*
fīlia–ae [f.] *daughter*
fīlius–ī [m.] *son*
fīniō [4] *end, set bounds to*
fīnis–is [m.] *end*
fīō, fierī, factus sum *become, happen, am made*
flagellum–ī [n.] *whip*
flāgitium–ī [n.] *crime*
flagrō [1] *blaze, burn*
fleō–ēre–ēvī–ētum *weep*
flōreō [2] *flourish*
flōs–ris [m.] *flower*
foedus–a–um *dirty, soiled*
fōns–ntis [m.] *fountain, spring*
forāmen–inis [n.] *opening, aperture*
foris–is [f.] *door, gate*
fōrma–ae [f.] *beauty, shape*
formīdō–inis [f.] *fear*
fōrmōsus–a–um *beautiful*
forte *by chance, perhaps*
fortūna–ae [f.] *fortune*
forum–ī [n.] *forum*
foveō–ēre, fōvī, fōtum *warm, cherish*
fragilis–e *fragile*
frangō–ere, frēgī, frāctum *break*
frāter–tris [m.] *brother*
frīgus–oris [n.] *cold*

frōns–ntis [f.] *forehead*
frūmentum–ī [n.] *corn*
frūstrā *in vain, not to be*
frūstror [1] *deceive*
frūx–gis [f.] *fruit, crop*
fugiō–ere, fūgī, fugitum *escape, flee*
fugō [1] *chase*
fūmus–ī [m.] *smoke*
Gallus–ī [m.] *a Gaul*
gallus–ī [m.] *cock*
garrulus–a–um *chattering*
gaudium–ī [n.] *joy*
gelidus–a–um *cool*
gemitus–ūs [m.] *groan*
gēns–ntis [f.] *race*
genus–eris [n.] *kind, race*
geōmetrēs–trae [m.] *surveyor*
gerō–ere, gessī, gestum *accomplish*
gladiātor–ōris [m.] *gladiator*
gladius–ī [m.] *sword*
gradus–ūs [m.] *step*
Graeculus–a–um *little Greek*
Graecus–a–um *Greek*
grāmen–inis [n.] *grass*
grammaticus–ī [m.] *teacher*
grātia–ae [f.] *thanks, favour*
grātulātiō–nis [f.] *congratulation*
grātus–a–um *pleasing*
gravis–e *heavy, serious*
gravitās–tātis [f.] *weight, severity*
grex–gis [m.] *flock*
habeō [2] *have, hold*
habitō [1] *live, dwell*
haedus–ī [m.] *young goat, kid*
harēna–ae [f.] *sand, arena*
haud *not*
hauriō, haurīre, hausī, haustum *drain, drink up*
hecyra–ae [f.] *mother-in-law*
heus *hey!*
hīc *here*
hic, haec, hoc *this, he, she, it*
hinc *here, from here*
hodiē *today*
homō–inis [m.] *man, human being, person*
honestās–tātis [f.] *reputation*
honestus–a–um *honourable*
honor–ōris [m.] *honour, favour*
hordeum–ī [n.] *barley*
horrendus–a–um *dreadful*
hortor [1] *encourage*
hortus–ī [m.] *garden*

hospes–itis [m.] *host, guest, stranger*
hostēs–ium [m. pl.] *enemy*
hostia–ae [f.] *sacrificial victim*
hūmānitās–tātis [f.] *civilisation, humanity*
hūmānus–a–um *civilised*
hypomnēma–tis [n.] *memorandum, note*
iaceō–ēre–cuī *lie down*
iaciō–ere, iēcī, iactum *throw*
iam *now, already, by this time*
ibī [ibĭ] *there*
īdem, eadem, idem *the same*
igitur *therefore*
ignāvus–a–um *idle, cowardly*
ignis–is [m.] *fire*
ignōminia–ae [f.] *disgrace*
ignōscō–ere–nōvī–nōtum [+dat.] *forgive*
īlex–icis [f.] *oak-tree*
ille, illa, illud *that, he, she, it*
imāgō–inis [f.] *likeness, bust, statue*
imbēcillus–a–um *weak*
imber–bris [m.] *rain-cloud, shower*
imbuō–ere–uī–ūtum *fill, taint*
immergō–ere–mersī–mersum *plunge*
immeritus–a–um *undeserving*
immodicus–a–um *excessive*
imperitō [+dat.] [1] *rule*
imperītus–a–um *ignorant*
imperium–ī [n.] *power*
impleō–ēre–ēvī–ētum *fill*
impōnō–ere–posuī–positum *impose*
impudēns, gen. impudentis *shameless, unscrupulous*
in *in, on* [+abl.]*; into, against* [+acc.]
incendium–ī [n.] *fire*
incendō–ere–cendī–cēnsum *burn, inflame*
incertus–a–um *uncertain*
incipiō–ere–cēpī–ceptum *begin*
incitō [1] *arouse*
incola–ae [c.] *inhabitant*
incolō–ere–coluī *inhabit*
incurrō–ere–cucurrī–cursum *run into*
inde *then, from there*
indignus–a–um *unworthy*
industria–ae [f.] *effort, attention*
īnfāns, gen. īnfantis *infant*
īnferō–erre, intulī, illātum *bring in, forward*
īnficiō–ere–fēcī–fectum *infect, stain*
īnflexibilis–e *inflexible*
ingēns, gen. ingentis *huge, great*
ingredior–ī, ingressus sum *enter, invade*
īnicio–ere–iēcī–iectum *impose*

inimīcus–a–um *hostile, unfriendly*
initium–ī [n.] *beginning*
inquam, inquit *I say, he/she says*
īnsānia–ae [f.] *madness*
īnscrīptiō–nis [f.] *inscription*
īnsidiae–ārum [f. pl.] *ambush*
īnsidiātor–ōris [m.] *trickster*
īnsociābilis–e *incompatible*
īnsolēns, gen. īnsolentis *wanton*
instituō–ere–stituī–stitūtum *begin, set up*
īnstrātus–a–um *covered*
īnsula–ae [f.] *island*
intellegentia–ae [f.] *understanding*
intellegō–ere–ēxī–ēctum *understand*
inter [+acc.] *among*
interdum *sometimes, now and then*
intereā *meanwhile*
interficiō–ere–fēcī–fectum *kill*
interim *meanwhile, sometimes*
intermittō–ere–mīsī–missum *leave off*
interrogō [1] *interrogate, question*
intestīnus–a–um *private, internal*
intrō [1] *enter*
inveniō–īre–vēnī–ventum *find*
inveterātus–a–um *long-standing*
invideō–ēre–vīdī–vīsum [+ dat.] *envy*
invidus–a–um *envious*
invīsus–a–um *hated*
invītō [1] *invite*
invītus–a–um *unwilling*
ipse, ipsa, ipsum *him/her/itself*
īrātus–a–um *angry*
iste–a–ud *that*
istūc *to that place*
ita *in such a way, like this, so*
iter, itineris [n.] *route, passage*
iterum *again*
iubeō–ēre, iussī, iussum *order*
iūdex–icis [m.] *judge*
iugulō [1] *cut a throat*
iugum–ī [n.] *summit, ridge*
iūmentum–ī [n.] *pack-animal*
iūs, iūris [n.] *justice*
iūstus–a–um *fair, reasonable*
iuvenis–e *young*
iuventa–ae [f.] *youth*
labefactus–a–um *shaken*
lābor–ī, lāpsus sum *fall*
labōs–ōris [m.] *toil*
labrum–ī [n.] *lip*
lac, lactis [n.] *milk*
lacer–era–erum *mutilated*

lacertus–ī [m.] *arm*
lacrima–ae [f.] *tear*
laetitia–ae [f.] *joy*
laetus–a–um *happy*
laniō [1] *tear apart*
lapidārius–a–um *stone-carrying*
largus–a–um *abundant*
lascīvus–a–um *playful*
latrōcinium–ī [n.] *robbery*
laudō [1] *praise*
lectīca–ae [f.] *litter*
lēctitō [1] *read repeatedly*
legō–ere, lēgī, lēctum *read*
lētum–ī [n.] *death*
levis–e *light*
lēx, lēgis [f.] *law*
libellus–ī [m.] *little book, handbill*
libenter *willingly*
līber–a–um *free*
liber–brī [m.] *book*
līberālis–e *noble*
līberī–ōrum [m. pl.] *children*
lībertās–tātis [f.] *freedom*
libertus–ī [m.] *freedman*
libet *it is pleasing*
librārius–ī [m.] *clerk*
licentia–ae [f.] *wantonness*
licet *although, granted, it is allowed*
līmen–inis [n.] *door, threshold*
lingua–ae [f.] *language, tongue*
liquō [1] *strain*
lītigium–ī [n.] *dispute*
littera–ae [f.] *letter (of the alphabet)*
litterae–ārum [f. pl.] *letter, correspondence, literature*
lītus–oris [n.] *shore*
locō [1] *place, contract*
locus–ī [m.]; pl.: loca [n.] *place*
longē *far*
longus–a–um *long*
loquor–ī, locūtus sum *speak*
lūctuōsus–a–um *sorrowful*
lūctus–ūs [m.] *grief*
lūdibrium–ī [n.] *mockery*
lūdō–ere, lūsī, lūsum *play*
lūdus–ī [m.] *school, game*
lūmen–inis [n.] *light*
luō–ere, luī *wash, atone for*
lūx–cis [f.] *light, daylight*
mactō [1] *slaughter*
madeō–ēre–duī *be wet*
magis *rather, more*

207

magister–trī [m.] *master, teacher*
magnus–a–um *great, large*
magus–ī [m.] *sorcerer*
māior, māius *greater (senior, ancestor)*
male *badly*
maledīcō–ere–īxī–ictum *to be cheeky to, abuse*
maledictum–ī [n.] *abuse*
malesuādus–a–um *evil-counselling*
mālō, mālle, māluī *prefer*
malus–a–um *bad*
mancipium–ī [n.] *slave*
mandō [1] *entrust*
māne *this morning, early*
maneō–ēre, mānsī, mānsum *remain*
manus–ūs [f.] *hand*
mappa–ae [f.] *napkin*
maritimus–a–um *by the sea*
marītus–ī [m.] *husband*
marmor–oris [n.] *marble*
māter–tris [f.] *mother*
mātrōna–ae [f.] *lady, matron*
maximē *especially*
medicus–ī [m.] *doctor*
medullae–ārum [f. pl.] *innermost core*
melius *better*
meminī–isse *remember*
memorābilis–e *memorable*
mēns–ntis [f.] *mind*
mēnsa–ae [f.] *table*
mentior–īrī, mentītus sum *lie, cheat*
mercātūra–ae [f.] *business, profit*
mercēnārius–ī [m.] *mercenary*
mercēs–ēdis [f.] *pay*
mereō–ēre–uī–itum *deserve*
meretrīx–īcis [f.] *prostitute*
mergō–ere, mersī, mersum *sink*
merīdiēs–ieī [m.] *midday*
merum–ī [n.] *wine*
metus–ūs [m.] *fear*
meus–a–um *my*
migrō [1] *move*
mīles–itis [m.] *soldier*
mīlle *thousand*
minimē *not at all*
ministerium–ī [n.] *service*
ministra–ae [f.] *deaconess*
minor [1] *threaten*
minus *less*
mīror [1] *wonder at*
mīrus–a–um *extraordinary*
miser–a–um *wretched*

mittō–ere, mīsī, missum *send*
modo [and modō] *now, recently*
modus–ī [m.] *way, method, measure*
mollis–e *soft, delicate*
moneō [2] *warn, advise*
mōns–ntis [m.] *mountain*
mōnstrō [1] *show*
morbus–ī [m.] *disease*
morior–ī, mortuus sum *die*
moror [1] *delay*
mors–tis [f.] *death*
mortālis–e *mortal*
mōs, mōris [m.] *custom (pl. character)*
mox *soon*
mufrius–ī [m.] *mutton-head*
mūgītus–ūs [m.] *bellowing*
muliebris–e *female*
mulier–is [f.] *woman*
multum [adverb] *much*
multus–a–um *much, many*
mūlus–ī [m.] *mule*
mundus–ī [m.] *world*
mūnus–eris [n.] *gift, show*
murmur–is [n.] *growling, humming*
mūs, mūris [c.] *mouse*
mūtō [1] *change*
nam *for*
nārrō [1] *tell, recount*
nātiō–nis [f.] *nation*
nātus–a–um *born*
nātus–ī [m.] *son*
nauta–ae [m.] *sailor*
nāvigō [1] *sail*
nāvis–is [f.] *ship*
-ne attached to the first word of a sentence introduces a question
nē *that not, lest*
nē . . . quidem *not even . . .*
nebula–ae [f.] *mist*
nec, nec . . . nec *and not, neither . . . nor*
necessārius–a–um *indispensable*
nefās [indecl. adj.] *wrong, forbidden*
neglegēns, gen. neglegentis *careless*
negō [1] *deny, refuse, say that . . . not*
negōtium–ī [n.] *affair, business*
nēmō–inis *no one*
neque, neque . . . neque *and not, neither . . . nor*
nesciō–īre–īvī–ītum *be ignorant, not know*
neuter–tra–trum *neither*
nī *if not*
niger–gra–grum *black*

nihil, nīl   *nothing*

nimis   *excessively*

nimium   *too much*

nisi   *except, unless*

niveus–a–um   *snow-white*

nōbilis–e   *noble, well-born, famous*

nōdus–ī [m.]   *knot*

nōlō, nōlle, nōluī   *not want, be unwilling*

nōmen–inis [n.]   *name*

nōn   *not*

nōn modo   *not only*

nōndum   *not yet*

nōnne   *surely*

nōnnumquam   *sometimes*

nōnus–a–um   *ninth*

nōscō–ere, nōvī, nōtum   *know*

noster–tra–trum   *our*

nota–ae [f.]   *social grading*

nōtus–a–um   *known*

novem   *nine*

novus–a–um   *new*

nox–ctis [f.]   *night*

noxius–a–um   *guilty*

nūllus–a–um   *no one, not any*

numerus–ī [m.]   *number*

nummus–ī [m.]   *coin*

numquam   *never*

nunc   *now*

nūntiō [1]   *announce*

ob [+acc.]   *because of*

oblīviō–nis [f.]   *neglect*

obscēnus–a–um   *foul, offensive*

observō [1]   *observe*

obstinātiō–nis [f.]   *obstinacy*

obstinātus–a–um   *stubborn*

obstō–āre, obstitī, obstātum   *stand in the way of*

occidō–ere–cidī   *fall, perish*

occīdō–ere–cīdī–cīsum   *kill*

occupō [1]   *occupy*

octō   *eight*

oculus–ī [m.]   *eye*

odor–ōris [m.]   *smell*

offēnsiō–nis [f.]   *trouble, offence*

offerō–erre, obtulī, oblātum   *offer*

ōlim   *previously, once upon a time*

omnīnō   *altogether, entirely*

omnis–e   *all, every*

opera–ae [f.]   *task*

opprimō–ere–pressī–pressum   *repress, put down, destroy*

ops, opis [f.]   *wealth*

opulentus–a–um   *lavish*

opus–eris [n.]   *work*

ōra–ae [f.]   *shore*

ōrātiō–nis [f.]   *speech*

orbis–is [m.]   *world*

orbitās–tātis [f.]   *bereavement*

orīgō–inis [f.]   *source*

ōrnāmentum–ī [n.]   *ornament*

ōrnō [1]   *decorate*

ōrō [1]   *beg*

ortus–a–um   *born, descended*

ōs, ōris [n.]   *mouth, face*

os, ossis [n.]   *bone*

ostendō–ere–endī–entum   *reveal*

ostentō [1]   *show*

ōstiārius–ī [m.]   *door-keeper*

ōtiōsus–a–um   *inactive*

ōtium–ī [n.]   *leisure, inactivity*

paene   *almost*

pallēns, gen. pallentis   *pallid-making*

pālum–ī [n.]   *stake*

pantomīmus–ī [m.]   *pantomime artist*

pār, paris   *equal*

parcō–ere, pepercī, parsum [+dat.]   *spare*

parēns–ntis [m.& f.]   *parent*

pāreō [+dat.] [2]   *obey*

pariter   *in like manner, equally*

parō [1]   *prepare*

pars–tis [f.]   *part*

partus–ūs [m.]   *birth*

parum   *not enough*

parvus–a–um   *small*

pāscō–ere, pāvī, pāstum   *feed*

pater–tris [m.]   *father*

paternus–a–um   *belonging to a father*

patior–ī, passus sum   *suffer, endure*

patria–ae [f.]   *country*

paucī–ae–a   *few*

paulātim   *little by little*

paulō   *a little*

pauper, gen. pauperis   *impoverished*

pāx–cis [f.]   *peace*

pecūnia–ae [f.]   *money*

pēius   *worse*

pellis–is [f.]   *skin*

penātēs–ium [m. pl.]   *spirits of the household*

pendō–ere, pependī, pēnsum   *hang, weigh*

penus–ī [m. & f.]   *provisions*

per [+acc.]   *through, across, by means of*

perditus–a–um   *ruined*

perfundō–ere–fūdī–fūsum   *drench*

perīculōsus–a–um *dangerous*
perīculum–ī [n.] *danger*
perpetior–ī, perpessus sum *endure*
persevērō [1] *persist*
pertimēscō–ere–uī *fear very much*
pertinācia–ae [f.] *perseverance*
pertināx, gen. pertinācis *persistent*
pervādō–ere–vāsī–vāsum *go through*
perveniō–īre–vēnī–ventum *reach*
pēs, pedis [m.] *foot*
petō–ere–īvī–ītum *seek*
philosophia–ae [f.] *philosophy*
pictor–ōris [m.] *painter*
pius–a–um *dutiful*
placeō [+dat.] [2] *please, satisfy*
plānē *clearly*
plēbēs–eī [f.] *ordinary people*
plēnus–a–um *full*
plērīque *for the most part*
plērumque *very often*
plūrimus–a–um *very many*
poena–ae [f.] *punishment, penalty*
poēta–ae [m.] *poet*
polītus–a–um *refined*
pōnō–ere, posuī, positum *place, put*
pōns–ntis [m.] *bridge*
populus–ī [m.] *people*
porticus–ūs [f.] *colonnade*
portō [1] *carry*
possum, posse, potuī *be able*
post [+acc.] *after*
posteā *afterwards*
posteritās–tātis [f.] *posterity*
postulō [1] *demand*
potestās–tātis [f.] *power*
potior–īrī, potītus sum [+abl.] *take
  possession of*
pōtō [1] *drink*
prae [+abl.] *before*
praeceptor–ōris [m.] *teacher*
praeceptum–ī [n.] *maxim, precept*
praeclārus–a–um *magnificent*
praecō–nis [m.] *herald*
praeda–ae [f.] *plunder, loot*
praeeō–īre–iī–itum *go before*
praeferō–ferre–tulī–lātum *carry before*
praehibeō [2] *supply*
praemium–ī [n.] *reward*
praesēns *here and now*
praeses–idis [m.] *governor*
praeter [+acc.] *besides, except*
praetereā *moreover*

prāvus–a–um *depraved*
prīmō *at first*
prīmum [adverb] *first*
prīmus–a–um *first*
prīnceps–ipis [m.] *leader, emperor*
prīncipātus–ūs [m.] *control, leadership*
prīncipium–ī [n.] *beginning*
prīscus–a–um *ancient*
prīstinus–a–um *previous*
prō [+abl.] *in place of, before*
probitās–tātis [f.] *honesty*
probō [1] *approve*
procul *from afar*
prōcurrō–ere–cucurrī–cursum *run
  forward*
prōditus–a–um *betrayed*
proelium–ī [n.] *battle*
proficīscor–ī, profectus sum *set out, leave*
profiteor–ērī, professus sum *declare*
profugus–ī [m.] *fugitive*
prōgredior–ī, prōgressus sum *advance*
prōmittō–ere–mīsī–missum *promise*
prope *almost, near*
properō [1] *hurry*
propinquus–ī [m.] *relative*
prōpōnō–ere–posuī–positum *put forward,
  display*
propter [+acc.] *because of*
prōsequor–ī, prōsecūtus sum *follow after*
prosperus–a–um *favourable*
prōspiciō–ere–spexī–spectum *be on the
  watch*
proximus–a–um *next*
prūdentia–ae [f.] *good sense*
pūblicus–a–um *public*
pudendus–a–um *shameful*
pudor–ōris [m.] *shame*
puella–ae [f.] *girl*
puer–ī [m.] *boy, slave*
pugna–ae [f.] *battle*
pugnō [1] *fight*
pulcher–chra–chrum *beautiful*
pulsō [1] *beat*
pulvīnar–āris [n.] *couch*
pūniō [4] *punish*
putō [1] *think*
quadrāns–ntis [m.] *quadrant, quarter of
  an as*
quaerō–ere–sīvī–sītum *search for*
quālis–e *just like, as*
quam *than, as, how, which*
quamquam *although*

quandō *when, since*
quantus–a–um *how great*
quārē *why*
quārtus–a–um *fourth*
quattuor *four*
-que *and (to be understood before the word to which -que is attached)*
querimōnia–ae [f.] *complaint*
quī [archaic] *how*
quī, quae, quod *who, which*
quis *who*
quia *because, that*
quid *what, why*
quīdam, quaedam, quoddam *somebody, something, a certain . . .*
quidem *indeed (emphasising the previous word)*
quiēs–tis [f.] *rest, peace*
quiētus–a–um *quiet, peaceful*
quīngentī–ae–a *five hundred*
quīnque *five*
quis *who*
quisquam, quidquam *anyone, anything*
quisque, quaeque, quodque *each, every*
quisquis, quidquid *whoever, whatever*
quō *to where, by which*
quod *because, which*
quondam *formerly*
quotiēns *how often*
radius–ī [m.] *rod, radius*
rapiō–ere, rapuī, raptum *take, snatch*
rārus–a–um *rare, unusual*
rāsus–a–um *shaved*
recēns, gen. **recentis** *fresh*
recipiō–ere–cēpī–ceptum *accept*
rēctē *properly*
recumbō–ere–cubuī–cubitum *lie down*
reddō–ere–didī–ditum *restore*
redimō–ere–dēmī–dēmptum *buy back, set free*
redūcō–ere–dūxī–ductum *bring back*
referō–erre, rettulī, relātum *bring back, refer*
reficiō–ere–fēcī–fectum *remake*
refugiō–ere–fūgī–fugitum *flee back*
regiō–nis [f.] *region*
rēgnō [1] *rule, reign*
rēgnum–ī [n.] *kingdom*
regō–ere, rēxī, rēctum *rule, guide*
rēgula–ae [f.] *rule*
religiō–nis [f.] *scruple, awe, religion*
relinquō–ere–īquī–ictum *leave*

reliquus–a–um *remaining*
remedium–ī [n.] *cure*
reor, rērī, ratus sum *think*
repente *suddenly*
repōnō–ere–posuī–positum *put back*
reprehendō–ere–hendī–hēnsum *seize, blame*
reprimō–ere–pressī–pressum *check, restrain*
requīrō–ere–quīsīvī–sītum *search for*
rēs, reī [f.] *thing*
rēs pūblica [f.] *republic*
resecō–āre–secuī–sectum *cut back*
resistō–ere, restitī [+dat.] *resist, oppose*
respondeō–ēre–spondī–spōnsum *reply*
respōnsum–ī [n.] *answer*
restituō–ere–stituī–stitūtum *restore*
retineō–ēre–tinuī–tentum *keep*
reus–ī [m.] *defendant*
revellō–ere–vellī–vulsum *tear back*
rēx–gis [m.] *king*
rhētor–oris [m.] *professor*
rīdeō–ēre, rīsī, rīsum *laugh*
rigō [1] *soak, drench*
rīvus–ī [m.] *stream*
rōdō–ere, rōsī, rōsum *gnaw*
rubeō [2] *be red*
ruber–bra–brum *red*
rudis–e *impressionable, inexperienced*
rūmor–ōris [m.] *rumour*
rumpō–ere, rūpī, ruptum *break*
rūrsum *again*
rūs, rūris [n.] *land, countryside*
sacculus–ī [m.] *purse*
saeculum–ī [n.] *age, era*
saepe *often*
saepius *more often, quite often*
saevitia–ae [f.] *cruelty*
saevus–a–um *cruel, savage*
sāl–is [m.] *salt, wit*
salutātor–ōris [m.] *visitor*
salūtō [1] *greet*
sānē *certainly*
sanguis–inis [m.] *blood*
saniēs–ēī [f.] *slaver, poison*
sānus–a–um *healthy, sane*
sapiēns, gen. **sapientis** *wise, discreet*
sapiō–ere–īvī *taste, be sensible*
satis *enough*
saucius–a–um *wounded*
scaenicus–a–um *theatrical*
scelerātus–a–um *accursed, wicked*

211

scīlicet *of course*
sciō–īre, scīvī, scītum *know*
scrībō–ere, scrīpsī, scrīptum *write*
scrīptor–ōris [m.] *writer*
scrīpulum–ī [n.] *a small weight*
scutica–ae [f.] *strap*
sē, sēsē *himself, herself, themselves*
secō–āre–uī, sectum *cut*
secundum [+acc.] *according to, following*
secundus–a–um *second*
secūris–is [f.] *axe*
sed *but*
sedeō–ēre, sēdī, sessum *sit*
sēdō [1] *calm, stop*
segnitia–ae [f.] *sluggishness*
semper *always*
senātor–ōris [m.] *senator*
senātus–ūs [m.] *senate*
senectūs–ūtis [f.] *old age*
senex–is [m.] *old man*
sentiō–īre, sēnsī, sēnsum *perceive, realise*
septem *seven*
sequor–ī, secūtus sum *follow*
sērius–a–um *serious*
sermō–nis [m.] *speech, conversation*
serō–ere, sēvī, satum *sow*
serviō [4] *serve*
servitūs–tūtis [f.] *slavery*
servō [1] *keep*
servus–ī [m.] *slave*
sescentī–ae–a *six hundred*
sēstertiārius–a–um *worth a sesterce*
sevērus–a–um *austere, strict*
sex *six*
sexus–ūs [m.] *sex, gender*
sī *if*
sīdus–eris [n.] *star*
silentium–ī [n.] *silence*
silva–ae [f.] *wood, forest*
simul *at the same time*
simulācrum–ī [n.] *statue*
simulō [1] *pretend, imitate*
sīn *but if*
sine [+abl.] *without*
sinō–ere, sīvī, situm *allow*
solitus–a–um *familiar, customary*
sōlus–a–um *only*
solūtus–a–um *released*
somnium–ī [n.] *dream*
sōpītus–a–um *sleeping*
soror–ōris [f.] *sister*
sospes, gen. **sospitis** *safe*

spatium–ī [n.] *space*
speciōsus–a–um *splendid*
spectāculum–ī [n.] *show*
spectō [1] *watch*
spēlunca–ae [f.] *cave*
spērō [1] *hope*
spēs–ēī [f.] *hope*
spīritus–ūs [m.] *breath*
spīrō [1] *breathe, blow*
splendidus–a–um *bright*
sponte *of one's own free will*
statim *immediately*
stō–āre, stetī, statum *stand*
strepitus–ūs [m.] *noise*
studium–ī [n.] *eagerness, pursuit, study*
subdō–ere–didī–ditum *lay under*
subiciō–ere–iēcī–iectum *suppress, subject*
subinde *then*
subolēs–is [f.] *offspring*
subrēpō–ere–rēpsī–reptum *advance slowly*
subvertō–ere–vertī–versum *upset, overturn*
sūdō [1] *sweat*
sufferō–erre, sustulī, sublātum *suffer, endure*
sufficiō–ere–fēcī–fectum *supply, be sufficient*
sufflō [1] *blow*
sum, esse, fuī *be*
summus–a–um *utmost*
sūmō–ere, sūmpsī, sūmptum *take*
sūmptuōsus–a–um *extravagant*
superbus–a–um *proud*
superior–ius *upper*
superstitiō–nis [f.] *superstition*
supplicium–ī [n.] *death-penalty*
suprā [+acc.] *beyond*
suscitō [1] *revive*
suus–a–um *his, her, its, their*
syllaba–ae [f.] *syllable*
taceō [2] *be silent*
tam *so*
tamen *however*
tamquam *as if, as it were*
tandem *at last, pray*
tantus–a–um *such, so great*
taurus–ī [m.] *bull*
tellūs–ūris [f.] *earth, ground*
templum–ī [n.] *temple*
temptō [1] *test, try*
tempus–oris [n.] *time*

tenāx, gen. **tenācis** *clinging*
tendō–ere, tetendī, tēnsum *stretch out, extend*
teneō [2] *hold*
tener–a–um *tender*
tenuis–e *slender, insignificant*
terreō [2] *frighten*
terribilis–e *terrible*
terror–ōris [m.] *terror, fear*
tertius–a–um *third*
testāmentum–ī [n.] *will*
testimōnium–ī [n.] *evidence*
testor [1] *bear witness*
thēsaurus–ī [m.] *treasure, store-house*
timeō [2] *fear*
timidē *timidly*
tolerō [1] *endure*
tollō–ere, sustulī, sublātum *raise*
tonō–āre–uī *thunder*
tormentum–ī [n.] *torture*
tortor–ōris [m.] *torturer*
torus–ī [m.] *couch*
tōtus–a–um *whole, all*
trādō–ere–didī–ditum *hand over*
trānō [1] *swim across*
trānseō–īre–iī, trānsitum *go over, through*
trānsmūtō [1] *transfer, switch*
trānsverberō [1] *transfix, pierce*
trecentī–ae–a *three hundred*
trēs *three*
tribūnal–ālis [n.] *tribunal*
tribūnus–ī [m.] *tribune*
tribuō–ere–buī–būtum *give*
trīstis–e *sad, grim*
trucīdō [1] *murder*
tueor–ērī, tuitus sum *preserve*
tum *then*
tumultus–ūs [m.] *noise*
tunc *then, at that time*
turba–ae [f.] *crowd*
turgidus–a–um *swollen*
turpis–e *disgraceful*
tuus–a–um *your*
ubī [ubĭ] *when, where*
ūllus–a–um *any*
ultrā *more, beyond*
ultrīx, gen. **ultrīcis** *avenging*
unda–ae [f.] *wave*
unde *from where*
ūndecimus–a–um *eleventh*
undique *from all sides*
unguis–is [m.] *nail*

ūniversus–a–um *all*
ūnus–a–um, (gen. **ūnīus**) *one*
urbs–is [f.] *city*
ūrō–ere, ussī, ustum *burn*
ut *that, so that, as, when*
uterque, utraque, utrumque *each of two*
ūtilis–e *beneficial, useful*
utinam *if only*
ūtor–ī, ūsus sum [+abl.] *use*
uxor–ōris [f.] *wife*
vacō [1] *be empty*
vae *oh dear*
valēns, gen. **valentis** *powerful*
validus–a–um *strong*
varius–a–um *different*
vehō–ere, vēxī, vectum *carry*
vel *or*
vēna–ae [f.] *vein*
vēnābulum–ī [n.] *hunting-spear*
venēnum–ī [n.] *poison*
veniō–īre, vēnī, ventum *come*
ventus–ī [m.] *wind*
venus–eris [f.] *love*
venustus–a–um *charming*
verber–is [n.] *beating, blow*
verberō [1] *whip*
verbum–ī [n.] *word*
vereor–ērī, veritus sum *fear*
vērō *indeed, but*
verrō–ere *sweep*
vertō–ere, vertī, versum *turn*
vērum *but, however*
vērus–a–um *true, real*
vester–tra–trum *your*
vestibulum–ī [n.] *hall*
vestītus–a–um *clothed*
vetustās–tātis [f.] *age*
via–ae [f.] *road, way*
vīcīnus–a–um *neighbouring*
victor–ōris [m.] *winner*
victōria–ae [f.] *victory*
videō–ēre, vīdī, vīsum *see*
vigilō [1] *be awake*
vīgintī *twenty*
vīlis–e *base, cheap*
vīlla–ae [f.] *villa, farm*
vincō–ere, vīcī, victum *conquer, win*
vīnum–ī [n.] *wine*
vir–ī [m.] *man, husband*
vīrēs–ium [f. pl.] *resources, strength*
virgō, virginis [f.] *maiden, girl*
virtūs–tūtis [f.] *courage*

vīsō–ere, vīsī *visit*
vīta–ae [f.] *life*
vitium–ī [n.] *vice, defect*
vitrum–ī [n.] *glass; woad*
vitta–ae [f.] *headband*
vituperō [1] *disparage*
vīvārium–ī [n.] *pond, aquarium*
vīvō–ere, vīxī, vīctum *live*
vīvus–a–um *alive, living*
vix *scarcely*

volō, velle, voluī *want, be willing*
volō [1] *fly*
voluntās–tātis [f.] *will, inclination*
voluptās–tātis [f.] *pleasure*
vomō–ere–uī–itum *pour forth*
vōx–cis [f.] *voice*
vulgus–ī [n.] *crowd*
vulnus–eris [n.] *wound*
vultus–ūs [m.] *face*